Causality, Correlation and Artificial Intelligence for Rational Decision Making

Causality, Correlation and Artificial Intelligence for Rational Decision Making

Tshilidzi Marwala

University of Johannesburg, South Africa

World Scientific

NEW JERSEY • LONDON • SINGAPORE • BEIJING • SHANGHAI • HONG KONG • TAIPEI • CHENNAI

Published by

World Scientific Publishing Co. Pte. Ltd.
5 Toh Tuck Link, Singapore 596224
USA office: 27 Warren Street, Suite 401-402, Hackensack, NJ 07601
UK office: 57 Shelton Street, Covent Garden, London WC2H 9HE

Library of Congress Cataloging-in-Publication Data
Marwala, Tshilidzi, 1971–
Causality, correlation, and artificial intelligence for rational decision making / by Tshilidzi Marwala (University of Johannesburg, South Africa).
pages cm
Includes bibliographical references and index.
ISBN 978-9814630863 (alk. paper)
1. Decision making. 2. Artificial intelligence. I. Title.
T57.95.M375 2015
006.301'51--dc23
2014027464

British Library Cataloguing-in-Publication Data
A catalogue record for this book is available from the British Library.

In-house Editors: Sutha Surenddar/Chelsea Chin

Typeset by Stallion Press
Email: enquiries@stallionpress.com

Printed in Singapore by Mainland Press Pte Ltd.

Preface

Causality, correlation and artificial intelligence for rational decision making covers five significant areas of intellectual inquiry which are causality, correlation, artificial intelligence, rationality, and decision making. It gives new insights on causality and correlations machines and proposes that these form as a fundamental unit for rational decision making.

Causality has been a subject of study for many years and has often been confused with correlation. Human intuition has evolved such that it has learned to identify causality through correlation. This book proposes a model that claims that within any causality model is buried a correlation machine.

This study uses artificial intelligence to build correlation and causality machines. Artificial intelligence methods that are used are the multi-layer perceptron (MLP), radial basis function (RBF), fuzzy inference systems, support vector machines, genetic algorithms (GAs), and simulated annealing (SA). The concepts of causality, correlation and artificial intelligence are then applied in interstate conflict, condition monitoring and several biomedical applications.

This book introduces the concept of flexibly-bounded rationality and uses the correlation and causal machines to implement this. Flexibly-bounded rationality is a special case of bounded rationality.

Furthermore, this book introduces the theory of the marginalization of irrationality for decision making and applies this to the problem of breast cancer diagnosis.

This book is intended for philosophers, computer scientists, engineers, and other interested parties at both undergraduate and graduate levels as well as practitioners.

Acknowledgments

I would like to thank the following institutions for contributing toward the writing of this book: University of Cambridge, University of Pretoria, and University of Johannesburg.

I also would like to thank my students for their assistance in developing this manuscript more particularly Fholisani Mashegana.

I dedicate this book to the schools that gave me the foundation to always seek excellence in everything I do and these are: Mbilwi Secondary School, Case Western Reserve University, University of Pretoria, University of Cambridge (St. John's College), and Imperial College (London). I thank the Stellenbosch Institute of Advanced Study (STIAS) for the financial support as well as accommodation during the writing of this book.

This book is dedicated to the following people: Nhlonipho Khathutshelo, Lwazi Thendo, Mbali Denga Marwala as well as Dr. Jabulile Vuyiswa Manana.

Professor Tshilidzi Marwala, Ph.D.
Johannesburg
1 February 2014

Contents

Chapter 1

Introduction to Artificial Intelligence based Decision Making

Abstract. In this chapter, decision making which is based on causality, correlation and artificial intelligence is introduced. The concept of correlation is introduced and is applied to build a correlation function. Furthermore, it relates causality to correlation and uses it to build a causal function. Artificial intelligence methods are introduced and these include neural networks, particle swarm optimization, genetic algorithm and simulated annealing. It describes decision making and outlines the rest of the book.

1.1 Introduction

The problem of understanding causality has pre-occupied philosophers for a very long time. From the times of Plato and Aristotle and even before that period, mankind has been asking why and how they are on this planet and various answers to these questions involve causality. The very idea that a higher being, or a great architect of the universe created, mankind is squarely premised on the principle of causality. The significance of understanding causality to satisfy human curiosity and enhance the functioning of society is enormous. As an example, the medical field is based on the premise that some medicines cause healing of diseases. To link specific medicines to the curing of diseases requires a good understanding of causality and as long as this understanding is not complete the results of clinical studies will always be sub-optimal. One example to illustrate this, is the avocado pear that was thought to be dangerous because the causal relation between avocado pear consumption and cholesterol was poorly understood but today it is considered good for one's cholesterol.

There is an old Tshivenda saying that states: "Tsho bebiwaho tsho fa" (Marwala, 2013a). What this expression signifies is that there is a perfect correlation between birth and death and those who are born will necessarily die. Many have simplified and misinterpreted this allegory to purport that it alludes to the fact that birth causes death. In fact, there is an information flow from birth to death but this is not causal information. It might be that the actual causal relation for this case was between a road accident and death, therefore, the road accident caused death. This example illustrates a very simple explanation of what a cause is and what a correlation is. On trying to understand causality, it is vital to understand the principle of correlation because within any causal model lies a correlation function.

1.2 Correlation

In this section, we explore the concept of correlation, what it is and what it can be used for. To illustrate this, we invoke the relationship between obesity and heart attack. In this example, the two variables x indicating a person's weight and y indicating whether they had a heart attack. In this case, variable x is positively correlated to variable y.

1.2.1 What is correlation?

According to *www.dictionary.com* correlation is defined as: "the degree to which two or more attributes or measurements on the same group of elements show a tendency to vary together." This degree to which variables vary together can be quantified. Two variables are correlated if their underlying substructures are connected. For example, if one was to measure the heart rate and blood pressure of patient John, then these parameters may be correlated primarily because they are measurements from a common structure, and in this case a patient called John. In statistics this case is known as confounding.

1.2.2 Correlation function

In this book, we introduce a concept called a correlation function which is a conventional predictive system that is primarily based on mapping variables to themselves and this is called the auto-associative network (Kramer, 1992). It is a process through which a system is able to recreate a complete set of information from a small piece of information. For example, one could easily complete the following statement if one is familiar with the former USA President J.F. Kennedy: "Ask not what your country can do for you but . . . ." In order to achieve this task, the auto-associative memory is used. The auto-associative networks are sometimes called auto-encoders or memory networks. These networks have been used in a number of applications including novelty detection, image compression (Rios and Kabuka, 1995) and missing data estimation (Marwala, 2009). An illustration of the auto-associative network is shown in Figure 1.1.

Masuda *et al.* (2012) successfully applied auto-associative memories based on recurrent neural networks to maximize the number of correctly stored patterns whereas Miranda *et al.* (2012) successfully applied auto-associative neural networks

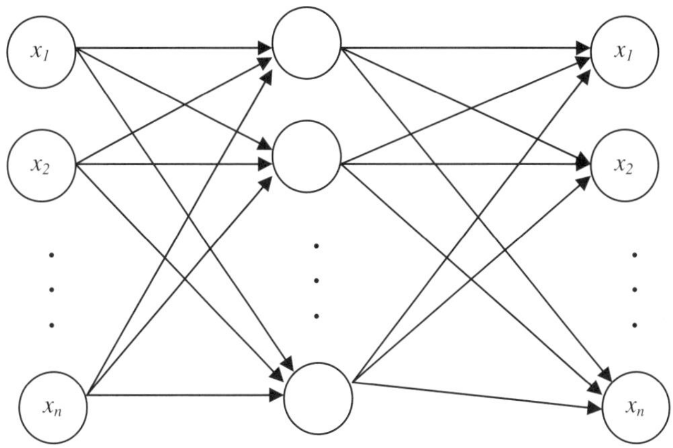

Figure 1.1 An auto-associative network

and mean shift for fault detection in power transformers. Valle and Grande Vicente (2011) successfully applied auto-associative networks to reconstruct color images corrupted by either impulsive or Gaussian noise, whereas Fernandes *et al.* (2011) successfully applied auto-associative pyramidal neural network for face verification, whereas Jeong *et al.* (2011) successfully applied auto-associative multilayer perceptron for laser spot detection based on computer interface system. Other successful applications of auto-associative network are in business failure (Chen, 2010) and gaze tracking (Proscevicius *et al.*, 2010).

The principles governing the auto-associative network are as follows (Marwala, 2009):

1. A correct model that describes inter-relationships that exist amongst the data variables and define the rules that govern the data, is identified. This is achieved using an auto-associative memory network.
2. In order to estimate unknown variable(s), the correct estimated variable(s) are those that when identified they obey all the inter-relationships that exist amongst the data as defined in Step 1 and the rules that govern the data. In order to ensure that the estimated values obey the inter-relationships in the data, an optimization method that treats the unknown variable(s) as design variable(s) and the inter-relationships amongst the data and rules that govern the data as the objective to be reached. Therefore, the unknown variable(s) estimation problem is fundamentally an optimization problem where the objective is to estimate unknown variable(s) by ensuring that the rules and inter-relationships governing the data are maintained.
3. It is vital to have a good idea of the bounds that govern the unknown variable(s) in order to aid the optimization process.

1.3 Causality

1.3.1 What is causality?

According to the Oxford English dictionary causality is defined as "the relationship between something that happens and the effect it produces" and defines a cause as "making something" while an effect is defined as "a change which is a result of an action". The cause does not necessarily have to be one-dimensional. For example, in a causal relationship between sunlight, minerals, air and water causing the tree to grow, the cause has 4 dimensions (sunlight, minerals, air and water). This book adopts the concept that for one variable to cause another, there has to be a flow of information from the cause to the effect. According to Suppes (1970), there are many different types of causes and these are *prima facie* causes, spurious causes, direct causes, supplementary causes, sufficient causes and negative causes.

According to Suppes (1970), the event B is the *prima facie* cause of event A if event A happened after event B has happened, the probability of event B happening $p(B)$ is greater than zero and the probability of event A happening given the fact that event B has happened $p(A \mid B)$ is greater than the probability of event A happening $p(A)$. Spurious cause is the cause of an event in which an earlier cause is the real cause of the event. According to Suppes (1970), "an event $B_{t'}$ is a spurious cause of A_t if and only if $t' > t''$ exists and that there is a partition $\pi_{t''}$ such that for all elements $C_{t''}$ of $\pi_{t''} t' < t$, $p(B_{t'}) > 0$, $p(A_t|B_{t'}) > p(A_t)$, $p(B_{t'}C_{t''}) > 0$ and $p(A_t|B_{t'}C_{t''}) = p(A_t|C_{t''})$." Again according to Suppes (1970), "an event $B_{t'}$ is a direct cause of A_t if and only if $B_{t'}$ is a *prima facie* cause of A_t and there is no t'' and no partition $\pi_{t''}$ such that for every $C_{t''}$ in $\pi_{t''} t' < t'' < t$, $P(B_{t'}C_{t''}) > 0$ and $p(A_t|B_{t'}C_{t''}) = p(A_t|C_{t''})$". Supplementary causes are more than one cause supplementing one another to cause an event. Suppes (1970) defines $B_{t'}$ and $C_{t''}$ as supplementary causes of A_t "if and only if $B_{t'}$ is a *prima facie* cause of A_t, $C_{t''}$ is a *prima facie* cause of A_t, $p(B_{t'}C_{t''}) > 0$, $p(A|B_{t'}C_{t''}) > \max(p(A_t|B_{t'}), p(A_t|C_{t''})$". Sufficient causes are causes that cause the event to definitely happen. Accordingly, Suppes (1970) defines that "$B_{t'}$ is a sufficient cause of A_t if and only if $B_{t'}$ is a *prima facie* cause of A_t and $p(A_t|B_{t'}) = 1$". Negative cause is an event that causes another event not to occur. According to Suppes (1970), "the event $B_{t'}$ is a *prima facie* negative cause of event A_t if and only if $t' < t$, $p(B_{t'}) > 0$ and $p(A_t|B_{t'}) < p(A_t)$."

1.3.2 Theories of causality

In this chapter, we use key terminologies one of which is a causal path that links an event (cause) to another event (effect) as well as a correlation path which links one variable to another. Hume (1896) advanced the following eight principles of causality:

1. The cause and effect are connected in space and time.
2. The cause must happen before the effect.
3. There should be a continuous connectivity between the cause and the effect.
4. The specific cause must at all times give the identical effect, and the same effect should not be obtained from any other event but from the same cause.
5. Where a number of different object give the same effect, it ought to be because of some quality which is the same amongst them.
6. The difference in the effects of two similar events must come from that which they are different.
7. When an object changes its dimensions with the change of its cause, it is a compounded effect from the combination of a number of different effects, which originate from a number of different parts of the cause.
8. An object which occurs for any time in its full exactness without any effect, is not the only cause of that effect, but needs to be aided by some other norm which may advance its effect and action.

Pećnjak (2011) demonstrated that unlike what Hume proposed under particular scenarios the same causes can have very different effects whereas Paoletti (2011) studied causes as contiguous events. McBreen (2007) studied realism and empiricism in Hume's account of causality and observed that the realist explanation of Hume by philosophers should be overruled because it is not consistent with empiricism. McBreen also observed that if the assumption that we cannot sense causality is tested then we can interpret causality both empirically and realistically. Other critical work on Hume and causality include by Rohatyn (1975), Rodríguez Sánchez (2004) and Watkins (2004).

The eight statements by Hume have been reduced by Granger (1969) to three principles with regards to causality and these are, that the cause and effect are associated or correlated, that the cause happens before the effect and that the cause and effect are connected. These three factors are in essence the necessary albeit not sufficient conditions for causality. Sections A–I study the different theories of causality.

A. *Transmission Theory of Causality*

In the transmission theory of causality, causal information is transmitted from the cause to the effect and this has been described in detail by Ehring (1986), Kistler (1998), Salmon (1984) and Dowe (1992). What this transmitted information is depends on the specific case being analyzed. Because of the transmission of such information from the cause to the effect, there should be a correlation between the cause at the time of the transmission of this information and the effect at the time of the arrival of the information. In simple terms, the effect at the time of the arrival of the information is correlated to the cause at the time of the departure of the information. It is because of this reason that whenever correlation is observed causality is wrongly inferred and human intuition has evolved such that it has learned to identify causality through correlation. This is because of the inability to detect a time lag between a cause and effect which necessarily implies causality.

This chapter proposes that within any causality model is buried a correlation function. Indeed, if x causes y then y at a later time must necessarily be correlated to x at the earlier time. This book uses Salmon's definition of causality which states that when x causes y then there has to be a flow of information between variable x and variable y. Of course causality is then easily detected if this information can be physically represented. As correlation is a vital part of causality, it is important to understand it.

B. *Probability Theory of Causality*

The probability theory of causality is based on the premise that some classes of causality are probabilistic. This of course is in violation of the principle advocated by Hume which states that the specific cause must at all times give the identical effect, and the same effect should not be obtained from any other event but from the same cause. For example, there is a controversial topic on whether *HIV causes AIDS*. There is clearly a correlation between HIV and AIDS, but not all people with HIV necessarily develop AIDS. In the deterministic world, HIV does not cause AIDS. Because all people who have HIV will not necessarily develop AIDS. However, in the probabilistic world indeed HIV causes AIDS. To be precise, the statement should be framed as follows: the probability of AIDS being there given that HIV is there is very high but not necessarily 100%. Therefore, a generalized causal model is necessarily probabilistic with the deterministic version being a special case when the probability is 100%.

Ten Kate (2010) as well as Schmidtke and Krawczak (2010) quantified causality probability on studying the delay in psychomotor development of offspring of father–daughter incest. Schmidtke and Krawczak studied a 20-year-old offspring of father–daughter incest who was looking for financial compensation for the delay in psychomotor development under the German federal act of victim indemnification. According to the law, the probability that the psychomotor development delay was caused by the incest should exceed 50% for her to qualify for compensation. The study revealed that indeed the probability of the incest being the cause was 65%.

Other studies of causality and probability were conducted by Plotnitsky (2009) who studied causality and probability in quantum mechanics, González Fernández

(2005) who studied probability and causality in the philosophy of Max Born, as well as Dawid (2004) who studied probability, causality and the empirical world using Bayes–de Finetti–Popper–Borel synthesis.

C. *Projectile Theory of Causality*

The projectile theory of causality is a generalized version of the transmission theory of causality. Like the transmission theory, it assumes that some information is transmitted from the cause to the effect. However, information is transmitted with a specific velocity (intensity and configuration). The information that is transmitted from the cause to the effect can, therefore, be viewed as a projectile. It leaves the point of cause with a certain velocity. Sometimes it reaches the point of effect, sometimes it falls short of the target and from this it is possible to build a probability distribution of causation. This theory is illustrated in Figure 1.2.

D. *Causal Calculus*

Causal calculus is derived from conditional probability theory and is premised on the idea of estimating interventional probability from conditional probabilities (Rebane and Pearl, 1987; Verma and Pearl, 1990; Pearl, 2000). Suppose we would like to estimate the hypothesis that HIV causes AIDS. Causal calculus allows us to estimate the interventional probability that a person who is forced to have HIV develops AIDS which is written as $P(AIDS|forced(HIV))$ from the conditional probability $P(AIDS|HIV)$ using Bayesian networks. When this process is defined on a directed acyclic graph, it is possible to infer causal relationships amongst variables. More details on this can be found in Pearl (2000), Ortigueira *et al.* (2012), Raginsky (2011) and Pommereau (2004). This causal calculus assumes that the structure that connects variables is in existence. There are cases where the structure does not exist and has to be identified from the observed data. This can be achieved by using the Bayesian networks. More details on causal calculus are in Chapter 6.

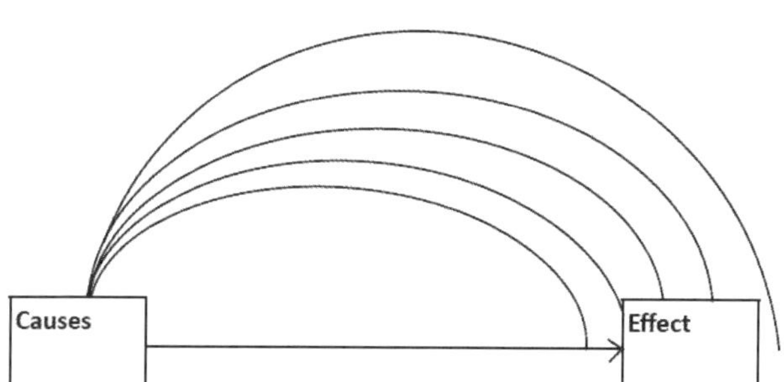

Figure 1.2 An illustration of the projectile theory of causality

E. *Granger Causality*

Granger causality is a technique for revealing directed functional connectivity based on time series analysis of causes and effect. Suppose we have variables observations $y_k, y_{k-1}, \ldots, y_1$ and $x_{k-1}, x_{k-2}, \ldots, x_1$ then there is a causal relationship between the variables if when solving the following linear regression problem then the coefficients β are non-zero (Granger, 1969):

$$y_k = \alpha_1 y_1 + \alpha_2 y_2 + \cdots + \alpha_{k-1} y_{k-1} + \beta_1 x_1 + \beta_2 x_2 + \cdots + \beta_{k-1} x_{k-1} + \varepsilon. \tag{1.1}$$

This relationship can then be generalized to become (Granger, 1969):

$$y_k = f(\alpha_{k-1} y_{k-1}, \ldots, \alpha_1 y_1, \beta_{k-1} x_{k-1}, \ldots, \beta_1 x_1, \varepsilon) \tag{1.2}$$

here α and β are hyper-parameters and are non-zero if there is a causal relationship between x and y and β is zero if there is no relationship between x and y. Candelon *et al.* (2013) applied and tested for Granger causality in distribution tails and applied this to the oil market integration. They observed that the integration level between crude oil markets decreases and that the price-setter markets also change during extreme periods. These findings imply the significance of an active energy policy in periods of extreme movements. Seth *et al.* (2013) applied Granger causality analysis and demonstrated that it was robust to a wide range of changes in hemodynamic response properties. Zhao *et al.* (2013) successfully applied NARX-based Granger linear and nonlinear casual influence detection technique to human EEG data analysis. Friston *et al.* (2013) successfully applied Granger causality and dynamic causal modelling to detect and estimate directed connectivity in neural networks whereas Croux and Reusens (2012) used Granger causality analysis in the frequency domain to evaluate whether stock prices contain predictive power for the future economic activity.

F. *Manipulation Theories*

The manipulation theories of causality consider causal relationships between causal variable x and effect variable y and consider changes in x called Δx and assess whether it leads to changes in $y(\Delta y)$ in the model $y = f(x)$. If it does, then there is a causal relationship between x and y. If this is not the case, then there is another variable which both x and y depend on.

Baedke (2012) demonstrated that interventionist notion of causality explains important elements of epigeneticists whereas Imai *et al.* (2013) applied experimental designs to identify causal mechanisms. Experimental approaches are, however, criticized because they do not reveal causal mechanisms and cannot identify the process through which causation happens.

Erisen and Erisen (2012) applied manipulation theories to study the effect of social networks on the quality of political thinking. They observed that small social networks produce "social bubbles" that limit communication. Silvanto and Pascual-Leone (2012) applied manipulation theory to assess causality between brain and behavior relations whereas Mazlack (2011) applied manipulation theories to study causality in bioinformatics.

G. *Process Theories*

Process theories of causality consider the causal relationship between variables x and y and identifies the actual process of causality not its mirror. Anderson and Scott (2012) studied process causality and social context. They presented a process perspective of causality that permitted qualitative researchers to infer causal relationships from the practice settings. Rodrigo *et al.* (2011) proposed a technique to identify hierarchical fibrillatory processes which used causal relations between neighboring electrodes to identify predominant propagation directions. Sia (2007) applied creative synthesis to build a process perspective of causality. Creative synthesis is a model of causality which resolves the determinism–indeterminism debate in philosophical discussions. It interprets effects as statistical averages and not as predictable results of the action of causal model. Samgin (2007) applied causality-based analytic assumptions to the theory of ion transport. This approach was found to give a unified procedure that included ionic oscillations in wells and classical-like escaping.

H. *Counterfactual Theory*

In counterfactual thinking given a factual with an antecedent (cause) and a consequence (effect), the antecedent is altered and the new consequence is derived (Byrne, 2005; Lewis, 1973; Miller and Johnson-Laird, 1976; Simon and Rescher, 1966). Suppose one would like to test what happens to a headache when aspirin is administered. Then one would observe what happens when one has a headache and nothing is administered and compare this to when aspirin is administered. In this instance not administering aspirin is called a factual while administering aspirin is called a counterfactual. Ideally for the efficacy of aspirin to be observed then not administering aspirin (factual) and administering aspirin (counterfactual) should happen at the same time which is physically impossible. The compromise is for the factual and counterfactual to happen at nearly identical conditions (Byrne and Tasso, 1999; De Vega *et al.*, 2007). Some successful applications of counterfactual theory to model causality include Shpitser (2013). There are different types of counterfactuals and these include directionality and additive/subtractive counterfactuals (Fillenbaum, 1974; Ferguson and Sanford, 2008; Ginsberg, 1986).

Directionality counterfactuals give direction and an example is: *if I had moved to London, I would have been wealthy* (factual) as opposed to *if I had not moved to London, I would have been poor* (factual). Additive/subtractive counterfactuals are the types where you add or subtract on the antecedent. An example is, *if I take too much sugar I develop diabetes* (factual) as opposed to if *I do not take too much sugar I do not develop diabetes* (counterfactual). The theory of counterfactuals will be used to describe the Neyman-Rubin causal model which is the subject of Chapter 6.

I. *Structural Learning*

Structural learning is a technique of identifying connections between a set of variables. Structural learning is based on the premise that there are three causal substructures that define causal relationships between variables and these were identified by Wright (1921) and they are direct and indirect causation ($X \rightarrow Z \rightarrow Y$), common cause confounding ($X \leftarrow Z \rightarrow Y$) and a collider ($X \rightarrow Z \leftarrow Y$). In the direct and indirect causation X and Y are conditionally dependent and furthermore, X and Y are conditionally independent given Z. For the common confounding, X and Y are conditionally dependent and furthermore, X and Y are conditionally independent given Z. In the collider, X and Y are independent and are dependent given Z and, therefore, can be uniquely identified from cross-sectional data. In structural learning, relationships between variables are identified using heuristic optimization techniques.

1.3.3 What is a causal function?

In this chapter, we define a causality function which takes an input vector (x) which is the cause and propagate it into the effect (y). This can be appropriately represented mathematically as follows:

$$y = f(x). \tag{1.3}$$

Here f is the functional mapping. This equation strictly implies that y is directly obtained from x. Of course this elegant equation is not strictly only applicable to the cause and effect but can still be valid if x and y are correlated. What this book argues is that a function philosophically and structurally assumes a causal model under certain conditions prescribed by Hume (1896) and these are that, x and y are connected in space and time, x must happen before y, as well as that there should be a flow of information between x and y. Flow of information implies connectivity and therefore the conditions that Equation 1.3 is a causal function are that x must happen before y and that there should be a flow of information from x to y.

1.3.4 How to detect causation?

One of the most important questions on causation is how do we detect causation and possibly measure it. If we are to adopt the projectile model of causation we could possibly observe whatever information is transmitted from the cause to the effect provided that such information is physically representable. Another way to sense causation is to frame a question differently by inquiring how relevant the cause is on the effect rather than asking how the cause is transmitted into the effect. By asking the question on how relevant the cause is on the determination of the effect and ruling out correlation can allow one to use relevance determination models such as factor analysis to possibly sense causality. The automatic relevance determination method for causality is a subject of Chapter 7.

1.4 Introduction to Artificial Intelligence

Artificial Intelligence (AI) is a field which is about the construction of intelligent systems with the ability to learn and think (Hopfield, 1982; Marwala and Lagazio, 2011). There are two kinds of AI systems and these are learning and optimization methods. The second class uses the contrivance of complex social organisms such as the flock of birds, colony of ants and school of fishes to design systems that are intelligent to adapt without human participation by representing dialectic relationships between individual and group intelligence.

In this chapter, we propose neural networks to create models that are capable of transmitting information from the cause to the effect and this is called a causal function provided that the cause happens before the effect and that there is transmission of information from the cause to the effect. This transmission process is enabled using neurons which transmit information from the cause to the effect. This in essence denotes that the effect depends on the cause. We also use neural networks to build an auto-associative memory network which is in essence a correlation function because it is primarily based on correlations between the data (Hopfield, 1982; Marwala, 2009). It is called auto-associative memory network because it is able to reveal a complete set of information by observing a small piece of information. It is an associative memory network because learning is based on association of the small piece of information to the whole. In cognitive psychology association is a powerful tool which is useful for learning complex patterns.

1.4.1 Neural networks

Neural networks are used to model the causal and correlation models in this book. Types of neural networks include the radial basis function (RBF) and the multi-layer perceptron (MLP) (Marwala, 2013). Neural networks have been applied effectively in numerous diverse areas of variable complexities including control of non-linear system (Chemachema, 2012), traffic sign classification (Cireşan *et al.*, 2012), dynamic portfolio optimization (Liu *et al.*, 2012) and for vibrant adaptation of wireless sensor and actor networks (Cañete *et al.*, 2012).

The MLP is feed-forward neural network model where the input variables are fed-forward until they become the effect. It, therefore, estimates a relationship between sets of input data (cause) and a set of appropriate output (effect). It is based on the standard linear perceptron and makes use of three or more layers of neurons (nodes) with non-linear activation functions, and is more powerful than the perceptron. This is because it can distinguish data that is not linearly separable, or separable by a hyper-plane. The MLP has been used to model many complex systems in areas such as estimating invasive cerebrospinal fluid pressure (Golzan *et al.*, 2012), monitoring electric load of residential buildings (Rababaah and Tebekaemi, 2012), separating nonlinear source (Elmannai *et al.*, 2012), monitoring gear dynamics (Sanz *et al.*, 2012), engineering sciences (Marwala, 2010), approximating the Vickers hardness of Mn–Ni–Cu–Mo austempered ductile iron (PourAsiabi *et al.*, 2012), estimating wind speed (Culotta *et al.*, 2012), automatically monitoring critical infrastructure (Marwala, 2012), and forecasting odorant chemical class from descriptor values (Bachtiar *et al.*, 2011).

The MLP neural network has multiple layers neural units, which are interconnected in a feed-forward configuration (Haykin, 1999; Marwala, 2013b). Each neuron in one layer is directly connected to the neurons of the subsequent layer. Two-layered MLP architecture is used in this book because of the universal approximation theorem, which states that a two layered architecture is adequate for MLP modelling (Haykin, 1999; Marwala, 2013a). The network can be described as follows by assuming a logistic function in the outer layer and a hyperbolic tangent function in the inner layer and is schematically shown in Figure 1.3:

$$y_k = \frac{1}{1 + e^{-\left(\sum_{j=1}^{M} w_{kj}^{(2)} \tanh\left(\sum_{i=1}^{d} w_{ji}^{(1)} x_i + w_{j0}^{(1)}\right) + w_{k0}^{(2)}\right)}}. \tag{1.4}$$

In Equation 1.4, $w_{ji}^{(1)}$ and $w_{ji}^{(2)}$ indicate weights in the first and second layer, respectively, going from input i to hidden unit j, M is the number of hidden units, d is the number of output units while $w_{j0}^{(1)}$ and $w_{k0}^{(2)}$ indicate the biases for the hidden unit j and the output unit k.

1.4.2 Hopfield networks

Hopfield networks are memory systems with binary threshold nodes and can be trained to converge to an optimal point (Hopfield, 1982). They are in essence models that allow for the comprehension of human memory. They are able to model

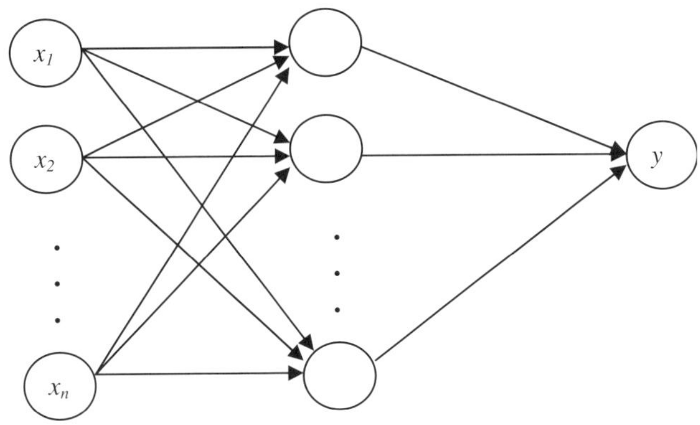

Figure 1.3 A MLP neural network

associative memory and there are two categories of processes: auto-association and hetero-association. Auto-association is when a vector is associated with itself while hetero-association is when two different vectors are associated. Auto-association is used in this chapter to build a correlation function. Hopfield networks have been applied quite extensively for economic dispatch with multiple options of fuel (Dieu *et al.*, 2013), in optimal control (Wang and Nakagiri, 2012), remote sensing (Santos *et al.*, 2012), spectrum and power distribution (Yang and Jiang, 2012), production planning (Su, 2012), solving load balancing problems (Fei and Ding, 2012) and fault diagnosis (Li *et al.*, 2012). The concept of a Hopfield network is used to create an auto-associative network.

1.4.3 Genetic algorithm

Genetic algorithm is a global optimization technique which is based on the principles of evolution as proposed by Darwin (1859). It consists of four motive forces and these are crossover where two members of a population mate to produce an offspring, mutation where a member of the population changes aspect of its genes and reproduces according to the principles of the survival of the fitness. Genetic algorithm was applied successfully to optimize resource levels in surgical services (Lin *et al.*, 2013), optimize stay cables in bridges (Hassan, 2013), optimize steel panels (Poirier *et al.*, 2013), schedule shop floor (Wang and Liu, 2013) and task teams of unmanned aerial vehicles (Darrah *et al.*, 2013). Genetic algorithm is used in this book to build a correlation function.

1.4.4 Particle swarm optimization

Particle swarm optimization technique is a stochastic, population-based evolutionary global optimization method that was motivated by algorithms that model the "flocking behavior" seen in birds (Kennedy and Eberhart, 1995). Within the optimization framework, the notion of birds identifying a roost is similar to a process of identifying an optimal solution. Its main feature is its socio-psychological characteristics derived from swarm intelligence and offers comprehension of social behavior and thus it is governed by two drivers and these are group and individual knowledge. Particle swarm optimization method has been applied successfully to predict foreign exchange rates (Sermpinis *et al.*, 2013), design bacterial foraging in power system stabilizers (Abd-Elazim and Ali, 2013), model elasto-plastic of unsaturated soils (Zhang *et al.*, 2013a), plan robot paths (Zhang *et al.*, 2013b) and design electronic enclosure (Scriven *et al.*, 2013). Particle Swarm Optimization is used to model a correlation model.

1.4.5 Simulated annealing

Simulated annealing is a probabilistic meta-heuristic global optimization technique that is based on natural annealing process (Kirkpatrick *et al.*, 1983). Critical elements of simulated annealing are the energy function which is a mathematical or heuristical representation of the objective function and the temperature. On implementing simulated annealing, the temperature is reduced gradually and this is called temperature schedule until it is frozen when the temperature is equal to 1. Simulated annealing has found many successful applications such as identification of order picking policy (Atmaca and Ozturk, 2013), vehicle routing (Baños *et al.*, 2013), design of pre-stressed concrete precast road bridges (Martí *et al.*, 2013), inferring maximum parsimony phylogenetic (Richer *et al.*, 2013) and mixed model assembly (Manavizadeh *et al.*, 2013). Simulated annealing is used to model a correlation model.

1.5 Rational Decision Making

In addition to causality and correlation, this book is also about decision making. This book basically proposes that the basic elements of rational decision making are causality and correlation. Correlation is important because it fills in the gaps that exist because of the limitation of information in decision making. Furthermore, causality is important in decision making because it is through causal loops (if this then act so) that an appropriate cause of action is chosen from many possible causes of actions and thus reducing the complexity of the problem. Rational decision making is a process of reaching a decision that maximizes the utility (Habermas, 1984) and decisions are arrived at based on relevant information and by applying sound logic and optimizing resources (Etzioni, 1988). Simon Herbert realized that on making a rational decision one does not always have all the information and the logic that is used is far from perfect and, consequently, he introduced the concept of bounded rationality (Simon, 1991; Gigerenzer and Selten, 2002).

In this book, it is established that advances in artificial intelligence are capable of increasing the amount of information that is otherwise limited and make otherwise inconsistent and complex decisions consistent. Consequently, artificial intelligence makes the theory of bounded rationality become the theory of flexibly-bounded rationality where the flexibility of the bounds are prescribed by the amount of artificial intelligence technology deployed in the decision making process.

Furthermore, the concept of decision making based on information and robust logic that globally optimize resources is most often than not possible and thus many decisions are made under irrational conditions. The surprising aspect of this assertion is that despite the fact that most decisions are made under irrational conditions, the world seems to work somewhat well. The reason for this is because in decision making processes there are rational and irrational actions and whether the decision will be sufficient and satisfactory, a process that Herbert Simon terms satisficing, depends on whether rational actions overwhelm irrational actions. The theory of satisficing based on whether irrational actions are overwhelmed by rational actions or vice versa is called the marginalization of irrationality theory (Marwala, 2013a).

1.6 Summary and Outline of the Book

In this chapter, four main themes were considered and these were causality, correlation, artificial intelligence and decision making. In Chapter 2, a correlation function is defined and built using various artificial intelligence tools whereas in Chapter 3 a causal function is defined and built using Bayesian framework and hybrid Monte Carlo methods. Chapter 4 introduces multi-layer perceptron and radial basis function techniques to build causal function and these are applied to create a Granger non-linear causality system whereas Chapter 5 introduces particle swarm and simulated annealing optimization techniques to build correlation functions and these are also applied to model non-linear Granger causal system. Chapter 6 studies the Neyman-Rubin, Pearl and Granger causal models and proposes how to unify these approaches. Chapter 7 introduces the automatic relevance determination, correlation and causal functions to extend Granger causality framework to the non-linear domain. Chapter 8 explores the concept of rational decision making, introduces the concept of flexibly-bounded rationality to extend the theory of bounded rationality and introduces the concept of the indivisibility of rationality. It explores the problem of imperfect and incomplete information and its impact on decision making within the context of the theory of bounded rationality. Chapter 9 introduces the theory of the marginalization of irrationality for decision making. This book is then concluded in Chapter 10.

1.7 Conclusions

This chapter presented causality, correlation and artificial intelligence. It described correlation and applied correlation to construct a correlation function. In addition, it presented causality and related it to correlation. It described causality and applied it to build a causal function. The artificial intelligence approaches presented in this chapter included neural networks, support vector functions, neuro-fuzzy system, particle swarm optimization, genetic algorithm and simulated annealing. It also introduced the concept of rational and irrational decision making.

References

Abd-Elazim, S.M., Ali, E.S. "A hybrid particle swarm optimization and bacterial foraging for optimal power system stabilizers design", *International Journal of Electrical Power and Energy Systems*, Vol. 46, No. 1, pp. 334–341, 2013.

Anderson, G.L., Scott, J. "Toward an intersectional understanding of process causality and social context", *Qualitative Inquiry*, Vol. 18, No. 8, pp. 674–685, 2012.

Atmaca, E., Ozturk, A. "Defining order picking policy: A storage assignment model and a simulated annealing solution in AS/RS systems", *Applied Mathematical Modelling*, Vol. 37, No. 7, pp. 5069–5079, 2013.

Bachtiar, L.R., Unsworth, C.P., Newcomb, R.D., Crampin, E.J. "Predicting odorant chemical class from odorant descriptor values with an assembly of multi-layer perceptrons", *Proceedings of the Annual International Conference of the IEEE Engineering in Medicine and Biology Society*, EMBS, art. no. 6090755, pp. 2756–2759, 2011.

Baedke, J. "Causal explanation beyond the gene: Manipulation and causality in epigenetics", *Theoria (Spain)*, Vol. 27, No. 2, pp. 153–174, 2012.

Baños, R., Ortega, J., Gil, C., Fernández, A., De Toro, F. "A simulated annealing-based parallel multi-objective approach to vehicle routing problems with time windows", *Expert Systems with Applications*, Vol. 40, No. 5, pp. 1696–1707, 2013.

Byrne, R.M.J. "The Rational Imagination: How People Create Counterfactual Alternatives to Reality", Cambridge, MA: MIT Press, 2005.

Byrne, R.M.J., Tasso, A. "Deductive reasoning with factual, possible, and counterfactual conditionals", *Memory & Cognition*, Vol. 27, pp. 726–740, 1999.

Candelon, B., Joëts, M., Tokpavi, S. "Testing for Granger causality in distribution tails: An application to oil markets integration", *Economic Modelling*, Vol. 31, No. 1, pp. 276–285, 2013.

Cañete, E., Chen, J., Marcos Luque, R., Rubio, B. "NeuralSens: A neural network based framework to allow dynamic adaptation in wireless sensor and actor networks", *Journal of Network and Computer Applications*, Vol. 35, No. 1, pp. 382–393, January 2012.

Chemachema, M. "Output feedback direct adaptive neural network control for uncertain SISO nonlinear systems using a fuzzy estimator of the control error", *Neural Networks*, Vol. 36, pp. 25–34, December 2012.

Chen, M.-H. "Pattern recognition of business failure by autoassociative neural networks in considering the missing values", *ICS 2010 — International Computer Symposium*, art. no. 5685421, pp. 711–715, 2010.

Cireşan, D., Meier, U., Masci, J., Schmidhuber, J. "Multi-column deep neural network for traffic sign classification", *Neural Networks*, Vol. 32, pp. 333–338, August 2012.

Croux, C., Reusens, P. "Do stock prices contain predictive power for the future economic activity? A Granger causality analysis in the frequency domain", *Journal of Macroeconomics*, Vol. 35, pp. 93–103, 2013.

Culotta, S., Messineo, A., Messineo, S. "The application of different model of multi-layer perceptrons in the estimation of wind speed", *Advanced Materials Research*, Vols. 452–453, pp. 690–694, 2012.

Darrah, M., Fuller, E., Munasinghe, T., Duling, K., Gautam, M., Wathen, M. "Using genetic algorithms for tasking teams of raven UAVs", *Journal of Intelligent and Robotic Systems: Theory and Applications*, Vol. 70, Nos. (1–4), pp. 361–371, 2013.

Darwin, C. "On the Origin of Species by Means of Natural Selection, or the Preservation of Favoured Races in the Struggle for Life, London: John Murray", 1859.

Dawid, A.P. "Probability, causality and the empirical world: A Bayes–de Finetti–Popper–Borel synthesis", *Statistical Science*, Vol. 19, No. 1, pp. 44–57, 2004.

De Vega, M., Urrutia, M., Riffo, B. "Canceling updating in the comprehension of counterfactuals embedded in narrative", *Memory & Cognition*, Vol. 35, pp. 1410–1421, 2007.

Dieu, V.N., Ongsakul, W., Polprasert, J. "The augmented Lagrange Hopfield network for economic dispatch with multiple fuel options", *Mathematical and Computer Modelling*, Vol. 57, Nos. 1–2, pp. 30–39, 2013.

Dowe, T.P. "Wesley Salmon's process theory of causality and conserved quantity theory", *Philosophy of Science*, Vol. 59, pp. 195–216, 1992.

Ehring, D. "The transference theory of causation", *Synthese*, Vol. 67, pp. 249–258, 1986.

Elmannai, H., Loghmari, M.A., Karray, E., Naceur, M.S. "Nonlinear source separation based on Multi-Layer Perceptron: Application on remote sensing analysis", *2012 2nd International Conference on Remote Sensing, Environment and Transportation Engineering*, RSETE 2012 — Proceedings, art. no. 6260640, 2012.

Erisen, E., Erisen, C. "The effect of social networks on the quality of political thinking", *Political Psychology*, Vol. 33, No. 6, pp. 839–865, 2012.

Etzioni, A. "Normative-affective factors: Towards a new decision-making model", *Journal of Economic Psychology*, Vol. 9, pp. 125–150, 1988.

Fei, C., Ding, F. "Solving the load balancing problem by adding decaying continuous Hopfield neural network", *2012 2nd International Conference on Applied Robotics for the Power Industry*, CARPI 2012, art. no. 6356299, pp. 276–279, 2012.

Ferguson, H.J., Sanford, A.J. "Anomalies in real and counterfactual worlds: An eye-movement investigation", *Journal of Memory Language*, Vol. 58, pp. 609–626, 2008.

Fernandes, B.J.T., Cavalcanti, G.D.C., Ren, T.I. "Autoassociative pyramidal neural network for face verification", *Proceedings of the International Joint Conference on Neural Networks*, art. no. 6033417, pp. 1612–1617, 2011.

Fillenbaum, S. "Information amplified: Memory for counterfactual conditionals", *Journal of Experimental Psychology*, Vol. 102, pp. 44–49, 1974.

Friston, K., Moran, R., Seth, A.K. "Analysing connectivity with Granger causality and dynamic causal modelling", *Current Opinion in Neurobiology*, Vol . 23, No. 2, pp. 172–178, 2013.

Gigerenzer, G., Selten, R. "Bounded Rationality: The Adaptive Toolbox", MIT Press, 2002.

Ginsberg, M.L. "Counterfactuals", *Artificial Intelligence*, Vol. 30, pp. 35–79, 1986.

Golzan, S.M., Avolio, A., Graham, S.L. "Non-invasive cerebrospinal fluid pressure estimation using multi-layer perceptron neural networks", *Proceedings of the Annual International Conference of the IEEE Engineering in Medicine and Biology Society*, EMBS, art. no. 6347185, pp. 5278–5281, 2012.

González Fernández, M.P. "Probability and causality in the philosophy of Max Born Logos", *Logos Annals of Metaphysics Seminar*, Vol. 38, pp. 241–269, 2005.

Granger, C.W.J. "Investigating causal relations by econometric models and cross-spectral methods", *Econometrica*, Vol. 37, pp. 424–438, 1969.

Habermas, J. "The Theory of Communicative Action Volume 1: Reason and the Rationalization of Society", Cambridge, Polity Press, 1984.

Hassan, M.M. "Optimization of stay cables in cable-stayed bridges using finite element, genetic algorithm, and B-spline combined technique", *Engineering Structures*, Vol. 49, pp. 643–654, 2013.

Haykin, S. "Neural Networks: A Comprehensive Foundation", 2nd Edition, Prentice-Hall, 1999.

Hopfield, J.J. "Neural networks and physical systems with emergent collective computational abilities", *Proceedings of the National Academy of Sciences of the USA*, Vol. 79, No. 8, pp. 2554–2558, 1982.

Hume, D. (Selby-Bigge (ed.)). *A Treatise of Human Nature*, Clarendon Press, 1896.

Imai, K., Tingley, D., Yamamoto, T. "Experimental designs for identifying causal mechanisms", *Journal of the Royal Statistical Society. Series A: Statistics in Society*, Vol. 176, No. 1, pp. 5–51, 2013.

Jeong, S., Jung, C., Kim, C.-S., Shim, J.H., Lee, M. "Laser spot detection-based computer interface system using autoassociative multilayer perceptron with input-to-output mapping-sensitive error back propagation learning algorithm", *Optical Engineering*, Vol. 50, No. 8, art. no. 084302, 2011.

Kennedy, J., Eberhart, R.C. "Particle swarm optimization," *Presented at the Proceedings of the IEEE International Joint Conference on Neural Networks*, 1995.

Kirkpatrick, S., Gelatt, C.D., Vecchi, M.P. "Optimization by simulated annealing", *Science*, Vol. 220, No. 4598, pp. 671–680, 1983.

Kistler, M. "Reducing causality to transmission", *Erkenntnis*, Vol. 48, pp. 1–24, 1998.

Kramer, M.A. "Autoassociative neural networks, *Computers & Chemical Engineering*", Vol. 16, No. 4, pp. 313–328, April 1992.

Lewis, D. "Counterfactuals", Blackwell Publishers, 1973.

Li, P., Xiong, Q., Chai, Y., Wang, K. "Analog fault diagnosis using hopfield network and multi-scale wavelet transform method", *Journal of Computational Information Systems*, Vol. 8, No. 23, pp. 9721–9728, 2012.

Lin, R.-C., Sir, M.Y., Pasupathy, K.S. "Multi-objective simulation optimization using data envelopment analysis and genetic algorithm: Specific application to determining optimal resource levels in surgical services", *Omega (United Kingdom)*, Vol. 41, No. 5, pp. 881–892, 2013.

Liu, Q., Guo, Z., Wang, J. "A one-layer recurrent neural network for constrained pseudoconvex optimization and its application for dynamic portfolio optimization", *Neural Networks*, Vol. 26, pp. 99–109, February 2012.

Manavizadeh, N., Hosseini, N.-S., Rabbani, M., Jolai, F. "A Simulated Annealing algorithm for a mixed model assembly U-line balancing type-I problem considering human efficiency and Just-In-Time approach", *Computers and Industrial Engineering*, Vol. 64, No. 2, pp. 669–685, 2013.

Martí, J.V., Gonzalez-Vidosa, F., Yepes, V., Alcalá, J. "Design of prestressed concrete precast road bridges with hybrid simulated annealing", *Engineering Structures*, Vol. 48, pp. 342–352, 2013.

Marwala, T., Lagazio, M. "Militarized conflict modeling using computational intelligence techniques", Springer-Verlag, London, 2011.

Marwala, T. "Computational intelligence for missing data imputation, estimation and management: Knowledge optimization techniques", Information Science Reference Imprint, IGI Global Publications, New York, USA, 2009.

Marwala, T. "Finite element model updating using computational intelligence techniques", Springer-Verlag, London, 2010.

Marwala, T. "Condition Monitoring Using Computational Intelligence Methods", Springer-Verlag, London, UK, 2012.

Marwala, T. "Flexibly-bounded Rationality and Marginalization of Irrationality Theories for Decision Making", arXiv:1306.2025 [cs.AI], 2013.
Marwala, T. "Causality, correlation and artificial intelligence: Implication on policy formulation", *The Thinker*, Vol. 49, pp. 36–37, 2013a.
Marwala, T. "Economic Modelling Using Artificial Intelligence Methods", Springer-Verlag, London, UK, 2013b.
Masuda, K., Fukui, B., Kurihara, K. "A weighting approach for autoassociative memories to maximize the number of correctly stored patterns", *Proceedings of the SICE Annual Conference*, art. no. 6318692, pp. 1520–1524, 2012.
Mazlack, L.J. "Approximate computational intelligence models and causality in bioinformatics", *Proceedings of the 6th IASTED International Conference on Computational Intelligence and Bioinformatics*, CIB 2011, pp. 1–8, 2011.
McBreen, B. "Realism and empiricism in Hume's account of causality", *Philosophy*, Vol. 82, No. 321, pp. 421–436, 2007.
Miller, G., Johnson-Laird, P.N. "Language and Perception", Cambridge: Cambridge University Press, 1976.
Miranda, V., Castro A.R.G., Lima S. "Diagnosing faults in power transformers with autoassociative neural networks and mean shift", *IEEE Transactions on Power Delivery*, Vol. 27, No. 3, art. no. 6176288, pp. 1350–1357, 2012.
Ortigueira, M.D., Rivero, M., Trujillo, J.J. "The incremental ratio based causal fractional calculus", *International Journal of Bifurcation and Chaos*, Vol. 22, No. 4, pp. 1–9, 2012.
Paoletti, C. "Causes as proximate events: Thomas Brown and the Positivist interpretation of Hume on causality", *Studies in History and Philosophy of Science Part A*, Vol. 42, Vol. 1, pp. 37–44. 2011.
Pearl, J. "*Causality: Models, Reasoning, and Inference*", Cambridge University Press, 2000.
Pećnjak, D. "Freedom of the will, causality and Hume Prolegomena", Vol. 10, No. 2, pp. 311–316, 2011.
Plotnitsky, A. "Causality and probability in quantum mechanics", *AIP Conference Proceedings*, Vol. 1101, pp. 150–160, 2009.
Poirier, J.D., Vel, S.S., Caccese, V. "Multi-objective optimization of laser-welded steel sandwich panels for static loads using a genetic algorithm", *Engineering Structures*, Vol. 49, pp. 508–524, 2013.
Pommereau, F. "Causal time calculus", *Lecture Notes in Computer Science (including subseries Lecture Notes in Artificial Intelligence and Lecture Notes in Bioinformatics)*, Vol. 2791, pp. 260–272, 2004.
PourAsiabi, H., PourAsiabi, H., AmirZadeh, Z., BabaZadeh, M. "Development a multi-layer perceptron artificial neural network model to estimate the Vickers hardness of Mn–Ni–Cu–Mo austempered ductile iron", *Materials and Design*, Vol. 35, pp. 782–789, 2012.
Proscevicius, T., Raudonis, V., Kairys, A., Lipnickas, A., Simutis, R. "Autoassociative gaze tracking system based on artificial intelligence", *Elektronika ir Elektrotechnika*, Vol. 5, pp. 67–72, 2010.
Rababaah, A.R., Tebekaemi, E. "Electric load monitoring of residential buildings using goodness of fit and multi-layer perceptron neural networks", *CSAE 2012 — Proceedings, 2012 IEEE International Conference on Computer Science and Automation Engineering*, 2, art. no. 6272871, pp. 733–737, 2012.
Raginsky, M. "Directed information and Pearl's causal calculus", *2011 49th Annual Allerton Conference on Communication, Control, and Computing*, Allerton 2011, art. no. 6120270, pp. 958–965, 2011.
Rebane, G., Pearl, J. "The Recovery of Causal Poly-trees from Statistical Data", *Proceedings, 3rd Workshop on Uncertainty in AI* (Seattle, WA), pp. 222–228, 1987.

Richer, J.-M., Rodriguez-Tello, E., Vazquez-Ortiz, K.E. "Maximum parsimony phylogenetic inference using simulated annealing", *Advances in Intelligent Systems and Computing*, Vol. 175, pp. 189–203, 2013.

Rios, A., Kabuka, M. "Image compression with a dynamic autoassociative neural network. Mathematical and Computer Modelling", Vol. 21, Nos. 1–2, pp. 159–171, January 1995.

Rodrigo, M., Liberos, A., Guillem, M.S., Millet, J., Climent, A.M. "Causality relation map: A novel methodology for the identification of hierarchical fibrillatory processes", *Computers in Cardiology*, Vol. 38, art. no. 6164530, pp. 173–176, 2011.

Rodríguez Sánchez, R.A. "Knowledge and causality in the thinking of David Hume", *Pensamiento*, Vol. 60, No. 226, pp. 145–161, 2004.

Rohatyn, D.A. "Kant, Hume and causality Journal for General Philosophy of Science", *Zeitschrift für Allgemeine Wissenschaftstheorie*, Vol. 6, No. 1, pp. 34–36, 1975.

Salmon, W. "Scientific explanation and the causal structure of the world", Princeton University Press, Princeton, 1984.

Samgin, A.L. "On an application of the causality principle to the theory of ion transport processes", *Journal of Physics and Chemistry of Solids*, Vol. 68, No. 8, pp. 1561–1565, 2007.

Santos, S., Castaneda, R., Yanez, I. "Hopfield and pulse coupled neural networks aggregation for enhanced change detection in remote sensing imagery", *World Automation Congress Proceedings*, art. no. 6320941, 2012.

Sanz, J., Perera, R., Huerta, C. "Gear dynamics monitoring using discrete wavelet transformation and multi-layer perceptron neural networks", *Applied Soft Computing Journal*, Vol. 12, No. 9, pp. 2867–2878, 2012.

Schmidtke, J., Krawczak, M. "Psychomotor developmental delay and epilepsy in an offspring of father-daughter incest: Quantification of the causality probability", *International journal of legal medicine*, Vol. 124, No. 5, pp. 449–450, 2010.

Scriven, I., Lu, J., Lewis, A. "Electronic enclosure design using distributed particle swarm optimization", *Engineering Optimization*, Vol. 45, No. 2, pp. 167–183, 2013.

Sermpinis, G., Theofilatos, K., Karathanasopoulos, A., Georgopoulos, E.F., Dunis, C. "Forecasting foreign exchange rates with adaptive neural networks using radial-basis functions and Particle Swarm Optimization", *European Journal of Operational Research*, Vol. 225, No. 3, pp. 528–540, 2013.

Seth, A.K., Chorley, P., Barnett, L.C. "Granger causality analysis of fMRI BOLD signals is invariant to hemodynamic convolution but not downsampling", *NeuroImage*, Vol. 65, pp. 540–555, 2013.

Shpitser, I. "Counterfactual graphical models for longitudinal mediation analysis with unobserved confounding", *Cognitive Science*, Vol. 37, No. 6, pp. 1011–1035, 2013.

Sia, S. "Creative synthesis: A process interpretation of causality", *Philosophia*, Vol. 36, No. 2, pp. 213–221, 2007.

Silvanto, J., Pascual-Leone, A. "Why the assessment of causality in brain-behavior relations requires brain stimulation", *Journal of Cognitive Neuroscience*, Vol. 24, No. 4, pp. 775–777, 2012.

Simon, H. "Bounded Rationality and Organizational Learning", *Organization Science*, Vol. 2, No. 1, pp. 125–134, 1991.

Simon, H., Rescher, N. "Cause and Counterfactual", *Philosophy of Science*, Vol. 33, pp. 323–340, 1966.

Su, J.-L. "Intelligence decision supporting algorithms of production planning based on Hopfield network", *Proceedings of the World Congress on Intelligent Control and Automation (WCICA)*, art. no. 6359166, pp. 4122–4125, 2012.

Suppes, P. "A probabilistic theory of causality", *North-Holland Publishing Company*, Amsterdam, 1970.

Ten Kate, L.P. "Psychomotor developmental delay and epilepsy in an offspring of father–daughter incest: Quantification of the causality probability International Journal of Legal Medicine", Vol. 124, No. 6, pp. 667–668, 2010.

Valle, M.E., Grande Vicente, D.M. "Some experimental results on sparsely connected autoassociative morphological memories for the reconstruction of color images corrupted by either impulsive or Gaussian noise", *Proceedings of the International Joint Conference on Neural Networks*, art. no. 6033232, pp. 275–282, 2011.

Verma, T., Pearl, J. "Equivalence and synthesis of causal models", *Proceedings of the Sixth Conference on Uncertainty in Artificial Intelligence* (July, Cambridge, MA), pp. 220–227, 1990.

Wang, Q.-F., Nakagiri, S.-I. "Sensitivity of optimal control for diffusion Hopfield neural network in the presence of perturbation", *Applied Mathematics and Computation*, Vol. 219, No. 8, pp. 3793–3808, 2012.

Wang, S., Liu, M. "A genetic algorithm for two-stage no-wait hybrid flow shop scheduling problem", *Computers and Operations Research*, Vol. 40, No. 4, pp. 1064–1075, 2013.

Watkins, E. "Kant's model of causality: Causal powers, laws, and Kant's reply to Hume", *Journal of the History of Philosophy*, Vol. 42, No. 4, pp. 449–488, 2004.

Wright, S. "Correlation and causation", *Journal of Agricultural Research*, Vol. 7, No. 3, pp. 557–585, 1921.

Yang, M., Jiang, M. "Hybrid spectrum access and power allocation based on improved hopfield neural networks", *Advanced Materials Research*, 588–589, pp. 1490–1494, 2012.

Zhang, Y., Gallipoli, D., Augarde, C., "Parameter identification for elasto-plastic modelling of unsaturated soils from pressuremeter tests by parallel modified particle swarm optimization", *Computers and Geotechnics*, Vol. 48, pp. 293–303, 2013a.

Zhang, Y., Gong, D.-W., Zhang, J.-H., "Robot path planning in uncertain environment using multi-objective particle swarm optimization", *Neurocomputing*, Vol. 103, pp. 172–185, 2013b.

Zhao, Y., Billings, S.A., Wei, H., He, F., Sarrigiannis, P.G., "A new NARX-based Granger linear and nonlinear casual influence detection method with applications to EEG data", *Journal of Neuroscience Methods*, Vol. 212, No. 1, pp. 79–86, 2013.

Chapter 2

What is a Correlation Machine?

Abstract. This chapter describes what a correlation machine is as well as the types of correlations machines. Correlations machines considered in this chapter are the auto-associative memory machine trained using genetic algorithm (GA), Expectation Maximization (EM) trained Gaussian mixed models and the principal component analysis (PCA) machine. These methods were used to model the antenatal HIV database. From this chapter, auto-associative memory machine is chosen as a correlation machine to be considered for the rest of this book.

2.1 Introduction

This book is on causality, correlation and artificial intelligence and the effect of these on decision making. It was described in Chapter 1 that the causal machine is a machine where the effect variable y is only derived from the causal variable x under the condition that x happens before y, x and y are connected in space and time and this connectivity is continuous. It was also described that because of this fact, the effect is correlated to the cause given a relevant time lag.

If one has three variables x, y and z and is aware that these variables are correlated then it is possible to predict any of these variables from the other 2 because all one needs to do is to make a prediction such that the existing correlation relationships are maintained.

This chapter considers three types of correlation machines and one is the auto-associative memory network where a vector is trained to recall itself. This of course can be viewed as training a network in order to identify the correlation relationships that exist amongst the data. Once this network is trained then whenever any of the variables are missing they can be identified by estimating them such that the correlation relationships are maintained. This can only be done with the help of an optimization technique.

The other correlation machine considered in this chapter is the principal component analysis (PCA) method which is trained using genetic algorithm (GA). If one was to take a matrix of data with one dimension corresponding to the number of variables and the other dimension corresponding to the number of observed cases then one can represent this in another space known as the eigenspace by calculating the eigensolution of the matrix. This then means that the data can be expressed in terms of eigenvalues and eigenvectors. This process is reversible. Once an observation has missing components this can be estimated by identifying the missing components so that the new completed data when added to the matrix does not distort the calculated eigensolution.

The other correlation machine applied in this chapter is the expectation maximization (EM) technique as applied to missing data estimation technique within the Gaussian mixture models (GMMs) framework. This essentially entails building GMMs describing the data and when an incomplete variable is introduced the free parameters of the GMMs are assumed and the missing values are estimated and using these missing values the GMMs parameters are re-estimated and this process is repeated until convergence.

This chapter describes these three methods and implement them for modeling the HIV phenomenon.

2.2 Correlation Machines

This section explores different types of correlation machines and these are the auto-associative memory network, PCA and GMMs based on the EM technique. The auto-associative memory network has been used quite extensively to model complex systems. Some of the applications of the auto-associative memory network include maximizing the number of correctly stored patterns (Masuda *et al.*, 2012a), reconstructing color images (Valle and Vicente, 2012), in neural binding problem (Hayworth, 2012), for memorization (Masuda *et al.*, 2012b) and for diagnosing power transformers (Miranda *et al.*, 2012). Some of the applications of the PCA include in brand power index (Bei and Cheng, 2013), structural assessment of zone subway performance assessment (Yang, 2013), testing analog circuits (Zhang and Chang, 2013), validating metabolic syndrome (Dusseault-Belanger *et al.*, 2013) and in canine hip dysplasia phenotypes (Duan *et al.*, 2013). The EM technique has been used widely for missing data estimation and some of these examples include in modeling forest growth (Mustafa *et al.*, 2012), evolving Electroencephalography (EEG) data (Kim *et al.*, 2011), estimating speed (Ramezani *et al.*, 2011), classifying volume (Yu *et al.*, 2010) and in medical application (Nelwamondo *et al.*, 2007).

2.2.1 Auto-associative memory network

The auto-associative variable estimation algorithms proposed in this chapter entails the use of a model which is built to remember its input as the output. As an example, suppose there is a set of data from the HIV database and it is a vector of

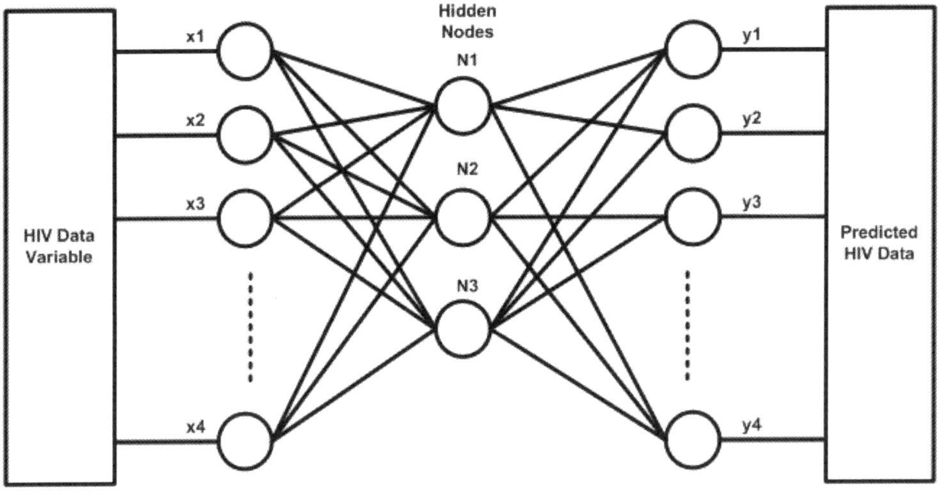

Figure 2.1 Auto-associative neural network

7 entries. Then a model can be constructed such that whenever this vector is presented a corresponding vector identical (nearly) to it is predicted. This model can be any viable mathematical model. For example, Figure 2.1 illustrates such a model which is based on neural networks (Marwala, 2009; Kakaei Lafdani *et al.*, 2013). Other models which can be used in this regard include support vector machines (He and Du, 2013; Liu *et al.*, 2013; Bifengrong, 2013) and rough sets (Marwala, 2009).

This model can be mathematically written as follows (Marwala, 2009):

$$\{Y\} = f(\{X\}, \{W\}). \tag{2.1}$$

In Equation 2.1, $\{Y\}$ is the output vector, $\{X\}$ the input vector and $\{W\}$ is the vector of network weights. Because in this framework a model is built to predict its own input vector, the input vector $\{X\}$ is approximately equal to output vector $\{Y\}$ and therefore$\{X\} \approx \{Y\}$.

Evidently, the input vector $\{X\}$ and output vector $\{Y\}$ will not always be exactly the same and, therefore, we will have an error function expressed as the difference between input and output vectors. Hence, the error can be formulated as:

$$\{e\} = \{X\} - \{Y\}. \tag{2.2}$$

Substituting the value of $\{Y\}$ from Equation 2.1 into Equation 2.2 the following expression is obtained:

$$\{e\} = \{X\} - f(\{X\}, \{W\}). \tag{2.3}$$

We intend for the error to be minimized and to be non-negative and therefore, the error function can be rewritten as a square of Equation 2.3:

$$\{e\} = (\{X\} - f(\{X\}, \{W\}))^2. \tag{2.4}$$

In the case of estimation, some of the values for the input vector $\{X\}$ may not be available. Therefore, we can divide the input vector elements into $\{X\}$ known vector represented by $\{X_k\}$ and $\{X\}$ unknown vector represented by $\{X_u\}$. Rearranging Equation 2.4 in terms of $\{X_k\}$and $\{X_u\}$ we have:

$$\{e\} = \left(\begin{Bmatrix} \{X_k\} \\ \{X_u\} \end{Bmatrix} - f\left(\begin{Bmatrix} \{X_k\} \\ \{X_u\} \end{Bmatrix}, \{W\} \right) \right)^2. \tag{2.5}$$

The error vector in Equation 2.5 can be reduced into a scalar by integrating over the size of the input vector and the number of training examples as follows:

$$E = \left\| \left(\begin{Bmatrix} \{X_k\} \\ \{X_u\} \end{Bmatrix} - f\left(\begin{Bmatrix} \{X_k\} \\ \{X_u\} \end{Bmatrix}, \{W\} \right) \right) \right\|. \tag{2.6}$$

In this book, Equation 2.6 is called the unknown data estimation equation. To approximate the missing input values, Equation 2.6 is minimized. The inter-relationships that exist in the data are thus stored in the function f and the network weights $\{W\}$. There are many types of optimization methods that can be applied to accomplish this task and in this chapter GA is used.

In this chapter, we apply the MLP to model the auto-associative memory network and this is referred to as f in the fitness function in Equation 2.6. The variable estimation model explained in this section is illustrated in Figure 2.2. In summary, the fitness function is derived from the error function of the input and output vector obtained from the trained auto-associative memory network. The error function is then minimized using GA to approximate the missing variables given the observed variables $\{X_k\}$, network weights $\{W\}$ and the model f describing the interrelationships and the rules describing the data.

2.2.2 Principal component analysis

PCA is a statistical procedure that is usually applied to identify patterns in high dimensional data expressed as eigenvectors and eigenvalues (Abdi and Williams, 2010; Jolliffe, 2002). The data can then be represented in a manner that emphasizes congruency and opposites. Further characteristics is that, after identifying the data patterns, the data set can be compressed without losing its essence. Parente and Sutherland (2013) applied the PCA on turbulent combustion data, Debelak and Tran (2013) applied the PCA in psychology, Zhang and Zhou (2013) applied it to

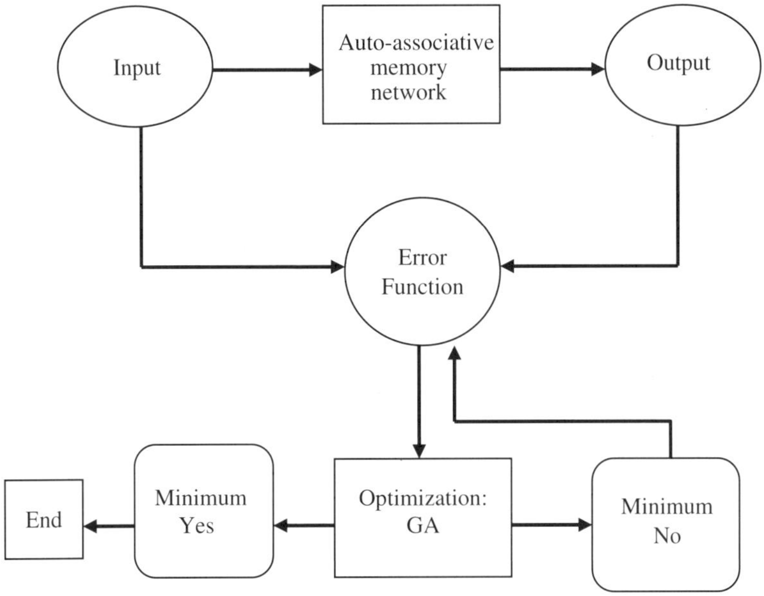

Figure 2.2 Unknown data estimation model key: GA, Genetic Algorithm

reconstruct spectral reflectance, Yingwang and Ying (2013) in process monitoring as well as Ji and Zhao (2013) for port logistics development.

The PCA is applied by following this procedure (Jolliffe, 2002):

1. Subtract the mean of each dimension of the data.
2. Compute the covariance matrix $[A]$ of the data.
3. Calculate the eigenvalues $[\Lambda]$ and eigenvectors $[V]$ of the covariance matrix.

The covariance matrix A of a matrix $[X]$ with a dimension m by n is as follows:

$$[A] = ([X] - [\mu])([X] - [\mu])^T. \tag{2.7}$$

Here n is the dimension corresponding to the number of observations and m corresponds to the size of each observation. The eigensolution of matrix $[A]$ is calculated by identifying the eigenvalue λ and eigenvector $\{v\}$ such that:

$$[A]\{v\} = \lambda\{v\}. \tag{2.8}$$

This equation can be generalized as follows:

$$[A][V] = [\Lambda][V]. \tag{2.9}$$

Combining Equations 2.7 and 2.9 gives the following equation:

$$[([X] - [\mu])([X] - [\mu])^T][V] = [\Lambda][V]. \tag{2.10}$$

The input data can be divided into the unknown component represented by subscript u as well as the known component represented by subscript k to give the following equation from Equation 2.10:

$$\left[\left(\begin{bmatrix}[X_u]\\ [X_k]\end{bmatrix} - [\mu]\right)\left(\begin{bmatrix}[X_u]\\ [X_k]\end{bmatrix} - [\mu]\right)^T\right][V] = [\Lambda][V]. \tag{2.11}$$

Equation 2.11 can be rearranged to give the following equation where $[e]$ is the error matrix:

$$[e] = \left[\left(\begin{bmatrix}[X_u]\\ [X_k]\end{bmatrix} - [\mu]\right)\left(\begin{bmatrix}[X_u]\\ [X_k]\end{bmatrix} - [\mu]\right)^T\right][V] - [\Lambda][V]. \tag{2.12}$$

Equation 2.12 can be reduced to a scalar by using the Euclidean norm to give the following expression:

$$E = \sum\sum\left(\left[\left(\begin{bmatrix}[X_u]\\ [X_k]\end{bmatrix} - [\mu]\right)\left(\begin{bmatrix}[X_u]\\ [X_k]\end{bmatrix} - [\mu]\right)^T\right][V] - [\Lambda][V]\right)^2. \tag{2.13}$$

Equation 2.13 implies that given the mean, eigenvalues and eigenvectors the missing component of the data can be estimated by minimizing Equation 2.13. The assumption of the PCA are that the data are randomly sampled, that the relationships between all observed data are linear and that each pair of observed variables should be bivariate normal distribution. The procedure outlined in this section is represented in Figure 2.3.

2.2.3 Expectation maximization algorithm

In this section, we apply the missing data framework called the EM algorithm to implement the correlation model. We characterize this as a correlation model because the problem is framed as consisting of a full vector of information with some components missing and thus the missing components are inferred from the observed components plus some model that characterizes the interrelationships that exist amongst the data.

The EM algorithm has been successfully applied to a number of important problems such as in the identification of system parameters in mixed models (Yao, 2013), to estimate parameters of nonlinear mixed-effects models (Fu *et al.*, 2013), to design a multilevel thresholding method (Liang and Yin, 2013), for channel estimation (Sheu and Sheen, 2013), for designing a proportional hazards model (Kim *et al.*, 2013), in land use models (Claassen *et al.*, 2013), and for modelling unconstrained latent variable models with categorical indicators (Weissman, 2013).

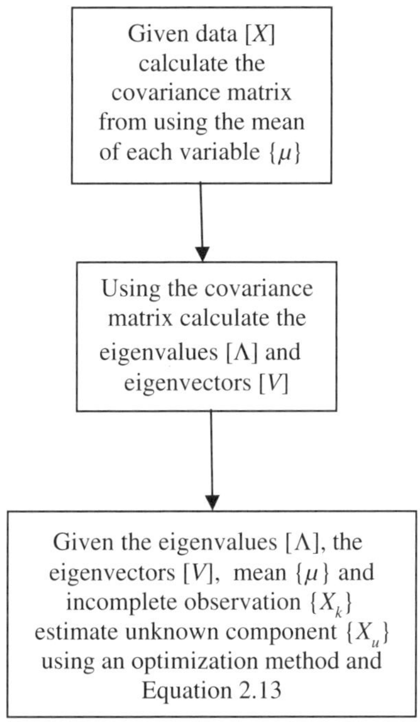

Figure 2.3 Unknown data estimation model using PCA

In the EM algorithm, the maximum likelihood estimation of the parameter vector is iteratively identified by repeating the following steps (Sundberg, 1974; Dempster *et al.*, 1977; Little and Rubin, 1987).

- *The expectation E-step*: In the existence of a set of parameter approximations, for instance a mean vector and covariance matrix for a multivariate normal distribution, the *E-step* approximates the conditional expectation of the complete-data log-likelihood in the presence of the observed data and the parameter approximations.
- *The maximization M-step:* The *M-step* finds the parameter approximations that maximize the complete-data log-likelihood from the *E-step* given a complete-data log-likelihood.

These steps are repeated until the algorithm converges. On implementing the EM algorithm, suppose $\{y\}$ denotes incomplete data which is composed of values of observable variables, and let $\{z\}$ be the missing data then $\{y\}$ and $\{z\}$ can be fused to create a complete data set. By setting p to be the joint probability density function of the complete data with parameters granted by the vector $\{\theta\} : p(\{y\}, \{z\}|\{\phi\})$ then this function can also be thought of as a complete data likelihood which is a function of $\{\phi\}$. Moreover, the conditional distribution of the missing data granted the observed data can be mathematically written as follows (Little and Rubin, 1987):

$$p(\{z\}|\{y\},\{\phi\}) = \frac{p(\{y\},\{z\}|\{\phi\})}{p(\{y\}|\{\phi\})} = \frac{p(\{y\}|\{z\},\{\phi\})p(\{z\}|\{\phi\})}{\int p(\{y\}|\{z\},\{\phi\})p(\{z\},\{\phi\})d\{z\}}. \tag{2.14}$$

Equation 2.14 is derived by using Bayes theorem and the law of total probability. This process necessitates the observation likelihood in the light of the unobservable data $p(\{y\}|\{z\},\{\phi\})$ and the probability of the unobservable data $p(\{z\}|\{\phi\})$. Accordingly, the EM algorithm recursively re-approximates missing values and as a result advances the initial approximation of the missing values by creating new estimations $\{\phi_n\}$, $\{\phi_{n+1}\}$, etc. This procedure can be written as follows (Little and Rubin, 1987):

$$\{\phi\}_{n+1} = \arg\max_{\phi} G(\{\phi\}). \tag{2.15}$$

Here $G(\{\phi\})$ is the expected value of the log-likelihood and can be expressed mathematically as follows (Little and Rubin, 1987):

$$G(\{\phi\}) = \sum_{z} p(\{z\}|\{y\},\{\phi\}_n) \log p(\{y\},\{z\}|\{\phi\}). \tag{2.16}$$

Simply expressed, the parameter $\{\phi\}_{n+1}$ is the value that maximizes the conditional expectation of the complete data log-likelihood in the light of the observed variables.

GMMs have been applied with the EM algorithm to solve for the missing data. Nelwamondo *et al.* (2006) classified bearing faults using GMMs while Yao and Liu (2013) applied GMM to extract robust distribution. Duarte-Carvajalino *et al.* (2013) applied GMM to task-driven adaptive statistical sensing whereas Rajkumar *et al.* (2013) applied GMM for color image segmentation. Pathak and Raj (2013) applied GMM for secure speaker verification and identification.

Suppose a sample of m data points is written as $\{y\}_1,\ldots,\{y\}_m$ and is sampled from one of the n Gaussian distributions and z_i which indicates which Gaussian y_i is from, the probability for $\{y\}$ can be written as follows (Little and Rubin, 1987):

$$P(\{y\}|z=i,\{\phi\}) = (2\pi)^{-D/2}|\sigma_i| \exp\{-1/2(\{y\}-\{\mu\}_i)^T\sigma_i^{-1}(\{y\}-\{\mu\}_i)\}. \tag{2.17}$$

In Equation 2.17, D is the dimension of the Gaussian distribution whereas $\{\mu\}_i$ and $\{\sigma\}_i$ are the mean and the variance of the ith Gaussian distribution vector. The objective of the EM algorithm is to approximate the unknown parameters $\{\phi\} = [\{\mu\}_1,\ldots,\{\mu\}_n,\{\sigma\}_1\ldots\{\sigma\}_n, P(\{z\}_{i=1}),\ldots,P(\{z\}_{i=n})]$ demonstrating the expected value and variance of each Gaussian in addition to the probability of sampling any Gaussian at any given time. The parameter n is the number of Gaussian distribution functions under deliberation.

In the E-step accordingly, the unobserved z may be estimated given the observed values using the last values as (Little and Rubin, 1987):

$$\begin{aligned} P(z_j = i|\{y\}_j, \{\phi\}_t) &= \frac{P(z_j = i, \{y\}_j|\{\phi\}_t)}{P(\{y\}_j|\{\phi\}_t)} \\ &= \frac{P(\{y\}_j|z_j = i, \{\phi\}_t)P(z_j = i|\{\phi\}_t)}{\sum_{k=1}^{n} P(\{y\}_j|z_j = k, \{\phi\}_t)P(z_j = k|\{\phi\}_t)}. \end{aligned} \tag{2.18}$$

In the M-step, the expected value of the log-likelihood of the joint event requires to be maximized. This expected value of the log-likelihood that is to be maximized can be expressed as follows (Dempster *et al.*, 1977):

$$\begin{aligned} G(\{\phi\}) &= E_z\left[\ln \prod_{i=1}^{m} P(\{y\}_j, \{z\}|\{\phi\})|\{y\}_j\right] \\ &= \sum_{j=1}^{m}\sum_{i=1}^{n} P(z_j = i|\{y\}_j, \{\phi\}_t)\ln P(z_j = i, \{y\}_j|\{\phi\}). \end{aligned} \tag{2.19}$$

The maximization of Equation 2.19 must be estimated given the following constraint (Dempster *et al.*, 1977):

$$\sum_{i=1}^{n} P(z_j = i|\{\phi\}) = 1. \tag{2.20}$$

The cost function in Equation 2.19 can be combined with the constraint in Equation 2.20 by calculating the Lagrangian, L, as indicated below (Dempster *et al.*, 1977):

$$L(\{\phi\})$$

$$= \left(\sum_{j=1}^{m}\sum_{i=1}^{n} P(z_j = i \left| \begin{array}{l} \{y\}_j, \{\phi\}_t)\left(-\frac{D}{2}\ln(2\pi) - \frac{1}{2}\ln|\sigma_i| \right. \\ \left. \quad -\frac{1}{2}(\{y\}_j - \{\mu\}_i)^T\sigma_i^T(\{y\}_j - \{\mu\}_i) + \ln(P(z_j = 1|\{\phi\})\right) \\ -\lambda\left(\sum_{i=1}^{n} P(z_j = i|\{\phi\}) - 1\right) \end{array} \right. \right) \tag{2.21}$$

Here λ is a parameter known as the Lagrangian multiplier. To solve for the new estimate $\{\phi\}_{n+1}$, Equation 2.21 can be maximized by calculating the gradient of the Lagrangian with respect to parameter $\{\phi\}$ and then equating this to zero as:

$$\frac{\partial L(\{\phi\})}{\partial\{\phi\}} = 0. \tag{2.22}$$

By calculating Equation 2.22, then the following expression is obtained (Dempster *et al.*, 1977):

$$\begin{aligned} P(\{z\}_j|\{\phi\}) &= \frac{1}{\lambda}\sum_{j=1}^{m} P(z_j = i|\{y\}_j, \{\phi\}_t) \\ &= \frac{\sum_{j=1}^{m} P(z_j = i|\{y\}_j, \{\phi\}_t)}{\sum_{k=1}^{n}\sum_{j=1}^{m} P(z_j = i|\{y\}_j, \{\phi\}_t)} \\ &= \frac{1}{m}\sum_{j=1}^{m} P(z_j = i|\{y\}_j, \{\phi\}_t). \end{aligned} \tag{2.23}$$

From this expression, ϕ_{n+1} can thus be estimated. This process is repeated until convergence is reached.

2.3 Genetic Algorithm

GA is applied in this chapter to minimize the objective function in Equations 2.6 and 2.13 and, thereby, estimate the missing information from the interrelationships that exist in the data. GAs are procedures applied to identify solutions to objective functions in an optimization problem by applying the philosophies of evolutionary biology to computer science (Michalewicz, 1996; Mitchell, 1996; Belevičius *et al.*, 2013). GA borrows concepts from evolutionary biology for instance inheritance, mutation, natural selection and recombination to estimate an optimal solution to difficult problems (Goldberg, 2002). In GA the identification of an optimal solution is viewed as a competition among a population of evolving potential solutions. An objective function estimates the objective state of each solution to evaluate whether it adds to the next generation of solutions. Using mechanisms related to gene transfer in sexual reproduction, the procedure produces a new population of potential solutions (Goldberg, 2002; Marwala, 2010; Xhafa *et al.*, 2013; Smolka, 2013).

Lin *et al.* (2013) successfully applied GA to solve a multi-objective simulation optimization problem in surgical services whereas Krishnamoorthi and Sathiya Devi (2013) successfully applied GA for image retrieval. Robles-Ortega *et al.* (2013) successfully applied GA to produce textured urban models whereas Zamani (2013) successfully applied GA for resource-constrained scheduling problem.

The three vital drivers of GAs are (Michalewicz, 1996): Description of the objective function, description as well as application of the genetic representation, and description and execution of the genetic operators. GA has been proven to be successful in optimization problems such as wire routing, scheduling, adaptive control, game playing, cognitive modeling, transportation problems, traveling salesman problems, optimal control problems, and database query optimization (Shieh and Chiou, 2013).

To implement GA, the following steps are followed: initialization, selection, reproduction, and termination.

2.3.1 Initialization

When GA is initiated, a specified number of possible individual solutions are randomly generated to form an initial population. It is ideally supposed to be a large number to include a fair representation of the solution space. The size of the population depends on the problem at hand and largely depends on the size of variables. For instance, if there are three variables that are missing, the size of the population must be higher than if there were two variables that were missing. The next sections describe the drivers of GA which are crossover, mutation, reproduction and termination.

2.3.2 Crossover

Given a population of possible solutions to the optimization problem, crossover operator is a method that combines different solutions thereby exchanging genetic information in the population. One way of doing this is by cutting pairs of chromosomes (i.e. possible solutions) at random positions along their lengths and swapping over the cut segments. Crossover takes place with a particular probability and this connects successful operators together.

Yuan *et al.* (2013) proposed a crossover method and applied this successfully to solve a traveling salesmen problem using GAs whereas Gunasekaran and Iruthayarajan (2013) applied binary crossover successfully for contour optimization of suspension insulators. Mudaliar and Modi (2013) successfully applied the m-crossover operator in a travelling salesman problem whereas Burjorjee (2013) successfully applied uniform crossover to optimize complex problems. Nagata and Kobayashi

(2013) successfully applied edge assembly crossover for the traveling salesman problem.

Simple crossover method is applied in this chapter and more details on this are in Goldberg (1989). The mechanism of simple crossover, involves selecting one crossover point and a binary string from beginning of chromosome to the crossover point and copy from one parent, and the remaining is copied from the second parent. For instance, when **11101**011 undergoes simple crossover with 11011**101** it becomes **11101101**.

2.3.3 Mutation

The mutation operator selects a binary digit of the chromosomes (i.e. solution) randomly and reverses it and this introduces to the population of solutions new information (Horng *et al.*, 2012). Mutation is conducted with a particular probability and normally the probability of mutation is low.

Rajakumar (2013) successfully applied static and adaptive mutation-based GA to model complex systems whereas Haga and Suehiro (2013) successfully applied mutation for automatic test case generation. Tang and Tseng (2013) successfully applied adaptive mutation to model complex systems. Bhattacharjee and Sarmah (2012) successfully applied genetic mutation for combinatorial optimization.

This chapter uses binary mutation and its mechanism includes writing a number in binary form and inverting it such that 1101**1**010 is muted to form 1101**0**010.

2.3.4 Reproduction

For each generation, a reproduction of the proportion of the current population is selected to breed a new population (Oh and Moon, 2010). Reproduction is executed using the fitness-based procedure, where solutions that have lower errors, as measured by the error function are assigned a higher probability of being reproduced.

Yan *et al.* (2011) successfully applied granular ranking and distant reproduction to optimize a complex function using multi-objective GA whereas Zhang *et al.* (2010) successfully applied sexual reproduction to create an adaptive GA based on the Baldwin effect.

In this chapter, we use the roulette reproduction method and in this technique each possible solution is allocated the error (Equations 2.6 and 2.13) which is used to assign the probability of reproduction for each possible solution (Zhang *et al.*, 2012; Hu *et al.*, 2012).

Given the fitness f_i (defined as the inverse of the error in Equations 2.6 and 2.13) of individual i in the population, the probability that this solution is reproduced can be mathematically written as follows (Hameed *et al.*, 2011; Laseetha and

Sukanesh, 2011):

$$p_i = \frac{f_i}{\sum_{j=1}^{N} f_j}. \tag{2.24}$$

Here N is the size of the population. GA guarantees that potential solutions with low errors have a high probability that they will be reproduced than those with higher errors.

2.3.5 Termination

The procedures of crossover, mutation and reproduction are reiterated until a stopping criterion is reached. This normally means that either a preferred solution is identified that fulfills the objective function or a stipulated number of generations has been achieved or the algorithm has converged.

GA procedure can be expressed algorithmically as follows (Goldberg, 1989; Marwala, 2009):

1. Choose the population size and generate an initial population.
2. Estimate the fitness of each individual in the population using Equations 2.6 or 2.13.
3. Iterate:
   a. Select individuals with lower error to reproduce.
   b. Produce a new population using a crossover technique.
   c. Mutate the resulting population to produce offspring.
   d. Estimate the fitness of each offspring.
   e. Substitute individual in the population with higher errors with individuals with low errors.
4. Repeat until the termination criterion is reached.

The missing data estimation technique described in this section can be summarized as in Figure 2.4.

2.4 Multi-layer Perceptron

Equation 2.1 is a function that maps some input vector $\{X\}$ to the output vector $\{Y\}$ using some weight vector $\{W\}$. In this chapter, such mapping is done using the MLP which will be described briefly in this section. The MLP contains hidden units and output units, as well as one hidden layer as shown in Figure 2.1 and can be

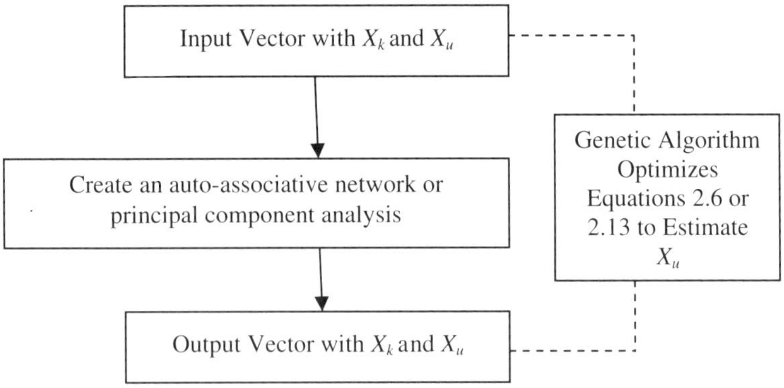

Figure 2.4 A missing data estimation technique using genetic algorithm

mathematically represented as follows (Bishop, 1995):

$$y_k = f_{outer}\left(\sum_{j=1}^{M} w_{kj}^{(2)} f_{inner}\left(\sum_{i=1}^{d} w_{ji}^{(1)} x_i + w_{j0}^{(1)}\right) + w_{k0}^{(2)}\right). \tag{2.25}$$

Here, $w_{ji}^{(1)}$ indicates weight in the first layer, going from input i to hidden unit j while $w_{j0}^{(1)}$ indicates the bias for the hidden unit j, M is the number of hidden units, d is he number of inputs, f_{inner} function represents the activation of the inner layer and in this chapter is the hyperbolic tangent function, f_{outer} function represents the activation of the outer layer and in this chapter a logistic function and the subscript 0 corresponds to a weight associated with a bias. Equation 2.25 is estimated using the scaled conjugate method and the details of the procedure followed are in Bishop (1995).

2.5 Experimental Comparison

In this section, we evaluate the so-called three correlation machines using data from the antenatal clinics in South Africa. Details of this are explained in Marwala (2009). The data was gathered by the Department of Health of South Africa and consists of multiple input variables. Data attributes used in this chapter are the HIV status, Education level, Gravidity, Parity, Age Group and Age Gap. The HIV status is represented in a binary form, where 0 and 1 represent negative and positive, respectively. The education level was measured using integers representing the highest grade successfully completed, with 13 representing tertiary education. Gravidity is the number of pregnancies, complete or incomplete, experienced by a female, and this variable is represented by an integer between 0 and 11. Parity is the number of instances the individual has given birth and multiple births are

Table 2.1 Summary of variables used from HIV data

Variable number	Variable	Type	Range
1	Age	Integer	14–50
2	Age Gap	Integer	1–7
3	Education level	Integer	0–13
4	Gravidity	Integer	0–13
5	Parity	Integer	0–14
11	HIV status	Binary	[0, 1]

Table 2.2 Results obtained from the implementation of NN-GA, PCA-GA and GMM-EM

	NN-GA (%)	PCA-GA (%)	GMM-EM (%)
HIV Classification	63	61	66
Education Level	28	40	62
Gravidity	89	65	32
Parity	79	80	61
Age	80	24	80
Age Gap	96	35	92

considered as one birth. Both parity and gravidity are vital, as they demonstrate the reproductive activity as well as the reproductive health state of the woman. Age gap is a measure of the age difference between the pregnant woman and the prospective father of the child. The data variables and their ranges are shown in Table 2.1.

The first model was an auto-associative neural networks trained using genetic algorithm (NN-GA), the second the PCA model which used genetic algorithm to estimate missing variables (PCA-GA) and the third was GMM trained using Expectation Maximization algorithm (GMM-EM). The details of all these can be found in Marwala (2009). A total of 100 instances were randomly extracted from the test dataset and variables therein removed. The resulting dataset, with missing values, was used to test the performance of the three missing data estimation schemes. The results obtained are shown in Table 2.2.

The NN-GA performed well except on estimating the education level whereas the PCA-GA performed well except on estimating the age gap, age of a mother and educational level and the GMM-EM performed well except on estimating gravidity. These results indicate that NN-GA gives the best results followed by GM-EM and then PCA-GA. The PCA-GA performed worse because of it assumes linear relations between variables and this is not valid for a complicated HIV problem.

2.6 Conclusions

This chapter described three types of correlation machines and these were an auto-associative neural network trained using genetic algorithm (NN-GA), the second was the PCA that used genetic algorithm to estimate missing variable (PCA-GA), and the third was GMM trained using Expectation Maximization algorithm (GMM-EM). When these methods were implemented to model the antenatal HIV database the NN-GA performed the best followed by the GMM-GA and then the PCA-GA.

References

Abdi, H., Williams, L.J. "Principal component analysis", *Wiley Interdisciplinary Reviews: Computational Statistics*, Vol. 2, pp. 433–459, 2010.

Bei, L.-T., Cheng, T.-C. "Brand power index-using principal component analysis", *Applied Economics*, Vol. 45, No. 20, pp. 2954–2960, 2013.

Belevičius, R., Jatulis, D., Šešok, D. "Optimization of tall guyed masts using genetic algorithms", *Engineering Structures*, Vol. 56, pp. 239–245, 2013.

Bhattacharjee, K.K., Sarmah, S.P. "A modified shuffled frog leaping algorithm with genetic mutation for combinatorial optimization" Lecture Notes in Computer Science (including subseries Lecture Notes in Artificial Intelligence and Lecture Notes in Bioinformatics), Vol. 7654 LNAI (PART 2), pp. 513–522, 2012.

Bifengrong, S. "Fault diagnosis of valve train of internal combustion engine based on the artificial neural network and support vector machine", *Advanced Materials Research*, Vols. 605–607, pp. 729–733, 2013.

Bishop, C.M. Neural Networks for Pattern Recognition. Oxford: Oxford University Press, 1995.

Burjorjee, K.M. "Explaining optimization in genetic algorithms with uniform crossover", FOGA 2013 — *Proceedings of the 12th ACM Workshop on Foundations of Genetic Algorithms*, pp. 37–49, 2013.

Claassen, R., Hellerstein, D., Kim, S.G. "Using mixed logit in land use models: Can expectation-maximization (EM) algorithms facilitate estimation?", *American Journal of Agricultural Economics*, Vol. 95, No. 2, pp. 419–425, 2013.

Debelak, R., Tran, U.S. "Principal Component Analysis of Smoothed Tetrachoric Correlation Matrices as a Measure of Dimensionality", *Educational and Psychological Measurement*, Vol. 73, No. 1, pp. 63–77, 2013.

Dempster, A.P. Laird, N.M., Rubin, D.B. "Maximum Likelihood from Incomplete Data via the EM Algorithm", *Journal of the Royal Statistical Society. Series B (Methodological)*, Vol. 39, No. 1, pp. 1–38, 1977.

Duan, F., Ogden, D., Xu, L., Liu, K., Lust, G., Sandler, J., Dykes, N.L., Zhu, L., Harris, S., Jones, P., Todhunter, R.J., Zhang, Z. "Principal component analysis of canine hip dysplasia phenotypes and their statistical power for genome-wide association mapping", *Journal of Applied Statistics*, Vol. 40, No. 2, pp. 235–251, 2013.

Duarte-Carvajalino, J.M., Yu, G., Carin, L., Sapiro, G. "Task-driven adaptive statistical compressive sensing of Gaussian mixture models", *IEEE Transactions on Signal Processing*, Vol. 61, No. 3, art. no. 6331558, pp. 585–600, 2013.

Dusseault-Belanger, F., Cohen, A.A., Hivert, M.-F., Courteau, J., Vanasse, A. "Validating metabolic syndrome through principal component analysis in a medically diverse, realistic cohort", *Metabolic Syndrome and Related Disorders*, Vol. 11, No. 1, pp. 21–28, 2013.

Fu, L., Lei, Y., Sharma, R.P., Tang, S. "Parameter estimation of nonlinear mixed-effects models using first-order conditional linearization and the EM algorithm", *Journal of Applied Statistics*, Vol. 40, No. 2, pp. 252–265, 2013.

Goldberg, D.E. "Genetic Algorithms in Search, Optimization, and Machine Learning. Reading", Addison-Wesley, MA, 1989.

Goldberg, D.E. "The Design of Innovation: Lessons from and for Competent Genetic Algorithms", Addison-Wesley, Reading, MA, 2002.

Gunasekaran, S., Iruthayarajan, M.W. "Contour optimization of suspension insulators using real coded genetic algorithm with simulated binary crossover", *Proceedings of the 2013 International Conference on Pattern Recognition, Informatics and Mobile Engineering*, PRIME 2013, art. no. 6496501, pp. 360–364, 2013.

Haga, H., Suehiro, A. "Automatic test case generation based on genetic algorithm and mutation analysis", *Proceedings — 2012 IEEE International Conference on Control System, Computing and Engineering*, ICCSCE 2012, art. no. 6487127, pp. 119–123, 2013.

Hameed, M.A., Ramachandram, S., Jadaan, O.A. "Information gain clustering through roulette wheel genetic algorithm (IGCRWGA): A novel heuristic approach for personalisation of cold start problem", *Proceedings — 2011 International Conference on Computational Intelligence and Communication Systems*, CICN 2011, art. no. 6112911, pp. 470–475, 2011.

Hayworth, K.J. "Dynamically partitionable autoassociative networks as a solution to the neural binding problem", *Frontiers in Computational Neuroscience*, pp. 1–22, 2012.

He, H., Du, X. "Distributed neural networks model based on support vector machine classifier for flatness recognition", *ICIC Express Letters*, Vol. 7, No. 1, pp. 235–239, 2013.

Horng, M.-F., Chen, Y.-T., Chu, S.-C., Pan, J.-S., Liao, B.-Y., Hsu, J.-P., Lin, J.-N. "A genetic algorithm with elite mutation to optimize cruise area of mobile sinks in hierarchical wireless sensor networks", Lecture Notes in Computer Science (including subseries Lecture Notes in Artificial Intelligence and Lecture Notes in Bioinformatics), Vol. 7654 LNAI (PART 2), pp. 402–412, 2012.

Hu, X., He, Y., Ni, W., Zhang, Y. "A privacy-preserving data publishing method based on genetic algorithm with roulette wheel", *Jisuanji Yanjiu yu Fazhan/Computer Research and Development*, Vol. 49, No. 11, pp. 2432–2439, 2012.

Ji, S., Zhao, L. "Key factors analysis of port logistics development based on principal component analysis", *Applied Mechanics and Materials*, Vols. 253–255 (PART 1), pp. 1522–1526, 2013.

Jolliffe, I.T. "Principal Component Analysis", Series: Springer Series in Statistics, 2nd edition, Springer, NY, 2002.

Kakaei Lafdani, E., Moghaddam Nia, A., Ahmadi, A. "Daily suspended sediment load prediction using artificial neural networks and support vector machines", *Journal of Hydrology*, Vol. 478, pp. 50–62, 2013.

Kim, S.H., Yang, H.J., Ng, K.S. "Incremental expectation maximization principal component analysis for missing value imputation for coevolving EEG data", *Journal of Zhejiang University: Science C*, Vol. 12, No. 8, pp. 687–697, 2011.

Kim, Y., Kim, J., Jang, W. "An EM algorithm for the proportional hazards model with doubly censored data", *Computational Statistics and Data Analysis*, Vol. 57, No. 1, pp. 41–51, 2013.

Krishnamoorthi, R., Sathiya Devi, S. "A simple computational model for image retrieval with weighted multifeatures based on orthogonal polynomials and genetic algorithm", *Neurocomputing*, Vol. 116, pp. 165–181, 2013.

Laseetha, T.S.J., Sukanesh, R. "Synthesis of linear antenna array using genetic algorithm with cost based roulette to maximize side lobe level reduction", *WSEAS Transactions on Communications*, Vol. 10, No. 12, pp. 385–394, 2011.

Liang, Y.-C., Yin, Y.-C. "A new multilevel thresholding approach based on the ant colony system and the EM algorithm", *International Journal of Innovative Computing, Information and Control*, Vol. 9, No. 1, pp. 319–337, 2013.

Lin, R.-C., Sir, M.Y., Pasupathy, K.S. "Multi-objective simulation optimization using data envelopment analysis and genetic algorithm: Specific application to determining optimal resource levels in surgical services", *Omega* (United Kingdom), Vol. 41, No. 5, pp. 881–892, 2013.

Little, R.J.A., Rubin, D.B. "Statistical Analysis with Missing Data", Wiley Series in Probability and Mathematical Statistics. New York: John Wiley & Sons. pp. 134–136, 1987.

Liu, M., Wang, M., Wang, J., Li, D. "Comparison of random forest, support vector machine and back propagation neural network for electronic tongue data classification: Application to the recognition of orange beverage and Chinese vinegar", *Sensors and Actuators, B: Chemical*, Vol. 177, pp. 970–980, 2013.

Marwala, T. "Computational intelligence for missing data imputation, estimation and management: Knowledge optimization techniques", *Information Science Reference Imprint, IGI Global Publications*, New York, USA, 2009.

Marwala, T. "Finite Element Model Updating Using Computational Intelligence Techniques", Springer-Verlag, London, UK, 2010.

Masuda, K., Fukui, B., Kurihara, K. "A weighting approach for autoassociative memories to maximize the number of correctly stored patterns", *Proceedings of the SICE Annual Conference*, art. no. 6318692, pp. 1520–1524, 2012a.

Masuda, K., Fukui, B., Kurihara, K. "A weighting approach for autoassociative memories to improve accuracy in memorization", *Proceedings of the International Joint Conference on Neural Networks*, art. no. 6252785, 2012b.

Michalewicz, Z. "Genetic Algorithms + Data Structures = Evolution Programs", Berling Heidelberg, New York: Springer-Verlag, 3rd Edition, 1996.

Miranda, V., Castro, A.R.G., Lima, S. "Diagnosing faults in power transformers with autoassociative neural networks and mean shift", *IEEE Transactions on Power Delivery*, Vol. 27, No. 3, art. no. 6176288, pp. 1350–1357, 2012.

Mustafa, Y.T., Tolpekin, V.A., Stein, A. "Application of the expectation maximization algorithm to estimate missing values in Gaussian Bayesian network modeling for forest growth", *IEEE Transactions on Geoscience and Remote Sensing*, Vol. 50, (5 PART 2), art. no. 6060908, pp. 1821–1831, 2012.

Mitchell, M. "An Introduction to Genetic Algorithms", MIT Press, Cambridge, MA, 1996.

Mudaliar, D.N., Modi, N.K. "Unraveling Travelling Salesman Problem by genetic algorithm using m-crossover operator", *International Conference on Signal Processing, Image Processing and Pattern Recognition 2013*, ICSIPR 2013, 1, art. no. 6497974, 2013.

Nagata, Y., Kobayashi, S. "A powerful genetic algorithm using edge assembly crossover for the traveling salesman problem", *INFORMS Journal on Computing*, Vol. 25, No. 2, pp. 346–363, 2013.

Nelwamondo, F.V., Marwala, T., Mahola, U. "Early classifications of bearing faults using hidden Markov models, Gaussian mixture models, Mel-frequency Cepstral coefficients and fractals", *International Journal of Innovative Computing, Information and Control*, Vol. 2, No. 6, pp. 1281–1299, 2006.

Nelwamondo, F.V., Mohamed, S., Marwala, T. "Missing data: A comparison of neural network and expectation maximization techniques", *Current Science*, Vol. 93, No. 11, pp. 1514–1521, 2007.

Oh, S., Moon, B.-R. "Automatic reproduction of a genius algorithm: Strassen's algorithm revisited by genetic search", *IEEE Transactions on Evolutionary Computation*, art. no. 5299113, Vol. 14, No. 2, pp. 246–251, 2010.

Parente, A., Sutherland, J.C. "Principal component analysis of turbulent combustion data: Data pre-processing and manifold sensitivity", *Combustion and Flame*, Vol. 160, No. 2, pp. 340–350, 2013.

Pathak, M.A., Raj, B. "Privacy-preserving speaker verification and identification using Gaussian mixture models", *IEEE Transactions on Audio, Speech and Language Processing*, Vol. 21, No. 2, art. no. 6289356, pp. 397–406, 2013.

Rajakumar, B.R. "Static and adaptive mutation techniques for genetic algorithm: A systematic comparative analysis", *International Journal of Computational Science and Engineering*, Vol. 8, No. 2, pp. 180–193, 2013.

Rajkumar, G.V.S., Rao, K.S., Rao, P.S. "Colour image segmentation with integrated left truncated bivariate Gaussian mixture model and hierarchical clustering", *Advances in Intelligent Systems and Computing*, 199 AISC, pp. 163–170, 2013.

Ramezani, A., Moshiri, B., Abdulhai, B., Kian, A.R. "Estimation of free flow speed and critical density in a segmented freeway using missing data and Monte Carlo-based expectation maximisation algorithm", *IET Control Theory and Applications*, Vol. 5, No. 1, pp. 123–130, 2011.

Robles-Ortega, M.D., Ortega, L., Feito, F.R. "A new approach to create textured urban models through genetic algorithms", *Information Sciences*, Vol. 243, pp. 1–19, 2013.

Sheu, J.-S., Sheen, W.-H. "An EM algorithm-based disintegrated channel estimator for OFDM AF cooperative relaying", *IEICE Transactions on Communications*, E96-B, No. 1, pp. 254–262, 2013.

Shieh, M.-Y., Chiou, J.-S. "Design of multi-sensory integrated interactive robot with genetic algorithm", *Advanced Science Letters*, Vol. 19, No. 9, pp. 2615–2617, 2013.

Smolka, J. "Genetic algorithm shape optimisation of a natural air circulation heating oven based on an experimentally validated 3-D CFD model", *International Journal of Thermal Sciences*, Vol. 71, pp. 128–139, 2013.

Sundberg, R. "Maximum likelihood theory for incomplete data from an exponential family", *Scandinavian Journal of Statistics*, Vol. 1, No. 2, pp. 49–58, 1974.

Tang, P.-H., Tseng, M.-H. "Adaptive directed mutation for real-coded genetic algorithms", *Applied Soft Computing Journal*, Vol. 13, No. 1, pp. 600–614, 2013.

Valle, M.E., Vicente, D.M.G. "Sparsely connected autoassociative lattice memories with an application for the reconstruction of color images", *Journal of Mathematical Imaging and Vision*, Vol. 44, No. 3, pp. 195–222, 2012.

Weissman, A. "Global Convergence of the EM Algorithm for Unconstrained Latent Variable Models with Categorical Indicators", *Psychometrika*, Vol. 78, No. 1, pp. 134–153, 2013.

Xhafa, F., Herrero, X., Barolli, A., Barolli, L., Takizawa, M. "Evaluation of struggle strategy in Genetic Algorithms for ground stations scheduling problem", *Journal of Computer and System Sciences*, Vol. 79, No. 7, pp. 1086–1100, 2013.

Yan, T.-S., Guo, G.-Q., Li, W. "An improved multi-objective genetic algorithm based on granular ranking and distant reproduction", *Proceedings — 2011 International Conference of Information Technology, Computer Engineering and Management Sciences*, ICM 2011, 1, art. no. 6113378, pp. 151–154, 2011.

Yang, H. "The application of principal component analysis in zone subway structural performance assessment", *Advanced Materials Research*, Vol. 639–640, No. 1, pp. 625–629, 2013.

Yao, W. "A note on EM algorithm for mixture models", *Statistics and Probability Letters*, Vol. 83, No. 2, pp. 519–526, 2013.

Yao, Z., Liu, W. "Extracting robust distribution using adaptive Gaussian Mixture model and online feature selection", *Neurocomputing*, Vol. 101, pp. 258–274, 2013.

Yingwang, X., Ying, D. "Combination method of kernel principal component analysis and independent component analysis for process monitoring", *Applied Mechanics and Materials*, Vols. 249–250, pp. 153–158, 2013.

Yu, L., Snapp, R.R., Ruiz, T., Radermacher, M. "Probabilistic principal component analysis with expectation maximization (PPCA-EM) facilitates volume classification and estimates the missing data", *Journal of Structural Biology*, Vol. 171, No. 1, pp. 18–30, 2010.

Yuan, S., Skinner, B., Huang, S., Liu, D. "A new crossover approach for solving the multiple travelling salesmen problem using genetic algorithms", *European Journal of Operational Research*, Vol. 228, No. 1, pp. 72–82, 2013.

Zamani, R. "A competitive magnet-based genetic algorithm for solving the resource-constrained project scheduling problem", *European Journal of Operational Research*, Vol. 229, No. 2, pp. 552–559, 2013.

Zhang, C., Chang, G. "Analog circuits test by using principal component analysis", *Applied Mechanics and Materials*, Vol. 278–280, pp. 709–713, 2013.

Zhang, L., Chang, H., Xu, R. "Equal-width partitioning roulette wheel selection in genetic algorithm", *Proceedings — 2012 Conference on Technologies and Applications of Artificial Intelligence*, TAAI 2012, art. no. 6395007, pp. 62–67, 2012.

Zhang, M.-M., Zhao, S.-G., Wang, X. "Sexual reproduction adaptive Genetic Algorithm based on Baldwin effect and simulation study", *Xitong Fangzhen Xuebao/Journal of System Simulation*, Vol. 22, No. 10, pp. 2329–2332, 2010.

Zhang, Y., Zhou, S. "Research on reconstruction of spectral reflectance based on principal component analysis", *Applied Mechanics and Materials*, Vol. 262, pp. 53–58, 2013.

Chapter 3

What is a Causal Machine?

Abstract. This chapter describes what a causal machine is as well as the types of causal machines. Machines that are framed as causal machines which are considered in this chapter are the multi-layer perceptron (MLP), radial basis function (RBF) and fuzzy inference system. These are framed as causal machines by ensuring that the cause happens before the effect, that the cause and the effect are connected and that there is a flow of information from the cause to the effect. The MLP was successfully used to identify the causal relationship between the militarized interstate dispute (MID) variables (causes) and conflict status (effect) whereas the RBF was used to identify the causal relationship between the dissolved gas analysis data (causes) and condition of bushings (effect) while fuzzy inference system was used to identify the causal relationship between causes (input fuel, air, reference level, and disturbance) and effect (steam flow rate).

3.1 Introduction

This book is on causality, correlation and artificial intelligence. It was described in Chapter 1, that the causal machine is a machine where the cause (x) is transmitted to the effect (y). It was also described that because of this fact, the effect is correlated to the cause. Bélaïd and Abderrahmani (2013) conducted a causal study between electricity consumption and economic growth in Algeria given the structural changes and they observed that there was a causal relationship between electricity consumption and economic growth. Sung and Song (2013) studied the causal link between public policies and exports of renewable energy technologies and found that there was a causal relationship between export and the contribution of renewable energy to the total energy supply.

Candelon *et al.* (2013) applied Granger causality model in distribution tails of oil markets and observed that the integration level between crude oil markets decreases during volatile periods and that this implied the need for dynamic energy policy in volatile conditions. Croux and Reusens (2013) studied the causal link between the stock prices and future economic activity and observed that stock prices predict future growth of the gross domestic product (GDP). Other applications of the concept of causality are to assess whether financial system activity affect tax revenues in Malaysia (Taha *et al.*, 2013) and to relate airfreight transport and economic development (Button and Yuan, 2013).

This chapter considers three types of a causal machines that are based on the extension of transmission theory of causality known as the projectile theory of causation. One of these is the multi-layer perceptrons (MLPs) where the input (cause) is transmitted to the output (effect). The MLP in this context is constructed using the measured data that have been gathered with repeated observations of the cause and the effect phenomena. The second type of a causal model is the radial basis function (RBF) where the input (cause) is transmitted into the output (effect). The RBF in this context is constructed using the measured data that have been gathered from the causal data with repeated observations of the cause and the effect phenomena. The third type of a causal model is fuzzy inference system. In this context, the output (effect) is obtained from the input (cause). The fuzzy inference system is identified using the cause and effect data as well as expert knowledge from a human observer who has some understanding of the cause and effect. This chapter describes three methods and implement them for modeling the HIV data.

3.2 Induction, Deduction, and Abduction

This section describes important concepts that were introduced by the philosopher Pierce which are induction, deduction and abduction (Moore and Robin, 1964; Kudo *et al.*, 2009; Kakas and Flach, 2009). These concepts are deemed important in our study of causality. Suppose we have a relationship between two variables x and y which can be mathematically expressed as follows:

$$y = f(x). \tag{3.1}$$

Here f is a model that describes this relationship. If you have observed data x and y then induction can be described as a process of extracting the model from the observed data. In engineering terminology, this concept is often described as system identification. In plain language, suppose x indicates that the grass is wet and y indicates the fact that it is has rained, then the model to be inducted from the observation is as follows: If the grass is wet then the probability that it has rained is positive. Within causality context this means that suppose you have observed that whenever x is observed then a particular y is observed and you have many observations that express multiple modes, then one can use the principle of induction to extract the causal model or within the context of this chapter a causal machine.

Suppose an observation y is made and a given model is known, then one can use abduction techniques to infer the value of x. In simple terms, if it is observed that the grass is wet, then one can use the general knowledge or model to infer what x is and this process is called abduction. In mathematical context, this is called an inverse problem and it is non-unique in the sense that there might be many values of x that can explain y. In simple terms, suppose you observe that the grass is wet and you have the model that says that the grass is wet if water has been poured into the grass, then the principle of abduction can be used to infer that perhaps the grass is wet because it rained. Of course it may be that the grass is wet because someone has poured water into it. The principles of probability may marginalize the explanations that are unlikely. Within causality perspective suppose you know the causal relationship that HIV causes AIDS. When you observe that the person has AIDS then you can be able to infer that he has HIV.

Suppose the input is x is known and that the causal model is known, then deduction can be used to infer y. Within the context of the grass, you know that it is raining and are aware of the causal relationship that the grass gets wet when it rains and there you can deduce that because it is raining then the grass is wet.

Minnameier (2010) explained that inductive reasoning is not necessarily creative because it generalizes information that already exist and that abduction is associated with creativity whereas Åsvoll (2013) applied abduction, deduction, and induction to understand the methodological processes in interpretative case studies, and Ing (2009) applied induction, abduction, and deduction to predict future innovation in service systems.

3.3 What is Causality?

In this chapter, we explore the concept of causality and use this to build causal machines. In Chapter 1, we explored what causality is and even reviewed different models of causality and explored the concept of a causal machine. We reviewed the transmission theory of causality where causal information is transmitted from the cause to the effect (Ehring, 1986; Kistler, 1998; Salmon, 1984). Artificial intelligence methods such as the MLPs, RBFs and fuzzy inference system which are described in this chapter are good examples of methods that are based on the concept of a projectile theory of causality where cause happens before the effect and there is information flow between the cause and the effect.

Furthermore, in Chapter 1, the projectile theory of causality was described as an extension of the transmission theory of causality. In this theory, information is transmitted with a specific velocity (intensity and configuration) and attributes in the same way as a projectile. The information leaves the cause with a certain velocity indicating a specific intensity of the cause and it either reaches the effect or falls short or overshoots the target and from this it is possible to build a probability distribution of causation. Attributes are intended to account for multi-variables causation.

In essence, in this chapter, we define causality as a process through which information from a variable called the cause which can have any number of dimensions is transmitted to (causes) another variable called the effect which can be multidimensional to happen. Causality is detected in a number of ways and the first mechanism is to evaluate whether there is a correlation between the cause and the effect. If there is no correlation at all then there is no causality between the cause and the effect. If there is a correlation then we investigate whether the cause happened before the effect. If this is true, then there is possibly causation otherwise there is no causation. Then the next step is to study whether there is an information flow from the cause to the effect as well as the mechanisms of this information flow. The procedure for determining causation is expressed in Figure 3.1.

Zhang *et al.* (2013) proposed a causal model for joint assessment of placebo and treatment-specific effects in clinical trials whereas Serbanuta *et al.* (2013) proposed the maximal causal models for sequentially consistent systems. Bennoui *et al.* (2012) applied cooperating behavioral Petri networks analysis for distributed causal model and implemented this for diagnosis whereas Dewey (2012)

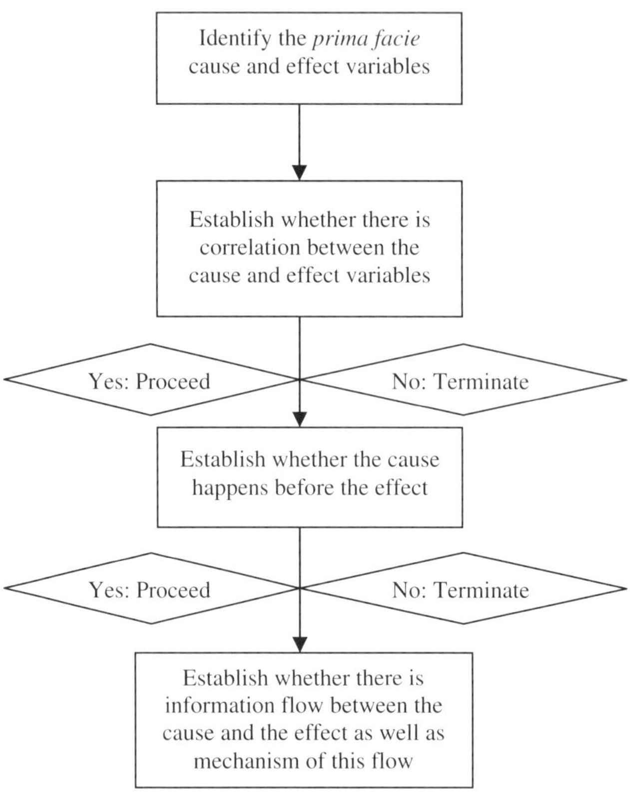

Figure 3.1 The procedure for establishing causation

applied representation theorem for assessing causal models. Agbloyor *et al.* (2013) investigated causal relations between financial markets and foreign direct investment (FDI) in Africa. They observed that a more advanced banking system causes more FDI flows.

Causality can be sensed by detecting the correlation between the cause and the effect or by evaluating how relevant the cause is in the determination of the effect and by tracking the information from the cause to the effect. Detection of causality by studying the correlation between the cause and the effect as well as by evaluating how relevant the cause is in the determination of the effect is a necessary condition but not a sufficient condition for causation. The sufficient condition for causality is for there to be an information flow from the cause to the effect.

3.4 Multi-layer Perceptron Causal Machine

In this section, we introduce the MLP which is used to build a causal machine by ensuring that the cause (input) is transmitted to the effect (output), the cause happens before the effect and that the cause and the effect are connected. More detail on the MLP can be found in Bishop (1995). In the chapter, the MLP is considered to be a broad structure for approximating the relationships between the cause and the effect. In this chapter, we consider supervised multi-layered perceptrons to map the cause to the effect.

Rababaah and Tebekaemi (2012) made an assumption that there was a causal relationship between the goodness of fit and electric load and applied this successfully to monitor residential buildings by mapping the goodness of fit to electric load using MLP neural networks.

Sanz *et al.* (2012) made an assumption that there was a causal link between torsional stiffness and condition of a gear. They then successfully applied MLP for condition monitoring.

Asl *et al.* (2011) assumed that there was a causal link between meteorological variables (air temperature, relative humidity, sunshine hours, evaporation, wind speed, and soil temperature) and global solar radiation. They then successfully applied MLP neural networks successfully to model this causal relationship.

Kitikidou and Iliadis (2010) assumed that there was a causal link between life expectancy, healthy life years, infant mortality, GDP as well as GDP growth rate (causes) and air quality (effect). They applied the MLP to map this relationship between the cause and the effect.

Vaferi *et al.* (2011) successfully applied MLP to identify a reservoir model whereas Achkar and Owayjan (2010) applied MLP to successfully control magnetic bearings.

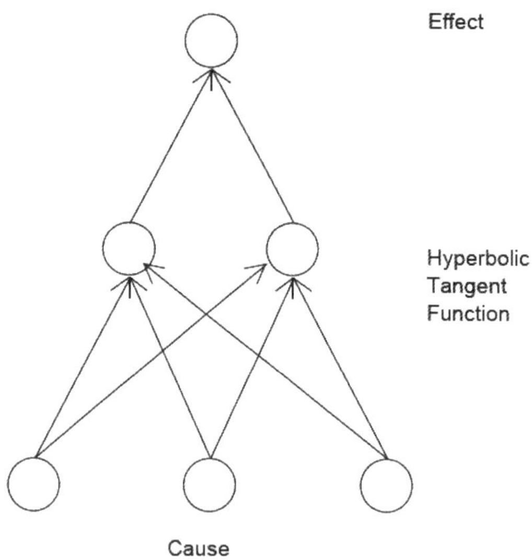

Figure 3.2 The MLP network with the hyperbolic tangent function in the hidden layer and a logistic function in the outer layer

3.4.1 The architecture of the MLP causal machine

In the MLP causal machine, the connections between the cause and the hidden layer as well as between the hidden layer and the effect are adjustable weight parameters also known as free parameters in statistics. The MLP network is shown in Figure 3.2. The MLP model is capable of estimating any relationship between the cause and the effect provided that the number of hidden neurons is sufficiently large.

In the MLP network, there are interconnected cross-couplings between the cause and the hidden nodes, and between the hidden nodes and the effect. If we assume that x is the cause and y is the effect, a mapping function between the input and the output may be expressed as follows for the MLP architecture with a hyperbolic tangent function in the hidden layer and logistic function in the output layer:

$$y = \frac{1}{1 + e^{-\left(\sum_{j=1}^{M} w_j \tanh\left(\sum_{i=0}^{N} w_{ij} x_i\right) + w_0\right)}}. \tag{3.2}$$

In Equation 3.2, N is the number of inputs units, M is the number of hidden neurons, x_i is the ith input unit, w_{ij} is the weight parameter between input i and hidden neuron j and w_j is the weight parameter between hidden neuron j and the output neuron. Within the context of the projectile theory of causality, Equation 3.2 indicates that the projectile either reaches the target or undershoots (either 0 or 1 or anything in between) but never overshoots.

Equation 3.2 is used to describe the causal relationship and this requires identifying the sizes of the hidden nodes and the estimation of the network weights. There are a number of critical concerns that ought to be considered to learn this causal relationship and these include generalization of the observed causal data. There are methods that have been suggested to handle this subject and they include cross-validation, early-stopping, and regularization.

There are two procedures that can be applied to train an MLP causal machine to learn the causal data. These methods are the maximum likelihood and Bayesian procedures. Maximum likelihood technique finds network weights that maximize the capacity of a trained MLP to better forecast the observed data whereas the Bayesian method creates the probability distribution of the network model given the causal data. The first objective which is to identify a vector of network weights that maximize the forecasting capacity of the MLP is to create an objective function. The objective function is, essentially, an extent of the difference between the forecasts of the model and the observed causal data.

In a two-class classification problem, the objective function is the difference between the MLP's estimated output and the target output, t, for all training causal data. E is the cross-entropy error function and is given by (Bishop, 1995):

$$E = -\sum_{p=1}^{P} \{t_p \ln(y_p) + (1 - t_p) \ln(1 - y_p)\}. \tag{3.3}$$

There are many benefits of using the cross-entropy function and these comprise the fact that it permits the output to be interpreted probabilistically and these are advantageous in the light of the probability interpretation of causation. The MLP causal machine is trained by iteratively fine-tuning the weight parameters, w, to minimize the objective function given by Equation 3.3. This is realized by randomly resetting the MLP network weights and then correcting the weight parameters using any optimization method and the details of these can be seen in (Marwala, 2013). One such optimization method is the scaled conjugate gradient technique which has the advantage that it is efficient in converging (Møller, 1993).

Generalization is the capability of a trained MLP neural network model to classify the causal data that were not used to train the MLP network. Essentially, on looking for a network that generalizes, one identifies a balance between ability of a network to remember the training data, i.e. training it with the capability of the network to forecast unseen data. The generalization of performance is a true reflection of the capability of an MLP network. One way of achieving this is to divide the causal data into training and testing data sets.

This section described the MLP network and how it is trained to generalize and how it can be used to characterize the data that relates the cause and the effect of any system as long as sufficient data of the cause and the effect are available. The MLP architecture was described and the general relationship between the cause x and the effect y was described within the context of the MLP network.

3.4.2 Interstate conflict

The MLP is used to identify the causal link between the Militarized Interstate Dispute (MID) variables and the conflict status. The MLP propagates information from the cause to the effect and thus is regarded to follow the projectile theory of causality. More details on interstate conflict are found in Marwala and Lagazio (2011). In the identification of the causal link between the MID and the conflict status, the MID variables which are used are the following:

- *Allies* which is a binary measure coded 1 if the two countries in question have any form of military alliance and a 0 if they do not have military alliance.
- *Contingency* is also binary, coded 1 if both countries share a border and 0 if they do not share a border.
- *Distance* measures the distance between the two countries' capitals.
- *Major power* is a binary variable coded 1 if either or both states are a major power and 0 if they are not.
- *Democracy* is measured on a scale where 10 is a maximum democracy and -10 is a maximum autocracy.
- *Dependency* is measured as the sum of the two countries' import and export with its partner divided by the GDP of the stronger country.
- *Capability* is the logarithm, to the base of 10, of the ratio of the total population plus the number of people in urban areas plus industrial energy consumption plus iron and steel production plus the number of military personnel in active duty plus military expenditure in dollars in the last 5 years measured on stronger country to weak country.

Politically relevant population which are dyads, having a major power, are selected for the reason that it sets a difficult test for prediction. Neglecting all distant dyads comprised of weak states imply that we overlook a great deal of the influence with variables that are not very responsive to policy intervention (distance and national power). Doing this reduces the predictive efficacy of such variables. Investigating this indicate a strong performance even when the analysis is limited to politically relevant group. By concentrating merely on dyads with major powers or are contiguous, the discriminative capacity of the MLP neural network on a difficult set of cases is tested. The MLP is trained with only informative data because every dyad is regarded as a risk of encountering a dispute. It is, however, difficult for the MLP to discriminate between the two classes (disputes dyad-years and the peaceful ones) because the politically relevant group is more similar than the all-dyad data set.

The COW data are used to generate training and testing sets. The MID data is collected such that the causes occur before the effect in that the input data are matched against the conflict/peace status the following year. It is also assumed that there is a connection between the input data and the output data and that there is information flow between the input and the output. For example, there is information flow from a variable dependency to whether the two countries go to war or not and in the event that they are heavily dependent then they will not go to war.

The training set for this chapter contained 1000 randomly chosen dyads (representing two countries) with 500 from conflict group and 500 from peace group. The test set contained 392 dyads which were conflict dyads and 392 which were non-conflict dyads.

The MLP neural network requires one to choose the best architecture to give good classification results and the best combination of the number of hidden units was 10, and activation functions were hyperbolic tangent function in the inner layer and logistic function in the outer layer. The MLP was trained using the scaled conjugate gradient method. The MLP predicted at the rates of 75% and 76%, respectively for conflict and peace with the averaged results for correct predictions of 75.5% for the MLP.

3.5 Radial Basis Function Causal Machine

3.5.1 Theoretical foundation

This section introduces RBF to build a causal machine. Similar to how it was described in the previous section, the RBF becomes a causal machine when the input happened before the output, the input and the output are connected and there is a flow of information between the input and the output. In this chapter, the RBF is viewed as a feed-forward network where the cause is transmitted forward into the effect and is trained using a supervised training algorithm (Bishop, 1995). Thus the RBF can be viewed as following the projectile theory of causality. The RBF is typically organized with a single hidden layer of units whose activation function is chosen from a type of function termed basis functions. The activation of the hidden units, in an RBF neural network, is given by a non-linear function of the distance between the input vector and a prototype vector (Bishop, 1995).

Tian *et al.* (2013) assumed the causal relationship between high temperature duration, degradation rate, nitrogen content, average oxygen concentration and maturity degree as causes and compost quality as the effect. When they applied the RBF, they found this technique to be feasible and effective. Sermpinis *et al.* (2013) applied

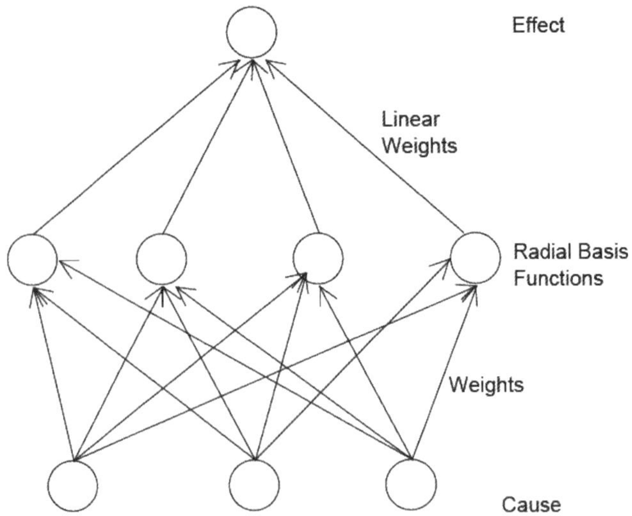

Figure 3.3 The RBF network with the Gaussian activation function in the hidden layer and a linear function in the outer layer

the RBF to successfully predict foreign exchange rates whereas Yuan *et al.* (2013) successfully applied the RBF to successfully predict classes of ion channel-targeted toxins. Chang (2013) successfully applied the RBF to successfully predict wind energy conversion system power whereas Shariati-Rad *et al.* (2013) successfully applied the RBF to model spectral interferences and nonlinearity and Rout *et al.* (2012) successfully applied the RBF to predict the stock indices.

Whereas alike the MLP in many ways, the RBF networks have a number of benefits. They are less disposed to problems of non-stationary inputs (causes) (Bishop, 1995). The RBF network can, therefore, be illustrated as presented in Figure 3.3 and can be written as follows:

$$y_k(\{x\}) = \sum_{j=1}^{M} w_{jk} \exp(-\beta(\{x\}) - \{c\}_j)^2. \tag{3.4}$$

In Equation 3.4, w_{jk} denotes the output weights, each corresponding to the connection between a hidden unit and an output unit, M denotes the number of hidden units, $\{c\}_j$ is the center for the jth neuron, $\phi_j(\{x\})$ is the jth non-linear activation function, $\{x\}$ the input vector, and $k = 1, 2, 3, \ldots, M$ (Bishop, 1995). Once more as for the MLP, the choice of the number of hidden nodes, M, is part of the model selection process. Some optimization approaches for instance genetic algorithms, simulated annealing, and particle swarm optimization have been applied to choose the optimal RBF design (Marwala, 2009).

The activation selected in this chapter for the hidden layers is the Gaussian distribution function (Marwala, 2009; Bishop, 1995). The RBF is different from the MLP in that it has weights in the outer layer only, while the hidden nodes have what are called the centers. Training an RBF network involves identifying two sets of parameters: The centers and the output weights which can both be looked at as free parameters in a regression framework.

The centers and network weights can both be identified concurrently using the full Bayesian method or can then again be identified using the maximization of expectation procedure (Bishop, 1995). In this chapter, a two-phase training process was used to first identify the centers, followed by a determination of the network weights. The first phase is to use a self-organizing map, the so-called the *k-means* clustering technique, to determine the centers (Marwala, 2009). The step of identifying the centers only contemplates the input space, while the identification of the network weights studies both the input and output space.

The *k-means* technique is intended to group objects based on attributes into k subdivisions. For the RBF, k is equal to the number of centers, M. The objective of the *k-means* algorithm is to identify the centers of natural clusters in the data and to assume that the object attributes form a vector space. It realizes this objective by minimizing the total intra-cluster variance, or, the squared error function which can be expressed as follows (Hartigan, 1975; Hartigan and Wong, 1979; Marwala, 2009):

$$E = \sum_{i=1}^{C} \sum_{x_j \in S_i} (\{x\}_j - \{c\}_i)^2. \tag{3.5}$$

In Equation 3.5, C is the number of clusters in S_i, $i = 1, 2, \ldots, M$ and $\{c\}_i$ is the center of all the points $x_j \in S_i$.

Lloyd algorithm (Lloyd, 1982) is applied to find the cluster centers. Lloyd algorithm is initialized by randomly dividing the input space into k initial sets or using heuristic data. The mean point is calculated for each set and then a new partition is built by associating each point with the closest center. The centroids are then re-calculated for the new clusters, and the process is repeated by changing these two steps until convergence. Convergence is attained when the centroids no longer change or the points no longer switch clusters.

The network weights are identified given the training data and the estimated centers using the Moore–Penrose pseudo inverse (Moore, 1920; Penrose, 1955; Ben-Israel and Greville, 2003). The approximation of the network weights given the centers is a linear process. The RBF equation can be written as follows after the centers have been identified:

$$[y_{ij}] = [\phi_{ik}][w_{kj}]. \tag{3.6}$$

Here, $[y_{ij}]$ is the output matrix, with i representing the number of training examples and j representing the number of outputs. Parameter $[\phi_{ik}]$ is the activation function matrix in the hidden layer, i represents the training examples, k is the number of hidden neurons while $[w_{kj}]$ is the weight matrix. The weight matrix, $[w_{kj}]$ can be identified by inverting the activation function matrix $[\phi_{ik}]$ if it is a square matric. Nevertheless, this matrix is not square and, consequently, it cannot be inverted using standard matrix methods. Fortunately, this matrix can be inverted using the Moore–Penrose pseudo-inverse technique which is expressed mathematically as follows (Penrose, 1955):

$$[\phi_{ik}]^* = ([\phi_{ik}][\phi_{ik}]^T)^{-1}[\phi_{ik}]^T. \tag{3.7}$$

This, consequently, indicates that the weight matrix may be approximated by using the pseudo inverse factor as follows (Marwala, 2009):

$$[w_{kj}] = [\phi_{ik}]^*[y_{ij}]. \tag{3.8}$$

3.5.2 Applications to condition monitoring

Bushings are vital components in electricity and are used in substation buildings, transformers, locomotives, and switchgears (Dhlamini and Marwala, 2004). Bushing failures normally lead to cataclysmic incident for instance a tank rupture, violent explosion of the bushing and fire (Lord and Hodge, 2003). Many diagnostic tools, e.g. on-line Partial Discharge analysis on-line power factor, and infra-red scanning, have been developed to diagnose transformer failure (Mojo, 1997).

This chapter applies the RBF to model the relationship between the cause and effect that is used for bushing condition monitoring. The cause variables are variables obtained from a Dissolve Gas-in-oil Analysis (DGA) test and the effect variable is the health state of bushings. The cause variables are described here as pseudo-cause variables because the data from the DGA are not direct causes but are proxies for the real cause. They are in essence the manifestation of the cause and because of this are deemed causes. Pseudo-causal variables as proxy causes happen before the effect, and they are connected albeit not directly to the effect and, however, even though there is no direct flow of information from the pseudo-cause to the effect as proxies for the cause then we will deem that there is a flow of information from the cause to the effect.

A DGA is the most frequently used diagnostic method for transformers bushings (Dhlamini and Marwala, 2004). A DGA is applied to identify oil breakdown, moisture presence and partial discharge activity. Fault gases are created by the degradation of the transformer and bushing oil and solid insulation such as paper and pressboard, which are all made of cellulose. The gases formed from the transformer and bushing operation are (Dhlamini and Marwala, 2004):

1. Hydrocarbons gases: hydrogen (H_2), methane (CH_4), ethane (C_2H_6), ethylene (C_2H_4), acetylene (C_2H_2), and hydrogen (H_2);
2. Carbon oxides: carbon monoxide (CO) and carbon dioxide (CO_2); and
3. Non-fault gases: nitrogen (N_2) and oxygen (O_2).

These 10 variables were used as causal variables and related to the health of the bushings using the RBF network. The RBF network had 10 pseudo-causal variables and 8 hidden units and 1 effect variable. The Gaussian activation function was used in the hidden layer. About 500 hundred faulty data and 500 not-faulty data were used to train the network and 500 faulty data and 500 not-faulty data were used to test the RBF causal machine and the results on the test data gave 95% accuracy on diagnosing the health status of bushings.

3.6 Fuzzy Inference System Causal Machine

3.6.1 Theoretical foundation

Fuzzy inference system is used as a causal machine in this chapter and this is achieved by ensuring that the input happens before the output, the input and the output are connected and that there is a flow of information from the input to the output. Fuzzy inference system in this section maps the cause to an effect by means of linguistic rules that involve the if-then statements (Zadeh, 1965; Novák *et al.*, 1999; Novák, 2005; Wright and Marwala, 2006; Marwala, 2013). Figure 3.4 displays the stages used to create a cause and effect mapping using fuzzy inference system. Because of the transmission of information from the cause to the effect, fuzzy inference system is viewed to follow the projectile theory of causality. Peña-Ayala and Mizoguchi (2012) successfully applied fuzzy inference system successfully to model causal behavior and approximate causal results in decision-making whereas Peña-Ayala *et al.* (2012) successfully applied fuzzy systems to model causal linkages of learning in the classroom. Chen *et al.* (2011) successfully applied fuzzy systems to model the causal model for decision-making model in information technology investment whereas Bouallegue *et al.* (2011) successfully applied fuzzy inference system to model causal relationships for on-line fault detection and isolation of bond graph.

Zhang *et al.* (2011) successfully applied fuzzy inference system to assess the causal relationship between health warnings and Australian smokers' psychosocial and quitting behaviors whereas Fiss (2011) successfully applied fuzzy theory to understand causal relationships.

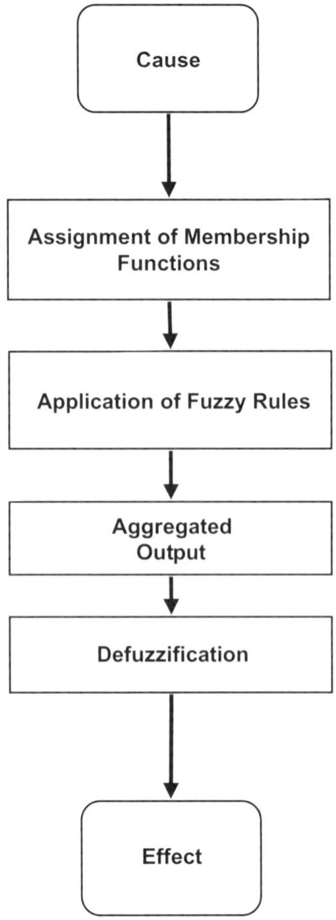

Figure 3.4 An illustration of fuzzy inference system to model a cause and effect relationship

In classical set theory, an object either belongs to or does not belong to a particular set and it is conceivable to define if an object is an element of a particular set for the reason that a set has separate boundaries. A different method of discriminating this is that an object's membership of a set is either true or false. For example, if a set x characterizes all possible heights of people, one could define a "tall" subset for any person who is above or equal to a specific height x, and anyone below x doesn't belong to the "tall" subset but to a "short" subset. This illustrates clearly that maybe a set does not have to be either tall or short and that there is a degree of tallness or shortness.

Fuzzy inference system as proposed by Zadeh (1965) ensures a relaxed representation of sets of objects and does not have as distinct boundaries as a classical set and the objects are characterized by a degree of membership to a specific set (Biacino and Gerla, 2002; Hájek, 1998). Accordingly, transitional values of objects can be characterized in a manner that is closer to the mode in which the human brain thinks contrasted to the crisp boundaries in classical sets.

A membership function describes the degree to which an object is a member of a certain set. The membership function is a function that maps the input (cause) to a number between 0 and 1, representing the degree that a particular input variable is a member of a particular set (Klir and Folger, 1988; Klir *et al.*, 1997; Klir and Yuan, 1995). A membership function can be a function of any shape.

The example above illustrates that there are two subgroups one for tall and one for short and they overlay. Like so, a person can have a fractional membership of a set, and consequently, responsible for the amount to which the person is both tall and short.

Logical operators produce new fuzzy sets from the current fuzzy sets. In set theory, there are operators to express logic and these are intersection, union, and the complement (Bocheński, 1959; Enderton, 2001; Hazewinkel, 2001; Humberstone, 2011). These operators are applicable to fuzzy inference system and have been modified to handle fractional memberships. The AND operator which is the intersection of two fuzzy sets is computed using a minimum operation whereas the OR operator which is the union of two fuzzy sets is computed by a maximum operation. These operators together with rules are used to compute the final output fuzzy set.

Fuzzy rules express the conditional declarations to model the cause–effect connection of a system using natural language. Linguistic rules are expressed in the *if-then* format and apply logical operators and membership functions to create an effect. A vital characteristic of fuzzy inference system is the application of linguistic variables which are variables that use words as a substitute of numbers (Zadeh, 1965). All linguistic variables consider linguistic values that match a fuzzy set, and the set of values that are factored are termed the term sets. For instance, a linguistic variable *height* may contain the following term set {*very tall, tall, medium, short, and very short*}. A single fuzzy rule is as follows:

$$\textbf{if } x \textbf{ is } M \textbf{ then } y \textbf{ is } N \tag{3.9}$$

here M and N are fuzzy sets defined for the cause and effect space correspondingly. Both x and y are linguistic variables, while M and N are linguistic values represented by membership functions. All rules contain two portions: the antecedent and the consequent. The antecedent is the constituent of the rule located between the *if-then* rules, and maps the cause x to the fuzzy set M, using a membership function. The consequent is the constituent of the rule after the then, and maps the effect y to a membership function. The input membership values can be viewed as weighting factors that regulate fuzzy output sets. A fuzzy system entails these *if-then* rules which are calculated separately and the inputs are shared using the *AND* operator.

Each rule is assessed for a cause set and the equivalent effect for the rule attained. If a cause matches two values of a linguistic variable then the rules related to these values are assessed. If the antecedent is true to an extent, the consequent will be true to an extent (Zadeh, 1965). The extent of each linguistic effect value is then calculated using a logical sum for each membership function (Zadeh, 1965) after which all the sums for a particular linguistic variable can be combined. These comprise the application of an inference technique which maps the result onto an output membership function (Zadeh, 1965).

To conclude de-fuzzification procedure is a process that calculates a single numeric value indicating the effect. One technique of calculating the degree of each linguistic output value is to choose the maximum of all rules describing this linguistic output value, and the output is considered the center of gravity of the area under the effected portion of the output membership function. The application of fuzzy rules and inference approach to create a de-fuzzified output is called a Fuzzy Inference System. The method described above is called the Mamdani fuzzy approach (Mamdani, 1974; Mamdani and Assilian, 1975).

In this chapter, we implement the Takagi–Sugeno–Kang neuro-fuzzy technique (Takagi and Sugeno, 1985; Araujo, 2008). This technique is alike the Mamdani technique besides the consequent part which is different. The *if-then* statement of a Sugeno fuzzy system articulates the output of each rule as a function of the input variables (Sugeno and Kang, 1988; Sugeno, 1985).

The *if-then* statement of a Sugeno fuzzy system articulates the output of each rule as a function of the input variables as follows (Wright and Marwala, 2006):

$$\textbf{if } x \textbf{ is } M \textbf{ AND } y \textbf{ is } N \textit{ then } z = \mathrm{f(x, y)}. \tag{3.10}$$

If the consequence of each rule is a linear combination of the causes plus a constant, then this is called first-order Sugeno fuzzy model and can be expressed as follows (Wright and Marwala, 2006):

$$z = px + qy + c. \tag{3.11}$$

Otherwise, the consequence of a rule can be a constant. The final output of the Sugeno fuzzy inference system is a weighted average of the outputs from each rule.

3.6.2 Application to a steam generator

This chapter models the cause–effect relationship of data obtained from a Steam Generator at Abbott Power Plant in the USA which is available online. The data set has 9600 samples. The cause–effect model contains 4 causes and 1 effect. The causes are the input fuel, air, reference level, and disturbance defined by the load level. The effect is the steam flow rate.

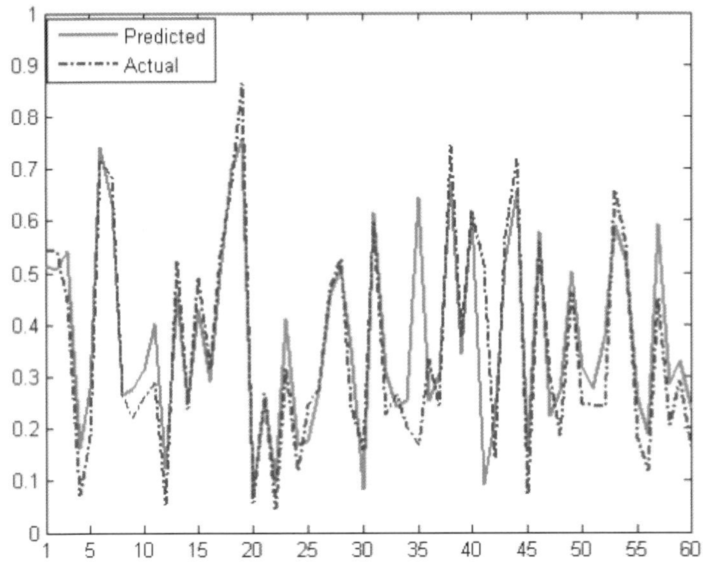

Figure 3.5 Predicted vs. actual values for the first 60 points of the test set

Fuzzy approach was applied to model the cause–effect relationship using the polynomial π function membership function and 16 fuzzy rules and the results for the prediction of the steam flow rate on the test data set are shown in Figure 3.5 (Wright and Marwala, 2006).

3.7 Conclusions

This chapter introduced three causal machines which are based on the principles of projectile theory of causality. These causal machines were based on the MLP, RBF and fuzzy inference system. The MLP was successfully used to identify the causal relationship between the MID variables (causes) and conflict status (effect) whereas the RBF was used to identify the causal relationship between the dissolved gas analysis data (causes) and condition of bushings (effect) while fuzzy inference system was used to identify the causal relationship between causes (input fuel, air, reference level, and disturbance) and effect (steam flow rate).

References

Achkar, R., Owayjan, M. "Control of an active magnetic bearing with multi-layer perceptrons using the torque method," *Proceedings of the 2010 10th International Conference on Intelligent Systems Design and Applications*, ISDA'10, art. no. 5687262, pp. 214–219, 2010.

Agbloyor, E.K., Abor, J., Adjasi, C.K.D., Yawson, A. "Exploring the causality links between financial markets and foreign direct investment in Africa," *Research in International Business and Finance*, Vol. 28, No. 1, pp. 118–134, 2013.

Araujo, E. "Improved Takagi–Sugeno Fuzzy Approach," In *Proceedings of the IEEE International Conference on Fuzzy Systems*, pp. 1154–1158, 2008.

Asl, S.F.Z., Karami, A., Ashari, G., Behrang, A., Assareh, A., Hedayat, N. "Daily global solar radiation modeling using multi-layer perceptron (MLP) neural networks", *World Academy of Science, Engineering and Technology*, Vol. 79, pp. 740–742, 2011.

Åsvoll, H. "Abduction, deduction and induction: Can these concepts be used for an understanding of methodological processes in interpretative case studies?", *International Journal of Qualitative Studies in Education*, Vol. 27, No. 3, pp. 289–307, 2013.

Bélaïd, F., Abderrahmani, F. "Electricity consumption and economic growth in Algeria: A multivariate causality analysis in the presence of structural change," *Energy Policy*, Vol. 55, pp. 286–295, 2013.

Ben-Israel, A., Greville, T.N.E. "Generalized Inverses", Springer-Verlag, 2003.

Bennoui, H., Chaoui, A., Barkaoui, K. "On structural analysis of interacting behavioral petri nets for distributed causal model-based diagnosis," *International Journal of Foundations of Computer Science*, Vol. 23, No. 7, pp. 1523–1541, 2012.

Biacino, L., Gerla, G. "Fuzzy logic, continuity and effectiveness," *Archive for Mathematical Logic*, Vol. 41, No. 7, pp. 643–667, 2002.

Bishop, C.M. "Neural Networks for Pattern Recognition," Oxford, UK: Oxford University Press, 1995.

Bocheński, J.M. "A Précis of Mathematical Logic, translated from the French and German editions by Otto Bird," Dordrecht, South Holland, D. Reidel, 1959.

Bouallegue, W., Bouslama Bouabdallah, S., Tagina, M. "Causal approaches and fuzzy logic in FDI of Bond Graph uncertain parameters systems," *2011 International Conference on Communications, Computing and Control Applications, CCCA 2011*, art. no. 6031220, 2011.

Button, K., Yuan, J. "Airfreight Transport and Economic Development: An Examination of Causality," *Urban Studies*, Vol. 50, No. 2, pp. 329–340, 2013.

Candelon, B., Joëts, M., Tokpavi, S. "Testing for Granger causality in distribution tails: An application to oil markets integration," *Economic Modelling*, Vol. 31, No. 1, pp. 276–285, 2013.

Chang, W.-Y. "Wind energy conversion system power forecasting using radial basis function neural network," *Applied Mechanics and Materials*, Vol. 284–287, pp. 1067–1071, 2013.

Chen, P.-C., Chern, C.-C., Tzeng, G.-H. "A fuzzy causal decision-making model for IT investment evaluation," *Proceedings of the 2011 International Conference on Artificial Intelligence*, ICAI 2011, Vol. 2, pp. 730–735, 2011.

Croux, C., Reusens, P. "Do stock prices contain predictive power for the future economic activity? A Granger causality analysis in the frequency domain," *Journal of Macroeconomics*, Vol. 35, No. 1, pp. 93–103, 2013.

Dewey, D. "A representation theorem for decisions about causal models," *Lecture Notes in Computer Science (including subseries Lecture Notes in Artificial Intelligence and Lecture Notes in Bioinformatics)*, 7716 LNAI, pp. 60–68, 2012.

Dhlamini, S.M., Marwala, T. "Bushing monitoring using MLP and RBF," In *Proceedings of the IEEE Africon 2004*, Gaborone, Botswana, pp. 613–617, 2004.

Ehring, D. "The transference theory of causation," *Synthese*, Vol. 67, pp. 249–258, 1986.

Enderton, H. "A Mathematical Introduction to Logic", 2nd Edition, Boston, Academic Press, MA, 2001.

Fiss, P.C. "Building better causal theories: A fuzzy set approach to typologies in organization research," *Academy of Management Journal*, Vol. 54, No. 2, pp. 393–420, 2011.

Hájek, P. "Metamathematics of fuzzy logic," Dordrecht: Kluwer, 1998.

Hartigan, J.A. "Clustering algorithms," John Wiley & Sons, Inc, 1975.

Hartigan, J.A., Wong, M.A. "Algorithm AS 136: A K-means clustering algorithm". *Journal of the Royal Statistical Society, Series C (Applied Statistics)*, Vol. 28, No. 1, pp. 100–108, 1979.

Hazewinkel, M. (ed.). "Propositional connective," Encyclopedia of Mathematics, Springer, 2001.

Humberstone, L. "The Connectives", MIT Press, 2011.

Ing, D. "Envisioning innovation in service systems: Induction, abduction and deduction," *53rd Annual Conference of the International Society for the Systems Sciences 2009: Making Liveable, Sustainable Systems Unremarkable*, Vol. 2, pp. 777–796, 2009.

Kakas, A., Flach, P. "Abduction and Induction in Artificial Intelligence," *Journal of Applied Logic*, Vol. 7, No. 3, p. 251, 2009.

Kistler, M. "Reducing causality to transmission," *Erkenntnis*, Vol. 48, pp. 1–24, 1998.

Kitikidou, K., Iliadis, L. "A multi-layer perceptron neural network to predict air quality through indicators of life quality and welfare," *IFIP Advances in Information and Communication Technology*, 339 AICT, pp. 395–402, 2010.

Klir, G.J., Folger, T.A. "Fuzzy Sets, Uncertainty, and Information", Englewood Cliffs, Prentice Hall, NJ, 1988.

Klir, G.J., St. Clair, U.H., Yuan, B. "Fuzzy Set Theory: Foundations and Applications", Englewood Cliffs, Prentice Hall, NJ, 1997.

Klir, G.J., Yuan, B. "Fuzzy Sets and Fuzzy Logic: Theory and Applications", Upper Saddle River, Prentice Hall, NJ, 1995.

Kudo, Y., Murai, T., Akama, S. "A granularity-based framework of deduction, induction, and abduction", *International Journal of Approximate Reasoning*, Vol. 50, No. 8, pp. 1215–1226, 2009.

Lloyd, S.P. "Least squares quantization in PCM," *IEEE Transactions on Information Theory*, Vol. 28, No. 2, pp. 129–137, 1982.

Lord, T., Hodge, G. "On-line monitoring technology applied to HV bushing", *Proceedings of the AVO Conference*, New Zealand, November (CD-ROM), 2003.

Mamdani, E.H., Assilian, S. "An experiment in linguistic synthesis with a fuzzy logic controller", *International Journal of man-machine studies*, Vol. 7, No. 1, pp 1–13, 1975.

Mamdani, E.H. "Application of Fuzzy Algorithms for the Control of a Dynamic Plant", In *Proceedings of IEE*, Vol. 121, pp. 1585–1588, 1974.

Marwala, T., Lagazio, M. "Militarized Conflict Modeling Using Computational Intelligence Techniques", Springer-Verlag, London, 2011.

Marwala, T. "Economic Modelling Using Artificial Intelligence Methods", Springer-Verlag, London, UK, 2013.

Marwala, T., Computational Intelligence for Missing Data Imputation, Estimation and Management: Knowledge Optimization Techniques. IGI Global Publications, Information Science Reference Imprint, IGI Global Publications, New York, 2009.

Minnameier, G. "Abduction, induction, and analogy: On the compound character of analogical inferences", *Studies in Computational Intelligence*, Vol. 314, pp. 107–119, 2010.

Mojo, B. "Transformer condition monitoring (non-invasive Infrared Thermography Technique)", University of the Witwatersrand Masters Thesis, Department of Electrical Engineering, 1997.

Møller, A.F. "A scaled conjugate gradient algorithm for fast supervised learning", *Neural Nets*, Vol. 6, pp. 525–533, 1993.

Moore, E.H. "On the reciprocal of the general algebraic matrix", *Bulletin of the American Mathematical Society*, Vol. 26, No. 9, pp. 394–395, 1920.

Moore, E.C., Robin, R.S. (eds.). "Studies in the Philosophy of Charles Sanders Peirce, Second Series", Amherst: University of Massachusetts Press, 1964.

Novák, V. "Are fuzzy sets a reasonable tool for modeling vague phenomena?" *Fuzzy Sets and Systems*, Vol. 156, pp. 341–348, 2005.

Novák, V., Perfilieva, I., Mockor, J. "Mathematical principles of fuzzy logic," Dodrecht: Kluwer Academic, 1999.

Peña-Ayala, A., Mizoguchi, R. "Intelligent decision-making approach based on fuzzy-causal knowledge and reasoning," *Lecture Notes in Computer Science (including subseries Lecture Notes in Artificial Intelligence and Lecture Notes in Bioinformatics)*, 7345 LNAI, pp. 534–543, 2012.

Peña-Ayala, A., Sossa-Azuela, H., Cervantes-Pérez, F. "Predictive student model supported by fuzzy-causal knowledge and inference," *Expert Systems with Applications*, Vol. 39, No. 5, pp. 4690–4709, 2012.

Penrose, R. "A generalized inverse for matrices", *Proceedings of the Cambridge Philosophical Society*, Vol. 51, pp. 406–413, 1955.

Rababaah, A.R., Tebekaemi, E. "Electric load monitoring of residential buildings using goodness of fit and multi-layer perceptron neural networks," *CSAE 2012 — Proceedings, 2012 IEEE International Conference on Computer Science and Automation Engineering*, Vol. 2, art. no. 6272871, pp. 733–737, 2012.

Rout, M., Majhi, B., Mohapatra, U.M., Mahapatra, R. "Stock indices prediction using radial basis function neural network', *Lecture Notes in Computer Science (including subseries Lecture Notes in Artificial Intelligence and Lecture Notes in Bioinformatics)*, 7677 LNCS, pp. 285–293, 2012.

Salmon, W. "Scientific Explanation and the Causal Structure of the World", Princeton University Press, Princeton, 1984.

Sanz, J., Perera, R., Huerta, C. "Gear dynamics monitoring using discrete wavelet transformation and multi-layer perceptron neural networks," *Applied Soft Computing Journal*, Vol. 12, No. 9, pp. 2867–2878, 2012.

Serbanuta, T.F., Chen, F., Rosu, G. "Maximal causal models for sequentially consistent systems", Lecture Notes in Computer Science (including subseries Lecture Notes in Artificial Intelligence and Lecture Notes in Bioinformatics), 7687 LNCS, pp. 136–150, 2013.

Sermpinis, G., Theofilatos, K., Karathanasopoulos, A., Georgopoulos, E.F., Dunis, C. "Forecasting foreign exchange rates with adaptive neural networks using radial-basis functions and Particle Swarm Optimization", *European Journal of Operational Research*, Vol. 225, No. 3, pp. 528–540, 2013.

Shariati-Rad, M., Irandoust, M., Amin, N., Shamsipur, M. "Solving matrix effect, spectral interferences and nonlinearity by generalized standard addition method coupled with radial basis functions-partial least squares: Application to simultaneous determination of drugs in urine", *Chemometrics and Intelligent Laboratory Systems*, Vol. 120, pp. 77–83, 2013.

Sugeno, M. "Industrial Applications of Fuzzy Control", Amsterdam: Elsevier Science, 1985.

Sugeno, M., Kang, G. "Structure Identification of Fuzzy Model," *Fuzzy Sets and Systems*, Vol. 28, pp. 15–33, 1988.

Sung, B., Song, W.-Y. "Causality between public policies and exports of renewable energy technologies", *Energy Policy*, Vol. 55, pp. 95–104, 2013.

Taha, R., Colombage, S.R.N., Maslyuk, S., Nanthakumar, L. "Does financial system activity affect tax revenue in Malaysia? Bounds testing and causality approach", *Journal of Asian Economics*, Vol. 24, pp. 147–157, 2013.

Takagi, T., Sugeno, M. "Fuzzy Identification of Systems and its Applications to Modeling and Control", *IEEE Transactions on Systems, Man, and Cybernetics*, Vol. 15, pp. 116–132, 1985.

Tian, J., Gao, M., Kong, C. "Sludge compost quality evaluation based on improved genetic algorithm and radial basis function neural network," *Journal of Convergence Information Technology*, Vol. 8, No. 1, 2013.

Vaferi, B., Eslamloueyan, R., Ayatollahi, S. "Automatic recognition of oil reservoir models from well testing data by using multi-layer perceptron networks", *Journal of Petroleum Science and Engineering*, Vol. 77, No. 3–4, pp. 254–262, 2011.

Wright, S., Marwala, T. "Artificial Intelligence Techniques for Steam Generator Modelling", arXiv:0811.1711, 2006.

Yuan, L.-F., Ding, C., Guo, S.-H., Ding, H., Chen, W., Lin, H. "Prediction of the types of ion channel-targeted conotoxins based on radial basis function network", *Toxicology in Vitro*, Vol. 27, No. 2, pp. 852–856, 2013.

Zadeh, L.A. "Fuzzy sets", *Information and Control*, Vol. 8, No. 3, pp. 338–353, 1965.

Zhang, J.Y., Borland, R., Coghill, K., Petrovic-Lazarevic, S., Young, D., Yeh, C.H., Bedingfield, S. "Evaluating the effect of health warnings in influencing Australian smokers' psychosocial and quitting behaviours using fuzzy causal network", *Expert Systems with Applications*, Vol. 38, No. 6, pp. 6430–6438, 2011.

Zhang, Z., Kotz, R.M., Wang, C., Ruan, S., Ho, M. "A causal model for joint evaluation of placebo and treatment-specific effects in clinical trials," *Biometrics*, Vol. 69, No. 2, pp. 318–227, 2013.

Chapter 4

Correlation Machines Using Optimization Methods

Abstract. In this chapter, we introduce a correlation machine which is a missing data estimation technique which is based on the multi-layered perceptron neural network and several optimization methods. Genetic algorithm (GA), simulated annealing (SA), and particle swarm optimization (PSO) methods are applied to minimize an error function resulting from an auto-associative multi-layer perceptron (MLP) neural network. These optimization approaches are tested in mechanical system and artificial beer taster.

4.1 Introduction

Using a correlation machine, which is created using an auto-associative network and optimization technique, to estimate missing data is a subject of considerable interest (Rubin, 1978; Allison, 2000; Marwala, 2009). There are many reasons why data are missing and these include sensors failure, unreachability of measuring surfaces, and so on. Within the context of rational decision-making, it is vital that the missing values be predicted as much as possible to enhance decision making. The concept of making rational decisions in the presence of missing data is what Nobel Laureate called bounded rationality for decision making.

Techniques have been developed to handle missing data and these include Expectation-Maximization (Dempster *et al.*, 1977; Little and Rubin, 1987; 2002; Marwala, 2009), auto-associative neural networks (Abdella and Marwala, 2005; Marwala and Chakraverty, 2006; Mistry *et al.*, 2009) and rough sets approach (Nelwamondo, 2008).

Shih *et al.* (2008) proposed a technique of approximating the mean of the data which included non-ignorable missing values whereas Keesing *et al.* (2007) presented missing data approximation method for 3D spiral CT image reconstruction. Wooldridge (2007) presented an inverse probability weighted method for missing data estimation whereas Mojirsheibani (2007) proposed a generalized empirical method to estimate missing data. Other missing data estimation methods are neural network and dynamic programming (Nelwamondo *et al.*, 2013), Bayesian principal component analysis (Shi *et al.*, 2013) and similarity measurement (Pati and Das, 2012).

These missing data estimation methods in essence are made up of two mechanisms: The auto-associative network module, which is a network that maps the input onto itself (Hines and Garvey, 2006; Makki and Hosseini, 2013; González and Villanueva, 2013) and the optimization component (Snyman, 2007). This chapter examines three optimization approaches for missing data approximation and compares them. Spiller and Marwala (2007) applied genetic algorithms (GAs), particle swarm optimization (PSO), and simulated annealing (SA) for warp control point placement and observed that PSO was better than the other procedures.

In this chapter, the optimization approaches that are studied are GA, SA, and PSO (Chen and Su, 2002; Güngör and Ünler, 2007; Liang *et al.*, 2013; Torrent-Fontbona *et al.*, 2013) and PSO (van den Bergh and Engelbrecht, 2006; Marwala, 2007; Jiang *et al.*, 2013; Setayesh *et al.*, 2013). In Chapter 8, missing data estimation is implemented to increase information that is used for decision thereby making Herbert Simon's theory of bounded rationality the theory of flexibly bounded rationality.

4.2 Multi-layer Perceptron Neural Network

This chapter applies a multi-layer perceptron (MLP) neural network and this will be briefly described below. The MLP is computational method which is intended to model input–output data (Marwala, 2001). The MLP has been successfully used in many diverse areas (Leke *et al.*, 2007; Marwala, 2001; Mohamed and Marwala, 2005). The MLP approximates the relations between sets of input data and output and a two layered network can be mathematically described as follows (Bishop, 1995):

$$y_k = f_{outer}\left(\sum_{j=1}^{M} w_{kj}^{(2)} f_{inner}\left(\sum_{i=1}^{d} w_{ji}^{(1)} x_i + w_{j0}^{(1)}\right) + w_{k0}^{(2)}\right) \tag{4.1}$$

here $w_{ji}^{(1)}$ and $w_{ji}^{(2)}$ are weights in the first and second layers, respectively, from input i to hidden unit j, M is the number of hidden units, d is the number of output units while $w_{j0}^{(1)}$ and $w_{k0}^{(2)}$ are the free parameters called the biases for the hidden unit j and the output unit k. The activation function $f_{outer}(\bullet)$ is linear whereas the activation function f_{inner} is the hyperbolic tangent function. The selection of these parameters allows modeling linear and non-linear data. Scaled conjugate gradient method is used to identify the network weights in Equation 4.1 and more details on this are found in Bishop (1995).

4.3 Missing Data Estimation Technique

The missing data estimation technique applied in this chapter uses a MLP auto-associative network to model the interrelationships that exist amongst the data. The missing data estimation equation can be mathematically represented as follows, was derived in Chapter 2 (Abdella, 2005; Abdella and Marwala, 2005; Marwala, 2009):

$$E = \left\| \left(\begin{Bmatrix} \{X_k\} \\ \{X_u\} \end{Bmatrix} - f\left(\begin{Bmatrix} \{X_k\} \\ \{X_u\} \end{Bmatrix}, \{W\} \right) \right) \right\| \tag{4.2}$$

here f is the MLP auto-associative network, $\{W\}$ is the network weight vector, $\{X_u\}$ is the missing variable and $\{X_k\}$ is the observed variables. In this chapter, this error function is optimized using GA, PSO, and SA to estimate missing variable $\{X_u\}$ given the observed variables $\{X_k\}$, the network weights $\{W\}$, and the MLP auto-associative network f describing the interrelationships and the rules characterizing the data.

4.4 Genetic Algorithms

GA is applied to minimize the objective function in Equation 4.2. GA is applied to identify solutions to objective functions using the philosophies of evolutionary biology to computer science (Michalewicz, 1996; Mitchell, 1996; Belevičius *et al.*, 2013). GA borrows concepts from evolutionary biology for instance inheritance, mutation, natural selection and recombination to estimate an optimal solution to difficult problems (Banzhaf *et al.*, 1998). In GA, the identification of an optimal solution is viewed as a competition among a population of evolving potential solutions. An objective function estimates the objective state of each solution to evaluate whether it adds to the next generation of solutions. Using mechanisms related to gene transfer in sexual reproduction, the procedure produces a new population of potential solutions (Goldberg, 1989; Xhafa *et al.*, 2013).

Lin *et al.* (2013) successfully applied a GA to solve a multi-objective simulation optimization problem in surgical services whereas Krishnamoorthi and Sathiya Devi (2013) successfully applied GA for image retrieval. Robles-Ortega *et al.* (2013) successfully applied GA to produce textured urban models whereas Zamani (2013) successfully applied GA for resource-constrained scheduling problem.

The three vital drivers on applying GAs are (Michalewicz, 1996): Description of the objective function, description as well as application of the genetic representation, and description and execution of the genetic operators. GAs have been proven to be successful in optimization problems such as wire routing, scheduling, adaptive control, game playing, cognitive modeling, transportation problems, traveling salesman problems, optimal control problems, and database query optimization (Michalewicz, 1996; Shieh and Chiou, 2013).

To implement GAs, the following steps are followed: Initialization, selection, reproduction, and termination and these are described in the next subsections.

4.4.1 Initialization

When GA is initiated, a specified number of possible individual solutions are randomly generated to form an initial population. It is ideally supposed to be a large number to include a fair representation of the solution space. The size of the population depends on the problem at hand and largely depends on the size of variables. For instance, if there are three variables that are missing, the size of the population must be higher than if there are two variables that are missing. The next sections describe the drivers of GA which are crossover, mutation, reproduction, and termination.

4.4.2 Crossover

Given a population of possible solutions to the optimization problem, crossover operator is a method that combines different solutions thereby exchanging genetic information in the population. One way of doing this is by cutting pairs of chromosomes (i.e. possible solutions) at random positions along their lengths and swapping over the cut segments. Crossover takes place with a particular probability and this connects successful operators together.

Yuan *et al.* (2013) proposed a crossover method and applied this successfully to solve a traveling salesmen problem using GAs whereas Gunasekaran and Iruthayarajan (2013) applied binary crossover successfully for contour optimization of suspension insulators. Mudaliar and Modi (2013) successfully applied the M-crossover operator in a traveling salesman problem whereas Burjorjee (2013) successfully applied uniform crossover to optimize complex problems. Nagata and Kobayashi (2013) successfully applied edge assembly crossover for the traveling salesman problem.

Simple crossover method is applied in this chapter and more details on this are in Goldberg (1989). The mechanism of simple crossover, involve selecting one crossover point and a binary string from beginning of chromosome to the crossover point is copied from one parent, and the remaining is copied from the second parent. For instance, when **11101**011 undergoes simple crossover with 11011**101** it becomes **11101101**.

4.4.3 Mutation

The mutation operator selects a binary digit of the chromosomes (i.e. solution) randomly and reverses it and this introduces to the population of solutions new information (Horng *et al.*, 2012). Mutation is conducted with a particular probability and normally the probability of mutation is low.

Rajakumar (2013) successfully applied static and adaptive mutation-based GA to model complex systems whereas Haga and Suehiro (2013) successfully applied mutation for automatic test case generation. Tang and Tseng (2013) successfully applied adaptive mutation to model complex systems. Bhattacharjee and Sarmah (2012) successfully applied genetic mutation for combinatorial optimization.

This chapter uses binary mutation and its mechanism includes writing a number in binary number is selected and inverted such that 1101**1**010 is muted to form 1101**0**010.

4.4.4 Reproduction

For each generation, a reproduction of the proportion of the current population is selected to breed a new population. Reproduction is executed using the fitness-based procedure, where solutions that have lower errors, as measured by the error function given in Equation 4.2, are assigned a higher probability of being reproduced.

Yan *et al.* (2011) successfully applied granular ranking and distant reproduction to optimize a complex function using multi-objective GA whereas Tran and Jin (2010) successfully applied multi-colony dynamic reproduction to create a GA method.

In this chapter, we use the roulette reproduction method and in this technique each possible solution is allocated the error (Equation 4.2) which is used to assign the probability of reproduction for each possible solution (Zhang *et al.*, 2012). Given the fitness f_i (defined as the inverse of the error in Equation 4.2) of individual i in the population, the probability that this solution is reproduced is mathematically written as follows (Laseetha and Sukanesh, 2011):

$$p_i = \frac{f_i}{\sum_{j=1}^{N} f_j}. \tag{4.3}$$

Here N is the size of the population. GA guarantees that potential solutions with low errors have a high probability that they will be reproduced than those with higher errors.

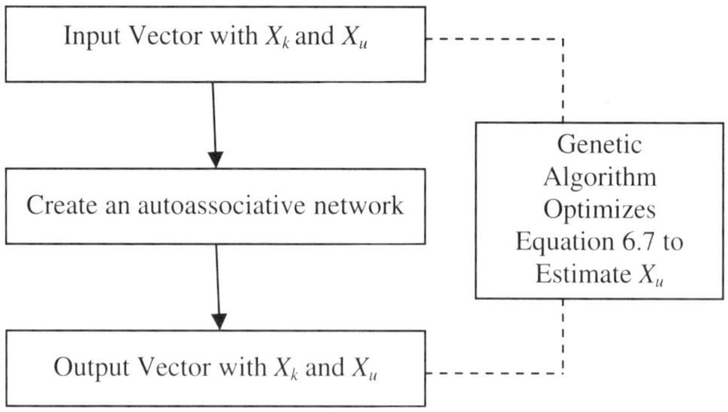

Figure 4.1 A missing data estimation technique

4.4.5 Termination

The procedure of crossover, mutation and reproduction is reiterated until a stopping criterion is reached. This normally means that either a preferred solution is identified that fulfills the objective function or a stipulated number of generations has been achieved or the algorithm has converged. The genetic procedure can be expressed algorithmically as follows (Goldberg, 1989):

1. Choose the population size and generate an initial population.
2. Estimate the fitness of each individual in the population using Equation 4.2.
3. Iterate:
   a. Select individuals with lower error according to Equation 4.2 to reproduce.
   b. Produce a new population using a crossover technique.
   c. Mutate the resulting population to produce offspring.
   d. Estimate the fitness of each offspring.
   e. Substitute individual in the population with higher errors (Equation 4.2) with individuals with low errors.
4. Repeat until the termination criterion is reached.

The missing data estimation technique described in this section can summarized as in Figure 4.1.

4.5 Particle Swarm Optimization

PSO technique is one of the two techniques that are applied to optimize Equation 4.2. PSO is a stochastic, population-based evolutionary technique that has been extensively applied to optimize complex functions and systems. It is inspired by the socio-psychological phenomena of swarm intelligence. Swarm intelligence allows for the understanding of social behavior. Society allows an individual to sustain cognitive capability through influence and learning, and thus individuals learn to solve complex problems by communicating and interacting with other individuals (Engelbrecht, 2005; Marwala and Lagazio, 2011). Therefore, swarm intelligence is enabled by two factors which are group and individual knowledge. Every element of a swarm behaves by balancing between its individual and group knowledge.

On applying PSO method to optimize complex problems, an objective function is built to estimate missing values and in this chapter this is represented by Equation 4.2. To estimate missing data, a social network expressing a population of possible solutions is specified randomly. These individuals in this social network are allocated neighbors to interrelate with and these individuals are so-called particles, therefore the expression PSO. Afterwards, a procedure to improve these particles is begun by assessing the error of each particle as indicated in Equation 4.2. Every particle recalls the location where it had its best success as measured by the error in Equation 4.2. The best solution of the particle is titled the *local best* and each particle shares this information on the local best to its neighbors and perceives its neighbors' success. The procedure of exploring the feasible space is directed by these successes and the population eventually converges on a minimum point of Equation 4.2.

The PSO was proposed by Kennedy and Eberhart (1995) and was inspired by procedures that model the "flocking behavior" observed in birds. Scientists in artificial intelligence have established simulations of bird flocking (Reynolds, 1987; Heppner and Grenander, 1990; Marwala and Lagazio, 2011). Within the perspective of optimization, the notion of birds identifying a roost is equivalent to a route of identifying an optimal solution in Equation 4.2. PSO has been successfully applied to optimize complex problems such as for molecular docking (Arumugam and Rao, 2008), model selection in neuro-fuzzy system (Arya *et al.*, 2007), in scheduling (Berlinet and Roland, 2008; Qi *et al.*, 2008), for conceptual design (Jiang *et al.*, 2007); in power systems (Kathiravan and Ganguli, 2007; Cao *et al.*, 2013); in inverse radiation problems (Lin *et al.*, 2008), data clustering (Jiang *et al.*, 2013), and image processing (Setayesh *et al.*, 2013).

Marwala (2005a) applied PSO to update finite element models to better reflect the measured data. This technique was compared to a finite element model updating method that applied SA and GA and these approaches were tested on a simple beam and an unsymmetrical H-shaped structure. It was observed that, on average, the PSO technique offered the most accurate results followed by SA and then GA.

Dindar (2004) as well as Dindar and Marwala (2004) effectively applied PSO to optimize the structure of the committee of neural networks. The results they attained from the optimized networks were better than both un-optimized networks and the committee of networks. Ransome *et al.* (2005) along with Ransome (2006) positively applied PSO to optimize the position of a patient during radiation therapy. They observed that the PSO was effective in dealing with problems in current solutions.

PSO is applied by identifying a balance between sampling for a good solution and using other particles' successes. If the sampling for a solution is inadequate, then the PSO converges to a local optimum solution. If the gains of other particles are not exploited then the PSO does not converge. The PSO is computationally efficient, is simple to implement, has few adjustable parameters when compared to other competing evolutionary programming methods such as GA and explores locally and globally.

When applying PSO technique, it is initialized with a population of random potential solutions, each hypothesized as particles. Each particle is allocated a random velocity and is iteratively moved through the particle space. For each stage, the particle is attracted in the direction of a region of the best fitness function by the location of the best fitness attained until now in the population.

On using the standard PSO, each particle is represented by two characteristics which are the position vector of particle i at step k denoted $p_i(k)$ and the corresponding velocity vector of particle i at step k denoted by $v_i(k)$. Positions and velocities of particles are initially randomly sampled and the following positions and velocities are computed using the position of the best solution that a specific particle has come across during the simulation termed $pbest_i$ and the best particle in the swarm, which is named $gbest(k)$. The succeeding velocity of a particle i can be computed using the following mathematical equation (Kennedy and Eberhart, 1995; Marwala, 2009; Marwala and Lagazio, 2011):

$$v_i(k+1) = \gamma v_i(k) + c_1 r_1 (pbest_i - p_i(k)) + c_2 r_2 (gbest(k) - p_i(k)). \tag{4.4}$$

Here the parameter γ is the inertia of the particle, the variables c_1 and c_2 are the 'trust' parameters, and the parameters r_1 and r_2 are randomly generated numbers between 0 and 1.

The first term in Equation 4.4 is the current motion, the second term is the influence of the particle memory and the third term is the swarm influence. For a particle i the position p_i at step $k+1$ can be computed from the position p_i at step k and velocity v_i at step $k+1$ as follows (Kennedy and Eberhart, 1995; Marwala, 2009; Marwala and Lagazio, 2011):

$$p_i(k+1) = p_i(k) + v_i(k+1). \tag{4.5}$$

The inertia of the particle regulates the influence of the previous velocity of the particle on the current velocity. These parameters regulate the exploratory characteristics of the PSO with a high inertia promoting global exploration while a low inertia promotes local exploration.

The trust parameter c_1 specifies the confidence the current particle has on itself also known as individual intelligence whereas the trust parameter c_2 specifies the confidence the current particle has on the population known as group intelligence. The parameters r_1 and r_2 are randomly generated numbers between 0 and 1 and they regulate the extent to which the simulation should explore the space. The PSO as implemented in this chapter can be summarized as follows (Marwala and Lagazio, 2011):

1. Reset a population of particles' positions and velocities. The positions of the particles are randomly distributed in the missing data parameter space.
2. Compute the velocity for each particle in the swarm using Equation 4.4.
3. Update the position of each particle using Equation 4.5.
4. Repeat steps 2 and 3 until convergence.

This process is represented diagrammatically in Figure 4.2.

4.6 Simulated Annealing

This section describes SA which is a Monte Carlo technique, which was inspired by the process of annealing where objects such as metals recrystallize or liquids freeze, and is applied to identify an optimal solution (Kirkpatrick *et al.*, 1983; Naderi *et al.*, 2009; Paya-Zaforteza *et al.*, 2009; Kannan and Zacharias, 2009).

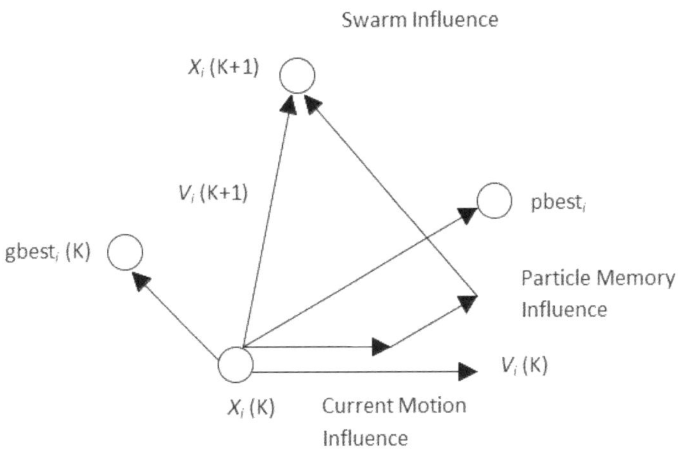

Figure 4.2 Illustration of velocity and particle update in PSO

Successful applications of SA include electricity demand (Chang, 2006), vibration control (Moita *et al.*, 2006), energy saving (Chang *et al.*, 2006), optimal packing problems (Gomes and Oliveira, 2006), to study of the pentacyclo-undecane cage amino acid tripeptides (Bisetty *et al.*, 2006), to optimize submarine maneuvering controllers (McGookin and Murray-Smith, 2006), solve large immobile location (Torrent-Fontbona *et al.*, 2013), to model shear capacity of beams (Gandomi *et al.*, 2013), to move clod boundaries on seedbed digital elevation model (Chimi-Chiadjeu *et al.*, 2013), and in sparse signal recover (Liang *et al.*, 2013).

For the reason that SA has been successfully applied to many different areas it is applied in this chapter to missing data estimation. SA is derived from the annealing process in physical systems. In the process of annealing, objects such as metals are heated until they are molten and then their temperatures are gradually lowered such that the metals, at any given time, are almost in thermodynamic equilibrium. As the temperature of the object is cooled, the system becomes more ordered as it moves towards a *frozen* state at $T = 0$. If the cooling process is done insufficiently or the initial temperature of the object is not satisfactorily high, the system forms prematurely, creating defects or freezing out in metastable states because it is stuck in a local minimum energy state.

SA procedure was first proposed by Metropolis *et al.* (1953) and it entails selecting an initial state using the objective function in Equation 4.2 and temperature, and maintaining this temperature constant, perturbing the initial formation and calculating the error at the new state. If the new error is lower than the old error then the new state is accepted, otherwise if the opposite is the case, then this state is accepted with a low probability. This is in essence a Monte Carlo technique.

SA substitutes for a candidate solution, with a "nearby" random solution with a probability that is a function of the difference between the objective function values derived from the current state and the previous state given a fixed temperature. The temperature is reduced during the process, so as temperature starts approaching zero then the solution converges. Theoretically SA converges on a global optimum solution as the number of simulation steps approaches infinity. The probability of accepting the reversal is defined by the Boltzmann's equation (Bryan *et al.*, 2006; Marwala and Lagazio, 2011):

$$P(\Delta E) = \frac{1}{Z}\exp\left(-\frac{\Delta E}{T}\right) \tag{4.6}$$

here ΔE is the difference in error (as calculated from the objective function described in Equation 4.2) between the old and new states. T is the temperature of the system; Z is a normalization factor that guarantees that when the probability function is integrated to infinity it becomes 1.

The cooling schedule chosen determines the rate at which the temperature decreases. There are many different types of temperature schedules. On applying SA, the main mechanism to do is to select its parameters.

4.6.1 SA parameters

On applying SA to missing data estimation problem a number of issues and that are considered are (Marwala and Lagazio, 2011):

- The state space which is defined in this chapter as a variable to be estimated;
- The objective function represented by Equation 4.2;
- A random number generator;
- The acceptance probability function; and
- The annealing temperature schedule.

The selection of these parameters has far reaching effect on the usefulness of the SA technique in so far as finding an optimal solution is concerned. Nevertheless, there is no optimal way that can be utilized to select these parameters that is perfect for all problems and there is no methodical process for optimally selecting these parameters. Accordingly, the selection of these parameters is subjective and a technique of trial and error is extensively used.

4.6.2 Transition probabilities

Random walk process is used to implement SA and this involves moving from one temperature to another. The transition probability is the probability of moving from one state to another. This probability is dependent on the present temperature, the order of generating the candidate moves, and the acceptance probability function. A Markov Chain Monte Carlo (MCMC) technique is applied to make a transition from one state to another and it generates a chain of possible missing data and accepts or rejects them using the Metropolis algorithm (Meer, 2007; Marwala and Lagazio, 2010).

4.6.3 Monte Carlo method

The Monte Carlo technique is a computational process that applies recurrent random sampling to estimate a result (Mathe and Novak, 2007; Cleveland *et al.*, 2013; Markhasin, 2013; Fabian *et al.*, 2013). Successful applications of the Monte Carlo procedure include in particle coagulation (Zhao and Zheng, 2009), in diffusion problems (Liu *et al.*, 2009), in nuclear design (Dunn and Shultis, 2009; Cetinel *et al.*, 2013), bacterial activities modeling (Oliveira *et al.*, 2009), in vehicle detection

(Jia and Zhang, 2009), in nitrogen absorption modeling (Rahmati and Modarress, 2009), simulating multivariate transformed Brownian motions (Zhang and Melnik, 2013), and to model degenerate plasma (Turrell *et al.*, 2013).

The Monte Carlo technique relies on recurrent calculations and random numbers and it is preferred if it is impractical to calculate precise solutions using deterministic procedure.

4.6.4 Markov Chain Monte Carlo

A MCMC technique is a process of mimicking a chain of states by using a random walk procedure and involves a Markov process and a Monte Carlo simulation (Liesenfeld and Richard, 2008). Successful applications of the MCMC include for tracking objects (Jing and Vadakkepat, 2009), optimal model identification (Gallagher *et al.*, 2009), DNA profiling (Curran, 2008), for optical cable flame retardancy tests (Kuandykov, 2013), approximating voltage sag (Hao *et al.*, 2013), and vehicle tracking (Kow *et al.*, 2012).

We now describe a system which can be characterized by a stochastic process comprising of random variables $\{x_1, x_2, x_3, \ldots, x_i\}$. A random variable x_i occupies a state x at discrete time i and a state space is a list of all possible orientations that a random variable can occupy. A Markov chain is a series of random variables where the probability that the system is in state x_{i+1} at time $i + 1$ depends completely on the fact that it was in state x_i at time i. In MCMC simulation, the transition between states is attained by randomly perturbing the present with a random noise (ε) as follows (Liesenfeld and Richard, 2008; Marwala and Lagazio, 2011):

$$x_{i+1} = x_i + \varepsilon. \tag{4.7}$$

4.6.5 Acceptance probability function: Metropolis algorithm

When sampling a probability distribution the current state (x) is accepted or rejected using the Metropolis algorithm (Metropolis *et al.*, 1953; Wang *et al.*, 2013; Zhu *et al.*, 2013). Metropolis algorithm has been applied widely to solve many complex problems such as simulating protein (Bazavov *et al.*, 2009; Tiana *et al.*, 2007), in nuclear power plants (Sacco *et al.*, 2008), and in hydrological modeling (Guo *et al.*, 2013).

On sampling a stochastic process $\{x_1, x_2, x_3, \ldots, x_i\}$ using Metropolis algorithm random changes to x, as explained in Equation 4.7, are considered and either accepted or rejected according to the following Metropolis criterion (Metropolis *et al.*, 1953):

$$\begin{aligned} &\textit{if } E_{new} < E_{old} \textit{ accept state } (s_{new}) \\ &\textit{else} \\ &\textit{accept } (s_{new}) \textit{ with probability} \\ &\exp\{-(E_{new} - E_{old})\} \end{aligned} \quad . \tag{4.8}$$

4.6.6 Cooling schedule

A *Cooling scheduling* is the procedure of reducing the temperature T when SA is applied (De Vicente *et al.*, 2003; Johannes and Puchta, 2010). The cooling rate should be satisfactorily low for the probability distribution to be approximately equal to the thermodynamic equilibrium (Das and Chakrabarti, 2005; Triki *et al.*, 2005). The time to reach equilibrium after a change in temperature is governed by the nature of the objective function (Equation 4.2), the current temperature and the random number generator. Thermodynamic SA avoids this problem by modifying the temperature at each step in the simulation, based on the difference in energy between the two states (Weinberger, 1990). The cooling schedule that is applied in this chapter is written as follows (Salazar and Toral, 2006; Tanimoto and Hagishima, 2005):

$$T(i) = \frac{T(i-1)}{1+\sigma} \tag{4.9}$$

where $T(i)$ is the current temperature; $T(i-1)$ is the previous temperature and σ is the cooling rate. The accuracy of numerical values used in SA has a significant impact on the efficacy of the algorithm. A technique to enhance SA's computational efficiency involve using fast simulated re-annealing or adaptive SA (Salazar and Toral, 2006).

This procedure is recurred until the sampling statistics for the present temperature is satisfactory and then the temperature is reduced, and the procedure is reiterated until a frozen state is realized when $T = 0$. SA was first used for optimization problems by Kirkpatrick *et al.* (1983).

4.7 Missing Data Estimation: Case Studies

The optimization approaches summarized above are tested on estimating missing data in a mechanical system and an artificial taster and these optimization approaches are then compared.

4.7.1 Mechanical system

In this section, the missing data estimation procedures based on GAs, PSO and SA are experimentally validated. The details of this problem are described in detail in Marwala (2012). This example involves measuring vibration data from a population of cylindrical shells and from these extracting 10 parameters to be used to estimate the physical integrity of these shells (Marwala, 2001).

The MLP auto-associative network with 10 inputs and 10 outputs are created and a number of numbers of hidden units are used. The auto-associative network is, as a result, trained to comprehend the interrelationships that exist in the measured variables.

Subsequent to the training of the auto-associative network then the investigation with 1, 2 and 3 missing variables is performed and the results for missing data estimation are then compared to the true values. The results that are attained are shown in Table 4.1. On the application of the missing data approximation process using GA, the maximum number of generations was set to 30 and a population of 10, for the PSO the maximum number of generations of 30 and a population of 10, and the initial number of particles also set to 30 while SA is applied with the cooling schedule in Equation 4.8, a random generator with the bounds of the maximum and minimum input values, an initial temperature of 1, a stopping temperature of 1 e^{-8}, a maximum number of consecutive rejection of 200 and a maximum number of successes within one temperature set to 0.

Table 4.2 shows that GA, PSO, and SA give similar results even though SA gives slightly better results while GA performs the worst.

Table 4.1 Accuracy in missing data estimation using GA, PSO and SA optimization methods

Method	Accuracy: 1 Missing variable (%)	Accuracy: 2 Missing variable (%)	Accuracy: 3 Missing variable (%)
GA	92.7	91.1	74.8
PSO	93.8	90.1	75.7
SA	93.7	91.3	76.0

Table 4.2 Percentage error

	Number of missing variables				
	1	2	3	4	5
GA	17.08	15.93	16.19	15.23	16.21
PSO	16.80	16.29	16.10	15.92	15.92
SA	15.21	14.87	15.63	15.33	15.62

4.7.2 Modeling of beer tasting

This section uses the auto-associative MLP neural network with 10 hidden neurons, 14 inputs, 10 hidden neurons and 14 outputs to estimate missing data from a Brewery in South Africa (Marwala, 2005b). Usually the factors that human beings are sensitive to when tasting beer are: (1) color of beer; (2) smell; and (3) chemical components. In human beings, the color of objects is captured using the eye; smell is captured using the nose and taste using the tongue. The following variables are under consideration in this section (Marwala, 2005b): alcohol; present extract; real extract; PE-LE, which is the present extract minus limit extract; pH; iron; acetaldehyde; DMS, which is dimethyl sulfide; ethyl acetate; iso-amyl acetate; total higher alcohols; color; bitterness and amount of carbohydrates. These variables capture the color, smell and chemical components of the beer and are normally used to predict the beer taste score, which is usually obtained from a panel of tasters. All these parameters are measured and sometimes one or more of these measurements may not be available due to problems such as instrumentation failure. In such a situation, it is essential to approximate these missing values because, otherwise, it is impossible to predict the taste score.

These beer characteristics variables are then used to train the neural networks with the architectures described earlier. These neural networks essentially maps all the 14 variables onto themselves, in an auto-associative fashion.

Examples of 1, 2, 3, 4 and 5 missing values in a single record were studied to examine the accuracy of the estimated values as the number of missing values within a single record increased (Draper and Smith, 1998). The results of the error measures obtained from the experiment are given in Table 4.2.

In Table 4.2, PSO is found to give better results than SA followed by GAs. In general, the accuracies of the results are found not to deteriorate as the number of missing values decrease.

4.8 Conclusions

This chapter applies and compares GA, PSO and SA methods to the missing data problem. These approaches are verified on mechanical system and artificial taster data. The results obtained from the mechanical system showed that PSO and SA give similar results albeit SA is marginally better and then GA. Additionally, it is observed that it is much easier to estimate one missing variables when compared to estimating two or three missing variables. The results obtained from the artificial taster data showed the PSO to give marginally better results than SA while GA performed marginally the worst.

References

Abdella, M. "The Use of Genetic Algorithms and Neural Networks to Approximate Missing Data in Database", Master Thesis, University of the Witwatersrand, 2005.

Abdella, M., Marwala, T. "The use of genetic algorithms and neural networks to approximate missing data in database", *Computing and Informatics*, Vol. 24, pp. 1001–1013, 2006.

Allison, P. "Multiple imputation for missing data: A cautionary tale", *Sociological Methods and Research*, Vol. 28, pp. 301–309, 2000.

Arumugam, M.S., Rao, M.V.C. "Molecular docking with multi-objective Particle Swarm Optimization", *Applied Soft Computing*, Vol. 8, pp. 666–675, 2008.

Arya, L.D., Choube, S.C., Shrivastava, M., Kothari, D.P. "The design of neuro-fuzzy networks using Particle Swarm Optimization and recursive singular value decomposition", *Neurocomputing*, Vol. 71, pp. 297–310, 2007.

Banzhaf, W., Nordin, P., Keller, R., Francone, F. "Genetic Programming — An Introduction: On the Automatic Evolution of Computer Programs and its Applications", 5th Edition, California: Morgan Kaufmann Publishers, 1998.

Bazavov, A., Berg, B.A., Zhou, H. "Application of biased metropolis algorithms: From protons to proteins", *Mathematics and Computers in Simulation*, doi: 10.1016/j.matcom.2009.05.005, 2009.

Belevičius, R., Jatulis, D., Šešok, D. "Optimization of tall guyed masts using genetic algorithms", *Engineering Structures*, Vol. 56, pp. 239–245, 2013.

Berlinet, A., Roland, C. "A novel Particle Swarm Optimization Algorithm for permutation flow-shop scheduling to minimize makespan", *Chaos, Solitons & Fractals*, Vol. 35, pp. 851–861, 2008.

Bhattacharjee, K.K., Sarmah, S.P. "A modified shuffled frog leaping algorithm with genetic mutation for combinatorial optimization", *Lecture Notes in Computer Science (including subseries Lecture Notes in Artificial Intelligence and Lecture Notes in Bioinformatics)*, Vol. 7654 LNAI (PART 2), pp. 513–522, 2012.

Bisetty, K., Corcho, F.J., Canto, J., Kruger, H.G., Perez, J.J. "Simulated Annealing Study of the Pentacyclo-undecane Cage Amino Acid Tripeptides of the Type [Ac-X-Y-Z-NHMe]", *Journal of Molecular Structure: THEOCHEM*, Vol. 759, pp. 145–157, 2006.

Bishop, C.M. "Neural Networks for Pattern Recognition", Oxford: Oxford University Press, 1995.

Bryan, K., Cunningham, P., Bolshkova, N. "Application of simulated annealing to the biclustering of gene expression data", *IEEE Transactions on Information Technology in Biomedicine*, pp. 10519–525, 2006.

Burjorjee, K.M. "Explaining optimization in genetic algorithms with uniform crossover", *FOGA 2013 — Proceedings of the 12th ACM Workshop on Foundations of Genetic Algorithms*, pp. 37–49, 2013.

Cao, H., Chen, W., Jia, L., Zhang, Y., Lu, Y. "Cluster analysis based on attractor particle swarm optimization with boundary zoomed for working conditions classification of power plant pulverizing system", *Neurocomputing*, Vol. 117, pp. 54–63, 2013.

Cetinel, H., Kayacan, O., Ozaydin, D. "Investigation of nucleation and grain growth in 2-dimensional systems by using generalized Monte Carlo simulations", *Physica A: Statistical Mechanics and its Applications*, Vol. 392, No. 18, pp. 4121–4126, 2013.

Chang, Y., Chen, W., Lee, C., Huang, C. "Simulated Annealing Based Optimal Chiller Loading for Saving Energy", *Energy Conversion and Management*, Vol. 47, pp. 2044–2058, 2006.

Chang, Y. "An innovative approach for demand side management — optimal chiller loading by simulated annealing", *Energy*, Vol. 31, pp. 1883–1896, 2006.

Chen, T.-Y., Su, J.-J. "Efficiency improvement of simulated annealing in optimal structural designs", *Advances in Engineering Software*, Vol. 33, No. 7–10, pp. 675–680, 2002.

Chimi-Chiadjeu, O., Vannier, E., Dusséaux, R., Le Hégarat-Mascle, S., Taconet, O. "Using simulated annealing algorithm to move clod boundaries on seedbed digital elevation model", *Computers and Geosciences*, Vol. 57, pp. 68–76, 2013.

Cleveland, M.A., Brunner, T.A., Gentile, N.A., Keasler, J.A. "Obtaining identical results with double precision global accuracy on different numbers of processors in parallel particle Monte Carlo simulations", *Journal of Computational Physics*, Vol. 251, pp. 223–236, 2013.

Curran, J.M. "A MCMC Method for Resolving Two Person Mixtures", *Science & Justice*, Vol. 48, pp. 168–177, 2008.

Das, A., Chakrabarti, B.K. "Quantum Annealing and Related Optimization Methods", *Lecture Notes in Physics*, Heidelberg: Springer, Vol. 679, 2005.

De Vicente, J., Lanchares, J., Hermida, R. "Placement by thermodynamic simulated annealing", *Physics Letters A*, Vol. 317, pp. 415–423, 2003.

Dempster, A., Liard, N., Rubin, D. "Maximum likelihood from incomplete data via the EM algorithm (with discussion)", *Journal of the Royal Statistical Society*, B39, pp. 1–38, 1977.

Dindar, Z.A., Marwala, T. "Option Pricing Using a Committee of Neural Networks and Optimized Networks", In *Proceedings of the 2004 IEEE International Conference on Systems, Man, and Cybernetics*, Vol. 1, pp. 434–438, 2004.

Dindar, Z.A. "Artificial Neural Networks Applied to Option Pricing", Unpublished Master Thesis, University of the Witwatersrand, Johannesburg, 2004.

Draper, N., Smith, H. "Applied Regression Analysis", 3rd Edition, New York: J. Wiley, 1998.

Dunn, W.L., Shultis, J.K. "Monte Carlo methods for design and analysis of radiation detectors", *Radiat Phys and Chem*, Vol. 78, pp. 852–858, 2009.

Engelbrecht, A.P. "Fundamentals of Computational Swarm Intelligence", Wiley, 2005.

Fabian, M., Svab, E., Pamukchieva, V., Szekeres, A., Todorova, K., Vogel, S., Ruett, U. "Reverse Monte Carlo modeling of the neutron and X-ray diffraction data for new chalcogenide Ge–Sb–S(Se)–Te glasses", *Journal of Physics and Chemistry of Solids*, Vol. 74, No. 10, pp. 1355–1362, 2013.

Gallagher, K., Charvin, K., Nielsen, S., Sambridge, M., Stephenson, J. "Markov Chain Monte Carlo (MCMC) sampling methods to determine optimal models, model resolution and model choice for earth science problems", *Marine and Petroleum Geology*, Vol. 26, pp. 525–535, 2009.

Gandomi, A.H., Alavi, A.H., Shadmehri, D.M., Sahab, M.G. "An empirical model for shear capacity of RC deep beams using genetic-simulated annealing", *Archives of Civil and Mechanical Engineering*, Vol. 13, No. 3, pp. 354–369, 2013.

Goldberg, D.E. "Genetic Algorithms in Search, Optimization, and Machine Learning. Reading", Addison-Wesley, MA, 1989.

Gomes, A.M., Oliveira, J.F. "Solving irregular strip packing problems by hybridising simulated annealing and linear programming", *European Journal of Operational Research*, Vol. 171, pp. 811–829, 2006.

González, J.P.N., Villanueva, P.P. "Vehicle lateral dynamics fault diagnosis using an autoassociative neural network and a fuzzy system", *Lecture Notes in Computer Science (including subseries Lecture Notes in Artificial Intelligence and Lecture Notes in Bioinformatics)*, Vol. 7630 LNAI (PART 2), pp. 236–246, 2013.

Gunasekaran, S., Iruthayarajan, M.W. "Contour optimization of suspension insulators using real coded genetic algorithm with simulated binary crossover", *Proceedings of the 2013 International Conference on Pattern Recognition, Informatics and Mobile Engineering*, PRIME 2013, art. no. 6496501, pp. 360–364, 2013.

Güngör, Z., Ünler, A. "K-harmonic means data clustering with simulated annealing heuristic", *Applied Mathematics and Computation*, Vol. 184, pp. 199–209, 2007.

Guo, J., Zhou, J., Song, L., Zou, Q., Zeng, X. "Uncertainty assessment and optimization of hydrological model with the Shuffled Complex Evolution Metropolis algorithm: An application to artificial neural network rainfall-runoff model", *Stochastic Environmental Research and Risk Assessment*, Vol. 27, No. 4, pp. 985–1004, 2013.

Haga, H., Suehiro, A. "Automatic test case generation based on genetic algorithm and mutation analysis", *Proceedings — 2012 IEEE International Conference on Control System, Computing and Engineering*, ICCSCE 2012, art. no. 6487127, pp. 119–123, 2013.

Hao, X.-H., Zhang, S.-Q., Chen, W., Xiao, J., Wang, W.-Z., Ma, Y. "Research on stochastic estimation of voltage sag based on MCMC method", *Dianli Xitong Baohu yu Kongzhi/Power System Protection and Control*, Vol. 41, No. 9, pp. 94–99, 2013.

Heppner, F., Grenander, U. "A Stochastic Non-linear Model for Coordinated Bird Flocks", In: Krasner S. (ed.), The Ubiquity of Chaos, 1st Edition, AAAS Publications, Washington DC, 1990.

Hines, J.W., Garvey, D. "Sensor fault detectability measures for autoassociative empirical models", *16th Annual Joint ISA POWID/EPRI Controls and Instrumentation Conference and 49th Annual ISA Power Industry Division*, POWID Symposium, Vol. 2, pp. 835–847, 2006.

Horng, M.-F., Chen, Y.-T., Chu, S.-C., Pan, J.-S., Liao, B.-Y., Hsu, J.-P., Lin, J.-N. "A genetic algorithm with elite mutation to optimize cruise area of mobile sinks in hierarchical wireless sensor networks", *Lecture Notes in Computer Science (including subseries Lecture Notes in Artificial Intelligence and Lecture Notes in Bioinformatics)*, Vol. 7654 LNAI (PART 2), pp. 402–412, 2012.

Jia, Y., Zhang, C. "Front-view Vehicle Detection by Markov chain Monte Carlo Method", *Pattern Recognition*, Vol. 42, pp. 313–321, 2009.

Jiang, Y., Hu, T., Huang, C., Wu, X. "Particle Swarm Optimization Based on Dynamic Niche Technology with Applications to Conceptual Design", *Advances in Engneering Software*, Vol. 38, pp. 668–676, 2007.

Jiang, B., Wang, N., Wang, L. "Particle swarm optimization with age-group topology for multimodal functions and data clustering", *Communications in Nonlinear Science and Numerical Simulation*, Vol. 18, No. 11, pp. 3134–3145, 2013.

Jing, L., Vadakkepat, P. "Interacting MCMC particle filter for tracking maneuvering target", *Digital Signal Processing*, doi: 10.1016/j.dsp.2009.08.011, 2009.

Johannes, J., Schneider, Puchta, M. "Investigation of acceptance simulated annealing — A simplified approach to adaptive cooling schedules", *Physica A: Statistical Mechanics and its Applications*, Vol. 389, No. 24, pp. 5822–5831, 15 December 2010.

Kannan, S., Zacharias, M. "Simulated annealing coupled replica exchange molecular dynamics — An efficient conformational sampling method", *Journal of Structural Biology*, Vol. 166, No. 3, pp. 288–294, 2009.

Kathiravan, R., Ganguli, R. "Particle Swarm Optimization for determining shortest distance to voltage collapse", *International Journal of Electrical Power & Energy Systems*, Vol. 29, pp. 796–802, 2007.

Keesing, D.B., O'Sullivan, J.A., Politte, D.G., Whiting, B.R., Snyder, D.L. "Missing data estimation for fully 3D spiral CT image reconstruction", *Progress in Biomedical Optics and Imaging — Proceedings of SPIE*, 6510, Paper 65105V, 2007.

Kennedy, J.E., Eberhart, R.C. "Particle Swarm Optimization", In *Proceedings of the IEEE International Conference on Neural Networks*, pp. 942–1948, 1995.

Kirkpatrick, S., Gelatt, C.D., Vecchi, M.P. "Optimization by Simulated Annealing", *Science, New Series*, Vol. 220, pp. 671–680, 1983.

Kow, W.Y., Chin, Y.K., Khong, W.L., Lau, H.K., Teo, K.T.K. "Implementing manifold learning in adaptive MCMC for tracking vehicle under disturbances", *Proceedings — 2012 IEEE International Conference on Control System, Computing and Engineering*, ICCSCE 2012, art. no. 6487186, pp. 440–445, 2012.

Krishnamoorthi, R., Sathiya Devi, S. "A simple computational model for image retrieval with weighted multifeatures based on orthogonal polynomials and genetic algorithm", *Neurocomputing*, Vol. 116, pp. 165–181, 2013.

Kuandykov, L. "Bayesian hierarchical model with MCMC for optical cable flame retardancy tests", *Expert Systems with Applications*, Vol. 40, No. 9, pp. 3574–3579, 2013.

Laseetha, T.S.J., Sukanesh, R. "Synthesis of linear antenna array using genetic algorithm with cost based roulette to maximize side lobe level reduction", *WSEAS Transactions on Communications*, Vol. 10, No. 12, pp. 385–394, 2011.

Leke, B., Marwala, T., Tettey, T. "Using inverse neural network for HIV adaptive control", *International Journal of Computational Intelligence Research*, Vol. 3, No. 1, pp. 11–15, 2007.
Liang, R., Du, X., Zhao, Q., Cheng, L. "Sparse signal recovery based on simulated annealing", *Applied Mechanics and Materials*, Vols. 321–324, pp. 1295–1298, 2013.
Liesenfeld, R., Richard, J. "Improving MCMC, using efficient importance sampling", *Computational Statistics & Data Analysis*, Vol. 53, pp. 272–288, 2008.
Lin, Y., Chang, W., Hsieh, J. "Application of Multi-phase Particle Swarm Optimization technique to inverse radiation problem", *Journal of Quantitative Spectroscopy & Radiativ Transfer*, Vol. 109, pp. 476–493, 2008.
Lin, R.-C., Sir, M.Y., Pasupathy, K.S. "Multi-objective simulation optimization using data envelopment analysis and genetic algorithm: Specific application to determining optimal resource levels in surgical services", *Omega* (United Kingdom), Vol. 41, No. 5, pp. 881–892, 2013.
Little, R., Rubin, D. "Statistical Analysis with Missing Data", 1st Edition, New York: John Wiley and Sons, 1987.
Little, R., Rubin, D. "Statistical Analysis with Missing Data", Wiley Publishers, 2002.
Liu, X., Newsome, D., Coppens, M. "Dynamic Monte Carlo simulations of binary self-diffusion in ZSM-5", *Microporous and Mesoporous Materials*, Vol. 125, pp. 149–159, 2009.
Makki, B., Hosseini, M.N. "Some refinements of the standard autoassociative neural network", *Neural Computing and Applications*, Vol. 22, Nos. 7–8, pp. 1461–1475, 2013.
Markhasin, L.Q. "Monte Carlo methods for integration of functions with dominating mixed smoothness in arbitrary dimension", *Journal of Complexity*, Vol. 29, No. 5, pp. 370–388, 2013.
Marwala, T. "Fault Identification Using Neural Networks and Vibration data", Ph.D. Thesis University of Cambridge, 2001.
Marwala, T. "Finite Element Model updating using Particle Swarm Optimization", *International Journal of Engineering Simulation*, Vol. 6, pp. 25–30, 2005a.
Marwala, T. "The artificial beer taster", Electricity + Control, pp. 22–23, May 2005b.
Marwala, T. "Computational Intelligence for Modelling Complex Systems", Research India Publications, Delhi, 2007.
Marwala, T. "Computational Intelligence for Missing Data Imputation, Estimation and Management: Knowledge Optimization Techniques", Information Science, Reference Imprint, IGI Global Publications, New York, 2009.
Marwala, T. "Condition Monitoring Using Computational Intelligence Methods", Springer-Verlag, Heidelberg, 2012.
Marwala, T., Chakraverty, S. "Fault classification in structures with incomplete measured data using autoassociative neural networks and genetic algorithm", *Current Science*, Vol. 90, No. 4, pp. 542–548, 2006.
Marwala, T., Lagazio, M. "Militarized Conflict Modeling Using Computational Intelligence Techniques", Springer-Verlag, Heidelberg, 2011.
Mathe, P., Novak, E. "Simple Monte Carlo and the Metropolis Algorithm", *Journal of Complex*, Vol. 23, pp. 673–696, 2007.
McGookin, E.W., Murray-Smith, D.J. "Submarine Manoeuvring Controllers' Optimisation using Simulated Annealing and Genetic Algorithms", *Control Engineering Practice*, Vol. 14, pp. 1–15, 2006.
Meer, K. "Simulated Annealing versus Metropolis for a TSP Instance", *Information Processing Letters*, Vol. 104, pp. 216–219, 2007.
Metropolis, N., Rosenbluth, A., Rosenbluth, M. "A. Teller, and E. Teller, Equation of State Calculations by Fast Computing Machines", *The Journal of Chemical Physics*, Vol. 21, pp. 1087–1092, 1953.
Michalewicz, Z. "Genetic Algorithms + Data Structures = Evolution Programs", Berling Heidelberg, 3rd Edition, New York: Springer-Verlag, 1996.

Mistry, J., Nelwamondo, F.V and Marwala, T. "Investigating Demographic Influences for HIV Classification Using Bayesian Autoassociative Neural Networks", *Lecture Notes in Computer Science*, Vol. 5507, pp. 752–759, 2009.

Mitchell, M. "An Introduction to Genetic Algorithms", MIT Press, Cambridge, MA, 1996.

Mohamed, S., Marwala, T. "Neural network based techniques for estimating missing data in databases", *Proceedings of the 16th Annual Symposium of the Pattern Recognition Society of South Africa*, Langebaan, South Africa, pp. 27–32, 2005.

Moita, J.M.S., Correia, V.M.F., Martins, P.G., Soares, C.M.M., Soares, C.A.M. "Optimal Design in vibration control of adaptive structures using a Simulated Annealing Algorithm", *Composite Structures*, Vol. 75, pp. 79–87, 2006.

Mojirsheibani, M. "Nonparametric curve estimation with missing data: A general empirical process approach", *Journal of Statistical Planning and Inference*, Vol. 137, No. 9, pp. 2733–2758, 2007.

Mudaliar, D.N., Modi, N.K. "Unraveling Travelling Salesman Problem by genetic algorithm using m-crossover operator", *International Conference on Signal Processing, Image Processing and Pattern Recognition 2013*, ICSIPR 2013, 1, art. no. 6497974, 2013.

Naderi, B., Zandieh, M., Khaleghi, A., Balagh, G., Roshanaei, V. "An Improved Simulated Annealing for hybrid flowshops with sequence-dependent setup and transportation times to minimize total completion time and total tardiness", *Expert Systems With Applications*, Vol. 36, pp. 9625–9633, 2009.

Nagata, Y., Kobayashi, S. "A powerful genetic algorithm using edge assembly crossover for the traveling salesman problem", *INFORMS Journal on Computing*, Vol. 25, No. 2, pp. 346–363, 2013.

Nelwamondo, F.V. "Computational Intelligence Techniques for Missing Data Imputation", Ph.D. Thesis, University of the Witwatersrand, 2008.

Nelwamondo, F.V., Golding, D., Marwala, T. "A dynamic programming approach to missing data estimation using neural networks", *Information Sciences*, Vol. 237, pp. 49–58, 2013.

Oliveira, R.G., Schneck, E., Quinn, B.E., Konovalov, O.V., Brandenburg, K., Seydel, U., Gill, T., Hanna, C.B., Pink, D.A., Tanaka, M. "Physical mechanisms of bacterial survival revealed by combined grazing-incidence X-ray Scattering and Monte Carlo Simulation", *Comptes Rendus Chimie*, Vol. 12, pp. 209–217, 2009.

Pati, S.K., Das, A.K. "Missing value estimation of microarray data using similarity measurement", *Lecture Notes in Computer Science*, Vol. 7677, pp. 602–610, 2012.

Paya-Zaforteza, I., Yepes, V., Hospitaler, A., Gonzalez-Vidosa, F. "CO_2-Optimization of reinforced concrete frames by Simulated Annealing", *Engineering Structures*, Vol. 31, pp. 1501–1508, 2009.

Qi, H., Ruan, L.M., Shi, M., An, W., Tan, H.P. "A combinatorial Particle Swarm Optimization for solving multi-mode resource-constrained project scheduling problems", *Applied Mathematics and Computation*, Vol. 195, pp. 299–308, 2008.

Rahmati, M., Modarress, H. "Nitrogen Adsorption on nanoporous Zeolites studied by Grand Canonical Monte Carlo simulation", *Journal of Molecular Structure: THEOCHEM*, Vol. 901, pp. 110–116, 2009.

Rajakumar, B.R. "Static and adaptive mutation techniques for genetic algorithm: A systematic comparative analysis", *International Journal of Computational Science and Engineering*, Vol. 8, No. 2, pp. 180–193, 2013.

Ransome, T. "Automatic Minimisation of Patient Setup Errors in Proton Beam Therapy", Unpublished Master Thesis, University of the Witwatersrand, Johannesburg, 2006.

Ransome, T.M., Rubin, D.M., Marwala, T., de Kok, E.A. "Optimising the Verification of Patient Positioning in Proton Beam Therapy", *In Proceedings of the IEEE 3rd International Conference on Computer Cybernetics*, pp. 279–284, 2005.

Reynolds, C.W. "Flocks, Herds and Schools: A Distributed Behavioral Model", *Computer Graphics*, Vol. 2, pp. 25–34, 1987.

Robles-Ortega, M.D., Ortega, L., Feito, F.R. "A new approach to create textured urban models through genetic algorithms", *Information Sciences*, Vol. 243, pp. 1–19, 2013.

Rubin, D.B. "Multiple imputations in sample surveys — A phenomenological Bayesian approach to non-response", *Proceedings of the Survey Research Methods Section of the American Statistical Association*, pp. 20–34, 1978.

Sacco, W.F., Lapa, C.M.F., Pereira, C.M.N.A., Filho, H.A. "A Metropolis Algorithm applied to a Nuclear Power Plant auxiliary feedwater system surveillance tests policy optimization", *Progress in Nuclear Energy*, Vol. 50, pp. 15–21, 2008.

Salazar, R., Toral, R. "Simulated Annealing Using Hybrid Monte Carlo", arXiv:cond-mat/9706051, 2006.

Setayesh, M., Zhang, M., Johnston, M. "A novel particle swarm optimisation approach to detecting continuous, thin and smooth edges in noisy images", *Information Sciences*, Vol. 246, pp. 28–51, 2013.

Shi, F., Zhang, D., Chen, J., Karimi, H.R. "Missing value estimation for microarray data by bayesian principal component analysis and iterative local least squares", *Mathematical Problems in Engineering*, 2013, art. no. 162938, 2013.

Shieh, M.-Y., Chiou, J.-S. "Design of multi-sensory integrated interactive robot with genetic algorithm", *Advanced Science Letters*, Vol. 19, No. 9, pp. 2615–2617, 2013.

Shih, W.J., Quan, H., Chang, M.N. "Estimation of the mean when data contain non-ignorable missing values from a random effects model", *Statistics and Probability Letters*, pp. 249–252, 2008.

Snyman, J.A. "Practical Mathematical Optimization: An Introduction to Basic Optimization Theory and Classical and New Gradient-Based Algorithms", Springer, New York, 2005.

Spiller, J.M., Marwala, T. "Evolutionary algorithms for warp control point placement", *The 2nd International Symposium on Intelligence Computation and Applications* (ISICA 2007), Wuhan, China, pp. 327–331, 2007.

Tang, P.-H., Tseng, M.-H. "Adaptive directed mutation for real-coded genetic algorithms", *Applied Soft Computing*, Vol. 13, No. 1, pp. 600–614, 2013.

Tanimoto, J., Hagishima, A. "State transition probability for the Markov Model dealing with on/off cooling schedule in dwellings", *Energy and Buildings*, Vol. 37, No. 3, pp. 181–187, March 2005.

Tiana, G., Sutto, L., Broglia, R.A. "Use of the metropolis Algorithm to simulate the dynamics of protein chains", *Physica A: Statistical Mechanics and its Applications*, Vol. 380, pp. 241–249, 2007.

Turrell, A.E., Sherlock, M., Rose, S.J. "A Monte Carlo algorithm for degenerate plasmas", *Journal of Computational Physics*, Vol. 249, ISSN: 0021-9991, pp. 13–21, 2013.

Torrent-Fontbona, F., Muñoz, V., López, B. "Solving large immobile location-Allocation by affinity propagation and simulated annealing. Application to select which sporting event to watch", *Expert Systems with Applications*, Vol. 40, No. 11, pp. 4593–4599, 2013.

Tran, T.-D., Jin, G.-G. "Genetic algorithm with multi-colony dynamic reproduction", *Proceedings of the 12th Annual Genetic and Evolutionary Computation Conference, GECCO'10 — Companion Publication*, pp. 2115–2116, 2010.

Triki, E., Collette, Y., Siarry, P. "A theoretical study on the behavior of simulated annealing leading to a new cooling schedule", *European Journal of Operational Research*, Vol. 166, No. 1, pp. 77–92, 1 October 2005.

van den Bergh, F., Engelbrecht, A.P. "Study of particle swarm optimization particle trajectories", *Information Sciences*, Vol. 176, No. 8, pp. 937–971, 2006.

Wang, S., Xing, Y., Tian, M., Qiu, X., Qi, J. "Hybrid evolutionary-Metropolis Monte Carlo algorithm for wet etching of silicon MEMS fabrication process", *Jixie Gongcheng Xuebao/Journal of Mechanical Engineering*, Vol. 49, No. 5, pp. 167–172, 2013.

Weinberger, E. Correlated and uncorrelated fitness landscapes and how to tell the difference. *Biological Cybernet*, Vol. 63, pp. 325–336, 1990.

Wooldridge, J.M. "Inverse probability weighted estimation for general missing data problems", *Journal of Econometrics*, Vol. 141, No. 2, pp. 1281–1301, 2007.

Xhafa, F., Herrero, X., Barolli, A., Barolli, L., Takizawa, M. "Evaluation of struggle strategy in Genetic Algorithms for ground stations scheduling problem", *Journal of Computer and System Sciences*, Vol. 79, No. 7, pp. 1086–1100, 2013.

Yan, T.-S., Guo, G.-Q., Li, W. "An improved multi-objective genetic algorithm based on granular ranking and distant reproduction", *Proceedings — 2011 International Conference of Information Technology, Computer Engineering and Management Sciences*, ICM 2011, 1, art. no. 6113378, pp. 151–154, 2011.

Yuan, S., Skinner, B., Huang, S., Liu, D. "A new crossover approach for solving the multiple travelling salesmen problem using genetic algorithms", *European Journal of Operational Research*, Vol. 228, No. 1, pp. 72–82, 2013.

Zamani, R. "A competitive magnet-based genetic algorithm for solving the resource-constrained project scheduling problem", *European Journal of Operational Research*, Vol. 229, No. 2, pp. 552–559, 2013.

Zhang, D., Melnik, R.V.N. "Computational aspects of Monte-Carlo simulations of the first passage time for multivariate transformed Brownian motions with jumps", *International Journal of Computational Methods*, art. no. 1350026, Vol. 10, No. 5, 2013.

Zhang, L., Chang, H., Xu, R. "Equal-width partitioning roulette wheel selection in genetic algorithm", *Proceedings — 2012 Conference on Technologies and Applications of Artificial Intelligence*, TAAI 2012, art. no. 6395007, pp. 62–67, 2012.

Zhao, H., Zheng, C. "Correcting the Multi-Monte Carlo method for particle coagulation", *Powder Technology*, Vol. 193, No. 1, pp. 120–123, 2009.

Zhu, H.-M., Li, R., Zeng, Z.-F., Yu, K.-M. "Bayesian analysis of Probit quantile regression models based on Metropolis–Hastings algorithm", *Hunan Daxue Xuebao/Journal of Hunan University Natural Sciences*, Vol. 40, No. 2, pp. 98–102, 2013.

Chapter 5

Neural Networks for Modeling Granger Causality

Abstract. The multi-layer perceptron (MLP) neural networks which is formulated in the Bayesian framework and trained using the Hybrid Monte Carlo (HMC) method as well as the radial basis function (RBF) trained using k-means and pseudo-inverse methods are used to build causal machines. These methods are then applied to extend Granger causality model to the non-linear domain and this is applied to model a simulated medical data in the form of chaotic time series.

5.1 Introduction

This chapter introduces the multi-layer perceptron (MLP) and radial basis function (RBF) for modeling Granger causality. In Chapter 3, the MLP and RBF were framed as causal machines by putting the conditions that the input happens before the output, the input and the output are connected and that there is a flow of information from the cause to the effect. The projectile theory of causality which was discussed in Chapter 1 was deemed to define the MLP and RBF causal machines.

The first part of this chapter introduces what is known as the Granger causality. In Granger causality, variable x is deemed to be a cause of variable y if previous values of variable y when used to predict future values of y performs worse than when past values of y and x are used to predict future values of y (Granger, 1969; Hacker and Hatemi, 2006). This is done by employing the statistical tools t-test and F-test (Rice, 2006). Granger causality is of course not real causality but it has been found to be useful in many areas including economics (Marwala, 2013).

This chapter basically combines Granger causality with the MLP and RBF neural networks. Combining neural networks with Granger causality has been explored in the past albeit in different context. Dong *et al.* (2012) successfully used Granger causality to identify feedback loops in neural networks. Wu *et al.* (2011) applied Granger causality to detect the neural network structure.

Attanasio and Triacca (2011) applied neural network and Granger causality to identify human influence on climate. They applied the MLP to create a non-linear Granger causality and observed that there was substantial unidirectional Granger causality from carbon dioxide to global temperature.

This chapter begins by describing the Granger causality model which in it, there is a function that models the cause and the effect. Granger's original proposal used linear autoregressive models and in this chapter, we apply the MLP which is trained using the Bayesian approach to describe the posterior probability as well as the RBF trained using k-means and inverse methods.

5.2 Granger Causality

In this section, we describe Granger causality which is a technique that was proposed by Nobel Laurate Clive Granger to detect the so-called Granger causality. Granger causality has found many uses in different disciplines. Hsueh *et al.* (2013) applied Granger causality successfully to relate financial development in Asia to economic growth and financial development. Candelon *et al.* (2013) applied Granger causality successfully to assess multiple risk levels across tail distributions in oil markets integration. Çağlayan and Güriş (2013) successfully applied Granger causality to relate consumption levels to CO_2 emission. Other applications of Granger causality are in the stock market (Croux and Reusens, 2013), in magnetic resonance imaging (Anwar *et al.*, 2012), and to relate technology progress to international trade (Yang, 2012).

Suppose we are given series of y values at time t as well as at earlier times, then an autoregressive linear model can be built using the following mathematical equation (Granger, 1969):

$$y(t) = \sum_{j=1}^{p} B_j y(t-j) + E_1(t). \tag{5.1}$$

Here p is the maximum number of past data points while E is the error of this model and B is a coefficient. Basically, Equation 5.1 implies that one can be able to predict future values of y using the past values of y. Equation 5.1 assumes that the history of y is available, stationary and can be modeled using linear relationships. Suppose we then introduce variable x which also has a time history available, is stationary and can be modeled to predict future values of y. Thus Equation 5.1 may then be re-written as follows (Granger, 1969):

$$y(t) = \sum_{j=1}^{q} A_j x(t-j) + \sum_{j=1}^{p} B_j y(t-j) + E_2(t). \tag{5.2}$$

Here A is a coefficient while q is the past time values to be included. Granger observed that given Equations 5.1 and 5.2, then variable x Granger causes variable y if the introduction of variable x to Equation 5.1 to form Equation 5.2 results in

Equation 5.2 being better at predicting variable y than Equation 5.2. In other words, x Granger causes y if E_2 is smaller than E_1.

Equations 5.1 and 5.2 can be generalized to form Equations 5.3 and 5.4 which can be written mathematically as follows:

$$y_{later} = f(y_{early}) + E_1 \tag{5.3}$$

$$y_{later} = f(y_{early}, x_{earlier}) + E_2. \tag{5.4}$$

Here f is the functional mapping, which in this chapter is approximated by the MLP and the RBF, while $y_{earlier}$ is a vector indicating the earlier version of y while $x_{earlier}$ is a vector indicating the earlier version of x and y_{later} is a vector indicating the later time history of y.

5.3 Multi-layer Perceptron for Granger Causality

As stated before, Equations 5.1 and 5.2 are limited in that they are linear and this chapter introduces the MLP neural network to model the functional mappings in Equations 5.3 and 5.4. Using the MLP equation that was described by Bishop (1995), Equations 5.3 and 5.4 can be extended to the non-linear domain to become:

$$y_{later} = f_{outer}\left(\sum_{j=1}^{M} w_{kj}^{(2)} f_{inner}\left(\sum_{i=1}^{d} w_{ji}^{(1)} x_i^{earlier} + w_{j0}^{(1)}\right) + w_{k0}^{(2)}\right) + E_1 \tag{5.5}$$

$$y_{later} = f_{outer}\left(\sum_{j=1}^{M} w_{kj}^{(2)} f_{inner}\left(\sum_{i=1}^{d} w_{ji}^{(1)} x_i^{earlier} + \sum_{i=d}^{e} w_{ji}^{(1)} y_i^{earlier} + w_{j0}^{(1)}\right) + w_{k0}^{(2)}\right) + E_2. \tag{5.6}$$

Here, $w_{ji}^{(1)}$ and $w_{kj}^{(2)}$ are the weights in the first and second layers, respectively, moving from input i to hidden unit j, M is the number of hidden units, d is the number of time units for the previous time history of x while e is the number of time units for the previous time history of y, whereas $w_{j0}^{(1)}$ designates the bias for the hidden unit j and $w_{k0}^{(2)}$ designates the bias for the output unit k. Given the availability of historical data x and y then the next step is to apply system identification techniques to identify the weights that will identify the network weights and in this chapter, we apply statistical technique based on Bayes' theorem.

There are two ways in which one can assess whether E_1 or E_2 are statistically different and this can be done using a t-test and Chi-squared test for variance. In a t-test, the test statistic is a t distribution if the null hypothesis is described and is applied to decide if two sets of data are considerably different from each other (Sawilowsky, 2005; Fay and Proschan, 2010; Blair and Higgins, 1980). The other way is to perform a Chi-squared test of the hypothesis that the data set in question is from a Gaussian distribution with a given variance, in contradiction to the alternative that the data set in question is from a Gaussian distribution of a dissimilar variance (Corder and Foreman, 2009; Greenwood and Nikulin, 1996; Nikulin, 1973; Bagdonavicius and Nikulin, 2011).

Tang and Srihari (2012) applied Chi-squared test to successfully trained Bayesian networks and applied this to multinomial data and found that the proposed method was more effective than the branch and bound algorithm and human experts. Katayama (2012) applied the Chi-squared test successfully in structural VARMA models with uncorrelated errors whereas Kakizawa (2012) successfully applied the Chi-squared test for a composite hypothesis.

Qi (2013) applied the t-test to analyze the effect of spreading of Western culture in China whereas Kumagai and Hayashi (2013) successfully applied the t-test for quantum hypothesis test on Gaussian states. Halperin and Klausner (2013) applied the t-test to improve frequency analyses in preclinical effectiveness studies whereas Wang *et al.* (2012) successfully applied the t-test for feature selection.

5.3.1 Bayesian statistics

The goal of learning the weights in Equations 5.5 and 5.6 is accomplished in this chapter using the Bayesian approach. Bayes' theorem can be written as follows (Bishop, 1995):

$$P(w|[D]) = \frac{P([D]|w)P(w)}{P([D])}. \tag{5.7}$$

Here $P(w)$ is the probability distribution function of the weight-space in the absence of the data (prior distribution function) and $[D] \equiv (y_1, \ldots, y_N)$ is a matrix of the data, $P(w|[D])$ is the posterior probability distribution function, $P([D|w])$ is the likelihood function and $P([D])$ is the evidence. Im and Park (2013) successfully used Bayesian approach for stochastic structural optimization whereas Schmelter *et al.* (2012) applied successfully Bayesian statistics to account for uncertainty in cumulative sediment transport. Marcoulaki *et al.* (2012) used Bayesian statistics to successfully forecast occupational accident statistics and work time loss distributions in the Greek Petrochemical Industry whereas Zhong *et al.* (2012) applied Bayesian statistics successfully to improve group assignment and annual average daily traffic estimation accuracy of short-term traffic counts using historical seasonal patterns. Other successful applications of Bayesian statistics are to predict order statistics for a Type-II censored Weibull distribution (Kundu and Raqab, 2012) as well as to examine the progress of white matter diffusivities in the splenium of the corpus callosum tract and the right internal capsule tract in new born babies (Hua *et al.*, 2012).

In a MLP neural network model, identification of the posterior probability of weights given the data may be written in the Bayesian framework as follows (MacKay, 1991; 1992; Bishop, 1995; Marwala, 2001; 2007; 2012):

$$P(w|[D]) = \frac{1}{Z_s} \exp\left(\beta \sum_{n}^{N} \sum_{k}^{K} \{t_{nk} - y_{nk}\}^2 - \sum_{j}^{W} \frac{\alpha_j}{2} w_j^2\right) \tag{5.8}$$

where t_{nk} is the target output with k being the index for the output units, n is the index for the training example, N is the number of training examples, K is the number of network outputs, W is the number of network weights, whereas α and β are hyper-parameters and

$$Z_S(\alpha, \beta) = \left(\frac{2\pi}{\beta}\right)^{\frac{N}{2}} + \left(\frac{2\pi}{\alpha}\right)^{\frac{W}{2}}. \tag{5.9}$$

Equation 5.9 is solved in this chapter by sampling the posterior probability space using the HMC which is based on the Markov principles (Markov, 1971) and is described in Section 5.3.2.

5.3.2 Hybrid Monte Carlo (HMC)

The HMC method is a sampling technique which can be applied to sample probability function in Equation 5.8. In crude terms, the HMC technique hybridizes the Markov Chain Monte Carlo and the gradient based optimization method. The infusion of the gradient information into the Markov Chain Monte Carlo (MCMC) procedure guarantees that the simulation samples through the areas of higher probabilities and, consequently, accelerates convergence to a stationary probability distribution function. The HMC technique is a Markov chain process and consists of dynamic moves which apply the Hamiltonian dynamics and permit sampling states with constant total energy and stochastic moves which permit the technique to sample states with different total energy.

Hammond *et al.* (2013) successfully applied the HMC to simulate titania/yttria-doped iron whereas Zhou *et al.* (2013) successfully applied the HMC sampling to identify a support vector machine model and implemented these to simulated data. Zhou *et al.* (2013) successfully applied the HMC to estimate digital planar curves whereas Bretz *et al.* (2012) applied the HMC to study ultra-high energy cosmic rays from their sources to the observer. Wu *et al.* (2012) successfully applied the HMC for reactor analysis whereas Misev *et al.* (2012) successfully applied the HMC to model condensed phases.

In this chapter, we apply Hamiltonian mechanics to implement the HMC method. The Hamiltonian of a system is the sum of the kinetic and potential energy of the system. The *Hamiltonian* of the system and can be mathematically written as follows

(Neal, 1993):

$$H(w, p) = \beta \sum^{N} \sum_{k}^{K} \{y_{nk} - t_{nk}\}^2 + \frac{\alpha}{2} \sum_{j=1}^{W} w_j^2 + \frac{1}{2} \sum_{i}^{W} p_i^2 \tag{5.10}$$

where, p_i is the momentum of the ith variable and p must not to be confused with P, which designates the probability. The parameter, p_i is an imaginary variable that contextualizes the method in a molecular dynamics setting. The weight vector $\{w\}$ and momentum vector $\{p\}$ have identical dimension. The potential energy of a system depends on its positions while the kinetic energy of the system depends on its momentum. The position of all molecules at a specific time in a physical system is known as the *state space*. Hamiltonian Mechanics has been applied successfully in many areas. Kunstatter *et al.* (2013) successfully applied Hamiltonian dynamics in black holes while Escalante and Tzompantzi (2012) applied Hamiltonian dynamics to describe Maxwell's equations. In Equation 5.10, the first two terms are the potential energy of the system and the last term is the kinetic energy. The distribution over the phase space, i.e. position and momentum, can be written as follows (Neal, 1993):

$$P(w, p) = \frac{1}{Z} \exp(-H(w, p)) = P(w|D)P(p). \tag{5.11}$$

The phase space can be expressed in the Hamiltonian dynamics by developing the derivative of the 'position' and 'momentum' in terms of time τ. The expression 'position' applied in this chapter is the neural network weights. The dynamics of the Hamiltonian consequently can be expressed as follows (Neal, 1993):

$$\frac{dw_i}{d\tau} = +\frac{\partial H}{\partial p_i} = p_i \tag{5.12}$$

$$\frac{dp_i}{d\tau} = +\frac{\partial H}{\partial w_i} = -\frac{\partial E}{\partial p_i}. \tag{5.13}$$

Equations 5.12 and 5.13 cannot be solved exactly and are thus discretized by applying a 'leapfrog' technique. The leapfrog discretization of Equations 5.12 and 5.13 may be expressed as follows (Neal, 1993):

$$\hat{p}_i\left(\tau + \frac{\varepsilon}{2}\right) = \hat{p}_i(\tau) - \frac{\varepsilon}{2}\frac{\partial E}{\partial w_i}(\hat{w}(\tau)) \tag{5.14}$$

$$\hat{w}_i(\tau + \varepsilon) = \hat{w}_i(\tau) + \varepsilon \hat{p}_i\left(\tau + \frac{\varepsilon}{2}\right) \tag{5.15}$$

$$\hat{p}_i(\tau + \varepsilon) = \hat{p}_i\left(\tau + \frac{\varepsilon}{2}\right) - \frac{\varepsilon}{2}\frac{\partial E}{\partial w_i}(\hat{w}(\tau + \varepsilon)). \tag{5.16}$$

Equation 5.14 allows the leapfrog changes a small half step for the momentum vector, $\{p\}$, and, Equation 5.15, changes a full step for the 'position', $\{w\}$, and, Equation 5.16, changes a half step for the momentum vector, $\{p\}$. These three steps combined offer a single leapfrog iteration that estimates the '*position*' and '*momentum*' of a system at time $\tau + \varepsilon$ from the '*position*' and 'momentum' at time τ. This discretization is reversible in time it almost conserves the Hamiltonian and conserves the volume in the phase space (Neal, 1993).

The HMC technique works by following a series of paths from an initial state, i.e. '*positions*' and '*momentum*', and moving in some direction in the state space for a given length of time and accepting the final state by applying the Metropolis Algorithm. In this regard, states with high probability form a high proportion of the Markov chain and those with a low probability form a low proportion of the Markov chain. The advantage of the HMC is influenced by these three properties of the Hamiltonian dynamics (Neal, 1993; Bishop, 1995; Marwala, 2009):

1. Time reversibility: It is invariant under $t \to -t$, $p \to -p$.
2. Conservation of energy: The $H(w, p)$ is the same at all times.
3. Conservation of state space volumes (Neal, 1993).

For a stated leapfrog step size, ε_0, and the number of leapfrog steps, L, the dynamic transition of the HMC method is applied as explained by Neal (1993) and Bishop (1995):

1. Randomly choose the direction of the trajectory, λ, to be either -1 for a backwards trajectory or $+1$ for forwards trajectory.
2. Starting from the first state, $(\{w\}, \{p\})$, perform L leapfrog steps with the step size $\varepsilon = \varepsilon_0(1 + 0.1k)$ leading to state $(\{w\}^*, \{p\}^*)$. Here, ε_0 is a selected fixed step size and k is a number selected from a uniform distribution and is between 0 and 1.
3. Reject or accept $(\{w\}^*, \{p\}^*)$ by using the Metropolis criterion. If the state is accepted then the new state becomes $(\{w\}^*, \{p\}^*)$. If rejected, the old state, $(\{w\}, \{p\})$, is reserved as the new state.

The Metropolis algorithm is as follows (Metropolis *et al.*, 1953; Marwala, 2010; Marwala and Lagazio, 2011):

- *if* $p_{new} > p_{old}$ *accept state* (s_{new}).
- Else generate a random value γ uniformly distributed between 0 and 1.
- *if* $\frac{p_{new}}{p_{old}} > \gamma$ then accept s_{new}.
- Otherwise reject and return to s_{old}.

These steps demonstrate that the HMC technique incorporates the gradient information in Step 2 so that the HMC trajectories move in the direction of high posterior probabilities, ensuing better acceptance rate of samples (Bishop, 1995).

Parameter L needs to be high to allow rapid search of the state space. The selections of ε_0 and L influence the time at which the simulation converges to a stationary posterior probability distribution and the correlation between the states accepted. Systematic errors are not introduced by the leapfrog discretization because of occasional rejection of states. In the HMC method, the step size $\varepsilon = \varepsilon_0(1 + 0.1k)$ where k is uniformly distributed between 0 and 1 is not static and this guarantees that the step size for each trajectory is changed in order to reject states that have high correlation. This can also be achieved by changing the leapfrog steps. The application of the Bayesian technique in neural networks results with weight vectors with corresponding mean and standard deviation. For that reason, the output parameters have a probability distribution. Applying probability theory, the distribution of the output vector $\{y\}$ given input vector $\{x\}$ can be written as follows (Bishop, 1995):

$$p(\{y\}|\{x\}, D) = \int p(\{y\}|\{x\}, \{w\})p(\{w\}|D)d\{w\}. \tag{5.17}$$

The HMC method is used to identify the distribution of the weight vectors, and consequently, of the output parameters. The integral in Equation 5.17 may be estimated as follows (Bishop, 1995; Neal, 1993):

$$I \equiv \frac{1}{L}\sum_{i=1}^{L} f(\{w\}_i). \tag{5.18}$$

Here, L is the number of reserved states and f is the MLP network. The application of a Bayesian method to the neural network results in the mapping of the weight vector between the input and the output having a probability distribution, within the context of this chapter, the conditional probability of the effect given the cause.

5.4 RBF for Granger Causality

This section describes the application of the RBF to extend Granger causality to the non-linear domain. As described earlier, Granger causality is a technique that can be used to evaluate whether a time series prediction can be improved by incorporating information from another time series, within the context of the RBF. Marinazzo *et al.* (2006) used a RBF method to construct nonlinear Granger causality. They applied this technique to time series of heart rate and blood pressure as well as in the feedback loop of a model of excitatory and inhibitory neurons. They observed symmetric causal relationships between heart rate and blood pressure and that feedback loop causality quantifies the joint effect of couplings and membrane time constants.

Cheung and Van Veen (2011) successfully applied the RBF to model the nonlinear dynamics of the cortical signals and evaluated connections between cortical regions of interest based on Granger causality technique. The results demonstrated that the cortical linkage measuring model offers better results than the decoupled method.

Liu *et al.* (2011) successfully applied the RBF for multi-variable systems using directional flow method that used Granger causality to identify pertinent information allied to the practical connectivity between different units in the system. They used this method in a brain computer interface and observed that the directions of causal relation of active brain regions were distinct with regard to the envisioned direction.

Ancona *et al.* (2004) applied a RBF approach to nonlinear Granger causality. In particular, they used Granger causality in nonlinear bivariate time series and found that this approach was able to identify casual structures through data analysis. Equations 5.1 and 5.2 are inadequate in that they are linear and this section introduces RBF neural network to model the functional mappings in Equations 5.3 and 5.5. Using the RBF Equations 5.3 and 5.4 can be extended to the non-linear domain to become (Buhmann, 2003; Press *et al.*, 2007):

$$y_{later}(\{x\}) = \sum_{j=1}^{M} w_{jk}\phi_j\left(\left\|\{x^{earlier}\} - \mu_j\right\|\right) + E_1 \tag{5.19}$$

$$y_{later}(\{x\}) = \sum_{j=1}^{M} w_{jk}\phi_j\left(\left\|\begin{Bmatrix} x^{earlier} \\ y^{earlier} \end{Bmatrix} - \mu_j\right\|\right) + E_2. \tag{5.20}$$

There are many basis functions ϕ that can be used and these include thin plate spline as well as multi-quadric and in this chapter, we use a Gaussian function (Lázaro *et al.*, 2003):

$$\phi_j(\{x\}) = \exp\left(-\frac{(\{x\} - \mu_j)^2}{2\sigma_j^2}\right). \tag{5.21}$$

Here, w is the weight, M is the number of hidden units, μ is the network center, σ is the standard deviation and β is the coefficient of the Gaussian. Given the availability of historical data x and y then the next step is to apply system identification techniques to identify the weights and centers that will identify the network weights given the data. In this chapter, we use the k-means algorithm to estimate the network centers and a pseudo-inverse method to estimate the RBF weights and this is described in detail in the next sub-sections.

5.4.1 The k-means

The methods which are used in this chapter to train the RBF thus identify the centers and the weights in Equations 5.19–5.21 are the k-means and pseudo-inverse methods. A two-stage training process which uses the k-means method to identify the centers and a pseudo-inverse method to identify the network weights are applied. The *k-means* clustering method is a self-organizing map technique that is used to identify the centers of mass of the input data x (Hartigan, 1975; Hartigan and Wong, 1979).

Sakashita and Osana (2011) successfully applied the k-means method to segment image and edge information whereas Ding *et al.* (2011) successfully applied the RBF-based on k-clustering technique for nonlinear system identification.

Shen and Sun (2011) successfully applied RBF based on the k-means clustering algorithm to estimate the daily maximum electric load whereas Zhang (2010) successfully applied the RBF-based on the k-means technique to predict quality of service of web service. Other successful applications of the RBF which is based on the k-means technique are to identify artifacts in scenery images using color and line information (Saito and Osana, 2010), to predict maximum power point in photovoltaic panels (Liao, 2010), and to predict sea clutter (Su and Suo, 2007).

The objective of the *k-means* technique is to identify the centers of mass of data by minimizing the squared error function which can be expressed as follows (Hartigan, 1975; Hartigan and Wong, 1979; Liu and He, 2009):

$$E = \sum_{i=1}^{C} \sum_{x_j \in S_i} (\{x\}_j - \{c\}_i)^2. \tag{5.22}$$

Here C is the number of clusters in S_i, $i = 1, 2, \ldots, M$ and $\{c\}_i$ is the center of all the points $x_j \in S_i$.

The Lloyd's procedure is applied to estimate the cluster centers (Lloyd, 1982) and is started by randomly distributing the input space into k initial sets. The centroid is computed for each set and then a new section is built by relating each point with the closest centroid. The centroids are then re-estimated for the new centroids and the procedure is recurred by varying these two steps until convergence. Convergence is attained when the centroids no longer change.

5.4.2 Pseudo-inverse methods

After the centers of the RBF have been extracted the following activity is to compute the network weights given the training data and the extracted centers. To achieve this goal, the Moore–Penrose pseudo-inverse (Moore, 1920; Penrose, 1955; Golub and Van Loan, 1996) was applied. Given the training data and the centers identified, the RBF equation can be modified as follows (Bishop, 1995):

$$[y_{ij}] = [\phi_{ik}][w_{kj}] \tag{5.23}$$

where $[y_{ij}]$ is the output matrix, with i indicates the number of training cases and j indicates the number of output nodes, $[\phi_{ik}]$ is the activation function matrix in the hidden layer, i indicates the training cases, k is the number of hidden neurons whereas $[w_{kj}]$ is the weight matrix.

Solving Equation 5.23 for the weight matrix $[w_{kj}]$, occurs is the inversion of the activation function matrix $[\phi_{ik}]$. This matrix is not square and consequently it cannot be inverted using standard matrix methods. This matrix can be inverted using the Moore–Penrose pseudo-inverse technique which is expressed mathematically as follows (Moore, 1920; Penrose, 1955):

$$[\phi_{ik}]^* = \left([\phi_{ik}][\phi_{ik}]^T\right)^{-1}[\phi_{ik}]^T. \tag{5.24}$$

This, consequently, points toward that the weight matrix may be approximated by using the pseudo-inverse factor as follows (Moore, 1920; Penrose, 1955):

$$[w_{kj}] = [\phi_{ik}]^*[y_{ij}]. \tag{5.25}$$

5.5 Example: Mackey–Glass System

In this chapter, we apply an example to illustrate the causal machine by applying the MLP and RBF to take linear Granger causality model into the non-linear domain. The example which is considered as the data generated from the Mackey–Glass time-delay differential equation.

The Mackey–Glass equation is a differential equation that is meant to model periodic and chaotic phenomena. In this chapter, we generate a time series from the Mackey–Glass equation and use this to test the MLP and RBF-based Granger causal models. The Mackey–Glass equation has found usage in modeling complex phenomena such as the dynamics of diseases (Bélair *et al.*, 1995). The Mackey–Glass equation can be expressed as follows (Mackey and Glass, 1977; Glass and Mackey; 1979):

$$\frac{dx(t)}{dt} = \beta\frac{x(t-\tau)}{1+x(t-\tau)^n} - \gamma x(t), \beta, \gamma, n > 0. \tag{5.26}$$

Berezansky *et al.* (2013) applied Mackey–Glass equation successfully to assess the stability, oscillation and control of hematopoiesis with non-monotone feedback whereas Enayatifar *et al.* (2013) applied Mackey–Glass to successfully hide Gray level image. Furthermore, Berezansky *et al.* (2012) successfully applied the

Mackey–Glass equation to model respiratory dynamics whereas Wan and Wei (2009) successfully applied the Mackey–Glass model for bifurcation analysis of electronic circuit model with delayed feedback while Shahmansoorian and Davoud (2007) applied neural-network model for Mackey–Glass time series prediction.

In this chapter, data is generated using the following parameters as it was done in the MATLAB Fuzzy Toolbox demonstration: $\beta = 0.2, \gamma = 0.1, n = 10, x(0) = 1.2$ and $\tau = 17$. In this chapter, we build a model that will ultimately predict $x(t + 6)$ from previous values at $x(t - 18), x(t - 12), x(t - 6)$ and $x(t)$. A total of 1000 data were collected and 500 were used for training and 500 were used for testing the MLP and RBF. The MLP and RBF neural networks were applied to model Granger causality by building the first network with 2 inputs and 1 output, second network with 3 inputs and 1 output, third network with 4 inputs and 1 output, and the fourth network with 8 inputs (4 inputs consisting of irrelevant data) and 1 output and testing whether adding additional inputs increases the accuracy of the model. These inputs are the values of the Mackey–Glass function at earlier times and are used to predict later value. The characteristics of the MLP network are shown in Table 5.1 while that for the RBF are in Table 5.2.

When the data set generated from the Mackey–Glass equation is used to evaluate the MLP and RBF-based Granger causal models the results in Table 5.3 are obtained.

Table 5.1 The characteristics of MLP neural networks

Number of inputs	Number of hidden nodes	A	B	Number of steps in the trajectory	Number of retained samples	Step size
2, 3, 4, and 8	5	0.001	100	100	500	0.002

Table 5.2 The characteristics of RBF neural networks

Number of inputs	Number of hidden nodes	Activation function	Training method
2, 3, 4, and 8	2, 3, 4, and 8	Gaussian	EM-Algorithm

Table 5.3 Results obtained from the modeling of the Mackey–Glass equation

Aspect	2 Inputs	3 Inputs	4 Inputs	8 Inputs
MLP Mean	3.4%	2.3%	1.6%	1.8%
MLP Variance	20	8.7	5.5	6.1
RBF Mean	2.8%	2.5%	1.3%	2.1%
RBF Variance	16.3	11.5	4.6	7.7

The t-test is used to evaluate whether the hypothesis that the error obtained has a zero mean is tested and these results show that indeed this causal hypothesis cannot be ruled out as the number of inputs increase.

When the variance test was conducted it was obtained that the addition of an additional input variable has impact from 2 to 3 but the fourth variable does not have an impact on the accuracy.

5.6 Conclusions

This chapter applied the MLP and RBF to create a causal machine. The MLP and RBF were successfully applied to extend the Granger causality model to the non-linear domain using a chaotic time series data as an example.

References

Ancona, N., Marinazzo, D., Stramaglia, S. "Radial basis function approach to nonlinear Granger causality of time series", *Physical Review E — Statistical, Nonlinear, and Soft Matter Physics*, art. no. 056221, Vol. 70, No. 5, pp. 056221-1–056221-7, 2004.

Anwar, A.R., Muthalib, M., Perrey, S., Galka, A., Granert, O., Wolff, S., Deuschl, G., Raethjen, J., Heute, U., Muthuraman, M. "Directionality analysis on functional magnetic resonance imaging during motor task using Granger Causality," *Proceedings of the Annual International Conference of the IEEE Engineering in Medicine and Biology Society*, EMBS, art. no. 6346419, pp. 2287–2290, 2012.

Attanasio, A., Triacca, U. "Detecting human influence on climate using neural networks based Granger causality," *Theoretical and Applied Climatology*, Vol. 103, No. 1, pp. 103–107, 2011.

Bagdonavicius, V., Nikulin, M.S. "Chi-square goodness-of-fit test for right censored data," *The International Journal of Applied Mathematics and Statistics*, pp. 30–50, 2011.

Bélair, J., Glass, L., van der Heiden, U., Milton, J. "Dynamical Disease: Mathematical Analysis of Human Illness," American Institute of Physics, Woodbury, New York, 1995.

Berezansky, L., Braverman, E., Idels, L. "The Mackey-Glass model of respiratory dynamics: Review and new results," *Nonlinear Analysis, Theory, Methods and Applications*, Vol. 75, No. 16, pp. 6034–6052, 2012.

Berezansky, L., Braverman, E., Idels, L. "Mackey-Glass model of hematopoiesis with non-monotone feedback: Stability, oscillation and control," *Applied Mathematics and Computation*, Vol. 219, No. 11, pp. 6268–6283, 2013.

Bishop, C.M. "Neural networks for pattern recognition," Oxford: Clarendon Press, 1995.

Blair, R.-C., Higgins, J.J. "A comparison of the power of Wilcoxon's rank-sum statistic to that of Student's t statistic under various nonnormal distributions," *Journal of Educational Statistics*, Vol. 5, No. 4, pp. 309–334, 1980.

Bretz, H.-P., Dolag, K., Erdmann, M., Kuempel, D., Mueller, G., Schiffer, P., Urban, M., Walz, D., Winchen, T. "A hybrid Monte Carlo generator for ultra-high energy cosmic rays from their sources to the observer," *Journal of Physics: Conference Series*, 396 (PART 2), art. no. 022036, 2012.

Buhmann, M.D. "Radial Basis Functions: Theory and Implementations", Cambridge University Press, 2003.

Çağlayan, E., Güriş, B. "Energy consumption and CO_2 emissions: A threshold error correction and threshold Granger Causality Analysis," *Energy Exploration and Exploitation*, Vol. 31, No. 1, pp. 109–118, 2013.

Candelon, B., Joëts, M., Tokpavi, S. "Testing for Granger causality in distribution tails: An application to oil markets integration," *Economic Modelling*, Vol. 31, No. 1, pp. 276–285, 2013.

Cheung, B.L.P., Van Veen, B.D. "Estimation of cortical connectivity from E/MEG using nonlinear state-space models", *ICASSP, IEEE International Conference on Acoustics, Speech and Signal Processing — Proceedings*, art. no. 5946517, pp. 769–772, 2011.

Corder, G.W., Foreman, D.I. "Nonparametric Statistics for Non-Statisticians: A Step-by-Step Approach Wiley," 2009.

Croux, C., Reusens, P. "Do stock prices contain predictive power for the future economic activity? A Granger causality analysis in the frequency domain," *Journal of Macroeconomics*, Vol. 35, No. 1, pp. 93–103, 2013.

Ding, S., Wu, Q., Yang, Y. "Research on the application of RBF neural network based on K-means clustering in system identification", *Proceedings of 4th International Workshop on Advanced Computational Intelligence,* IWACI 2011, art. no. 6159984, pp. 110–112, 2011.

Dong, C.-Y., Shin, D., Joo, S., Nam, Y., Cho, K.-H. "Identification of feedback loops in neural networks based on multi-step granger causality," *Bioinformatics*, Vol. 28, No. 16, art. no. bts354, pp. 2146–2153, 2012.

Enayatifar, R., Abdullah, A.H., Mirza, A.A., Mahmud, M. "Gray level image hiding by using Mackey–Glass series," *Research Journal of Applied Sciences, Engineering and Technology*, Vol. 5, No. 2, pp. 553–557, 2013.

Escalante, A., Tzompantzi, O.R. "Hamiltonian dynamics for an alternative action describing Maxwell's equations," *International Journal of Pure and Applied Mathematics*, Vol. 81, No. 5, pp. 701–713, 2012.

Fay, M.P., Proschan, M.A. "Wilcoxon–Mann–Whitney or t-test? On assumptions for hypothesis tests and multiple interpretations of decision rules," *Statistics Surveys*, Vol. 4, pp. 1–39, 2010.

Glass, L., Mackey, M.C. "Pathological physiological conditions resulting from instabilities in physiological control systems," *Annals of the New York Academy of Sciences*, Vol. 316, pp. 214–235, 1979.

Golub, G.H., Van Loan, C.F. "Matrix computations", 3rd Edition, Baltimore: Johns Hopkins, pp. 257–258, 1996.

Granger, C.W.J. "Investigating causal relations by econometric models and cross-spectral methods", *Econometrica*, Vol. 37, No. 3, pp. 424–438, doi: 10.2307/1912791, JSTOR 1912791, 1969.

Greenwood, P.E., Nikulin, M.S. "A guide to chi-squared testing," Wiley, New York, 1996.

Hacker, R.S., Hatemi, J.A. "Tests for causality between integrated variables using asymptotic and bootstrap distributions: Theory and application," *Applied Economics*, Vol. 38, No. 13, pp. 1489–1500, 2006.

Halperin, G., Klausner, Z. "Frequency analyses can be improved by a modified t-test in sample-based preclinical efficacy studies," *PDA Journal of Pharmaceutical Science and Technology*, Vol. 67, No. 1, pp. 74–78, 2013.

Hammond, K.D., Voigt, H.-J.L., Marus, L.A., Juslin, N., Wirth, B.D. "Simple pair-wise interactions for hybrid Monte Carlo-molecular dynamics simulations of titania/yttria-doped iron," *Journal of Physics Condensed Matter*, Vol. 25, No. 5, art. no. 055402, 2013.

Hartigan, J.A. "Clustering algorithms", John Wiley & Sons, Inc, 1975.

Hartigan, J.A., Wong, M.A. "Algorithm AS 136: A K-means clustering algorithm," "*Journal of the Royal Statistical Society", Series C (Applied Statistics)*, Vol. 28, No. 1, pp. 100–110, 1979.

Hsueh, S.-J., Hu, Y.-H., Tu, C.-H. "Economic growth and financial development in Asian countries: A bootstrap panel Granger causality analysis," *Economic Modelling*, Vol. 32, No. 1, pp. 294–301, 2013.

Hua, Z., Dunson, D.B., Gilmore, J.H., Styner, M.A., Zhu, H. "Semiparametric Bayesian local functional models for diffusion tensor tract statistics," *NeuroImage*, Vol. 63, No. 1, pp. 460–474, ISSN 1053-8119, 10.1016/j.neuroimage.2012.06.027, 15 October 2012.

Im, J., Park, J. "Stochastic structural optimization using particle swarm optimization, surrogate models and Bayesian statistics," *Chinese Journal of Aeronautics*, Vol. 26, No. 1, pp. 112–121, ISSN 1000-9361, 10.1016/j.cja.2012.12.022, February 2013.

Kakizawa, Y. "Improved chi-squared tests for a composite hypothesis," *Journal of Multivariate Analysis*, Vol. 107, pp. 141–161, 2012.

Katayama, N. "Chi-squared portmanteau tests for structural VARMA models with uncorrelated errors," *Journal of Time Series Analysis*, Vol. 33, No. 6, pp. 863–872, 2012.

Kumagai, W., Hayashi, M. "Quantum hypothesis testing for gaussian states: Quantum analogues of χ^2, t-, and F-Tests," *Communications in Mathematical Physics*, Vol. 318, No. 2, pp. 535–574, 2013.

Kundu, D., Raqab, M.Z. "Bayesian inference and prediction of order statistics for a Type-II censored Weibull distribution," *Journal of Statistical Planning and Inference*, Vol. 142, No. 1, pp. 41–47, ISSN 0378-3758, 10.1016/j.jspi.2011.06.019, January 2012.

Kunstatter, G., Maeda, H., Taves, T. "Hamiltonian dynamics of Lovelock black holes with spherical symmetry," *Classical and Quantum Gravity*, Vol. 30, No. 6, art. no. 065002, 2013.

Lázaro, M., Santamaría, I., Pantaleón, C. "A new EM-based training algorithm for RBF networks", *Neural Networks*, Vol. 16, No. 1, pp. 69–77, 2003.

Liao, C.-C. "Genetic k-means algorithm based RBF network for photovoltaic MPP prediction", *Energy*, Vol. 35, No. 2, pp. 229–236, 2010.

Liu, M., Kuo, C.-C., Chiu, A.W.L. "Statistical threshold for nonlinear Granger Causality in motor intention analysis", *Proceedings of the Annual International Conference of the IEEE Engineering in Medicine and Biology Society*, EMBS, art. no. 6091247, pp. 5036–5039, 2011.

Liu, H., He, J. "The application of dynamic K-means clustering algorithm in the center selection of RBF neural networks", *3rd International Conference on Genetic and Evolutionary Computing*, WGEC 2009, art. no. 5402788, pp. 488–491, 2009.

Lloyd, S.P. "Least squares quantization in PCM", *IEEE Transactions on Information Theory*, Vol. 28, No. 2, pp. 129–137, 1982.

MacKay, D.J.C. "Bayesian Methods for Adaptive Models," Ph.D. Thesis, California Institute of Technology, 1991.

MacKay, D.J.C. "A practical bayesian framework for backpropagation networks," *Neural Comp*, Vol. 4, pp. 448–472, 1992.

Mackey, M.C., Glass, L. "Oscillation and chaos in physiological control systems", *Science*, Vol. 197, No. 4300, pp. 287–289, 1977.

Marcoulaki, E.C., Papazoglou, I.A., Konstandinidou, M. "Prediction of occupational accident statistics and work time loss distributions using Bayesian analysis," *Journal of Loss Prevention in the Process Industries*, Vol. 25, No. 3, pp. 467–477, ISSN 0950-4230, 10.1016/j.jlp.2011.11.014, May 2012.

Marinazzo, D., Pellicoro, M., Stramaglia, S. "Nonlinear parametric model for Granger causality of time series", *Physical Review E — Statistical, Nonlinear, and Soft Matter Physics*, art. no. 066216, Vol. 73, No. 6, 2006.

Markov, A.A. "Extension of the limit theorems of probability theory to a sum of variables connected in a chain", Reprinted in Appendix B of: R. Howard. Dynamic Probabilistic Systems, Vol. 1: Markov Chains. John Wiley and Sons, 1971.

Marwala, T. "Fault Identification Using Neural Networks and Vibration Data," Ph.D. Thesis, University of Cambridge, 2001.

Marwala, T. "Bayesian Training of Neural Network Using Genetic Programming," *Pattern Recognition Letters*, doi: org/10.1016/j.patrec.2007.034, 2007.

Marwala, T. "Computational Intelligence for Missing Data Imputation, Estimation and Management: Knowledge Optimization Techniques", IGI Global Publications, Information Science Reference Imprint, IGI Global Publications, New York, 2009.

Marwala, T. "Condition Monitoring Using Computational Intelligence Methods," Springer-Verlag, London, 2012.

Marwala, T. "Economic Modeling Using Artificial Intelligence Methods," Springer, 2013.

Marwala, T., Lagazio, M. "Militarized Conflict Modeling Using Computational Intelligence Techniques," Springer-Verlag, London, 2011.

Metropolis, N., Rosenbluth, A.W., Rosenbluth, M.N., Teller, A.H., Teller, E. "Equations of state calculations by fast computing machines," *Journal of Chemical Physics*, Vol. 21, No. 6, pp. 1087–1092, 1953.

Misev, A., Sahpaski, D., Pejov, L. "Implementation of hybrid Monte Carlo (molecular dynamics) quantum mechanical methodology for modeling of condensed phases on high performance computing environment," *Advances in Intelligent and Soft Computing*, 150 AISC, pp. 269–277, 2012.

Mistry, J., Nelwamondo, F.V., Marwala, T. "Investigating a Predictive Certainty measure for Ensemble Based HIV Classification," *IEEE International Conference on Systems, Computational Cybernetics*, ICCC 2008, pp. 231–236, 27–29 November 2008.

Moore, E.H. "On the reciprocal of the general algebraic matrix", *Bulletin of the American Mathematical Society*, Vol. 26, No. 9, pp. 394–395, 1920.

Neal, R.M. "Probabilistic Inference Using Markov Chain Monte Carlo Methods," Toronto, Canada: University of Toronto Technical Report CRG-TR-93-1, 1993.

Nikulin, M.S. "Chi-squared test for normality," *In Proceedings of the International Vilnius Conference on Probability Theory and Mathematical Statistics*, v.2, pp. 119–122, 1973.

Penrose, R. "A generalized inverse for matrices", *Proceedings of the Cambridge Philosophical Society*, Vol. 51, pp. 406–413, 1955.

Press, W.H., Teukolsky, S.A., Vetterling, W.T., Flannery, B.P. "Section 3.7.1. Radial Basis Function Interpolation", *Numerical Recipes: The Art of Scientific Computing*, 3rd Edition, New York: Cambridge University Press, 2007.

Qi, X. "Analysis on double-sword effect of spreading of Western culture and traditional Chinese culture based on t-test law," *Lecture Notes in Electrical Engineering*, 209 LNEE, pp. 395–401, 2013.

Rice, J.A. "Mathematical Statistics and Data Analysis", Third Edition, Duxbury Advanced, 2006.

Saito, Y., Osana, Y. "Identification of artifacts in scenery images using color and line information by RBF network and K-means", *Proceedings — 2010 2nd World Congress on Nature and Biologically Inspired Computing*, NaBIC 2010, art. no. 5716275, pp. 540–545, 2010.

Sakashita, Y., Osana, Y. "Identification of artifacts in scenery images using color and line information by RBF network — Segmentation by K-means algorithm and edge information", *Conference Proceedings — IEEE International Conference on Systems*, Man and Cybernetics, art. no. 6083917, pp. 1704–1709, 2011.

Sawilowsky, S. "Misconceptions leading to choosing the *t* test over the Wilcoxon Mann-Whitney U test for shift in location parameter," *Journal of Modern Applied Statistical Methods*, Vol. 4, No. 2, pp. 598–600, 2005.

Schmelter, M.L, Erwin, S.O., Wilcock, P.R. "Accounting for uncertainty in cumulative sediment transport using Bayesian statistics," *Geomorphology*, Vol. 175–176, pp. 1–13, ISSN 0169-555X, 10.1016/j.geomorph.2012.06.012, 2012.

Shahmansoorian, A., Davoud, A.M.F. "An adaptable recursive Neural-Network model for Mackey-Glass time series prediction," *European Journal of Scientific Research*, Vol. 18, No. 4, pp. 655–662, 2007.

Shen, W., Sun, Y. "Daily maximum electric load forecasting with RBF optimized by AFSA in K-means clustering algorithm", *Key Engineering Materials*, Vol. 467–469, pp. 1225–1230, 2011.

Su, X., Suo, J. "Prediction of sea clutter based on chaos theory with RBF and K-mean clustering", *CIE International Conference of Radar Proceedings*, art. no. 4148260, 2007.

Tang, Y., Srihari, S.N. "Efficient and accurate learning of Bayesian networks using chi-squared independence tests," *Proceedings — International Conference on Pattern Recognition*, art. no. 6460728, pp. 2723–2726, 2012.

Wan, A., Wei, J. "Bifurcation analysis of Mackey-Glass electronic circuits model with delayed feedback," *Nonlinear Dynamics*, Vol. 57, Nos. 1–2, pp. 85–96, 2009.

Wang, D., Zhang, H., Liu, R., Lv, W. "Feature selection based on term frequency and t-test for text categorization," *ACM International Conference Proceeding Series*, pp. 1482–1486, 2012.

Wu, X., Zhou, C., Wang, J., Lu, J.-A. "Detecting the topology of a neural network from partially obtained data using piecewise granger causality," *Lecture Notes in Computer Science (including subseries Lecture Notes in Artificial Intelligence and Lecture Notes in Bioinformatics)*, 6675 LNCS (PART 1), pp. 166–175, 2011.

Wu, Z., Zhang, Q., Hany, A.-K. "Hybrid Monte Carlo-deterministic methods for reactor analysis," *Nuclear Technology*, Vol. 180, No. 3, pp. 372–382, 2012.

Yang, Y. "China's technology progress and international trade: Granger causality test on China's data," *Proceeding of 2012 International Conference on Information Management, Innovation Management and Industrial Engineering*, ICIII 2012, 3, pp. 9–12, 2012.

Zhang, J.-H. "A short-term prediction for QoS of Web Service based on RBF neural networks including an improved K-means algorithm", *ICCASM 2010 — 2010 International Conference on Computer Application and System Modeling, Proceedings*, 5, art. no. 5620138, pp. V5633–V5637, 2010.

Zhong, M., Bagheri, E., Christie, J. "Improving Group Assignment and AADT Estimation Accuracy of Short-term Traffic Counts using Historical Seasonal Patterns & Bayesian Statistics", *Procedia — Social and Behavioral Sciences*, Vol. 43, pp. 607–617, ISSN 1877-0428, 10.1016/j.sbspro.2012.04.134, 2012.

Zhou, Y., Li, J., Liu, L. "Hybrid Monte Carlo sampling implementation of Bayesian support vector machine," *Advances in Information Sciences and Service Sciences*, Vol. 5, No.1, pp. 284–290, 2013.

Chapter 6

Rubin, Pearl and Granger Causality Models: A Unified View

Abstract. In this chapter, the Neyman-Rubin, Pearl and Granger causality models are described. The Neyman-Rubin causal model is described particularly within the context of missing data estimation framework and directed acyclic graphs (DAGs). The Granger causality is described within the context of the identification of the causal relations. The frameworks are applied to a simulated example.

6.1 Introduction

The issue of causality has concerned philosophers for many years. As described in earlier chapters, for there to be causality is the transmission of information from one point called the cause (x) to another called the effect (y). The aggregation of information from the cause to the effect forms a probability distribution. This book also proposes that this transmission occurs in the form of a projectile. It also proposes that a function $y = f(x)$ becomes a causal function when x happens before y, x and y are connected (to rule out spurious correlation) and that there is a flow of information from x to y (to rule out confounding). This chapter explores three existing causal models which are the Neyman-Rubin, Pearl, and Granger causal models. The Neyman-Rubin model is based on the concept of factual and counterfactuals and these concepts present the problem of causality to be in essence a problem of missing data estimation (Neyman, 1923; Rubin, 1974; 1977; 1978; 2005; Heckman, 2005; 2008). Because of this fact a review of missing data estimation techniques is done in this chapter, particularly within the context of causality. The second model which is explored in this chapter is the Pearl's causal model which is based on the concepts of do-calculus, directed acyclic graphs (DAGs) and conditional probability (Pearl, 1988; 1998). Basically, Pearl causality is a technique for transforming conditional probability distribution which is a statistical concept into interventional probability which is a causal concept (Elwert, 2013; Pearl, 1995; 2000; 2010). The last aspect that will be studied is Granger causality which is at best a correlation concept even though it is derived from the principles of causality (Granger, 1969).

6.2 Neyman-Rubin Causal Model

This section describes the Newman-Rubin causal model which fundamentally assumes that for there to be a causal relationship between a decision action to administer a particular action and an effect then there has to be a difference between the result of admistering an action and not adminstering an action. The difficulty with this procedure is that it is impossible to administer an action on a particular object and not administer an action on the same object at the same time. In the definition derived from the Neyman-Rubin causal model, the decision of administering an action is called a counterfactual while the decision not to administer an action is called a factual.

West and Thoemmes (2010) compared the Campbell and Rubin causal models. Campbell's model identifies the counter arguments to the validity and the inclusion of design variables that may stop those counter arguments from happening or make them improbable. The results obtained indicated that the strengths of both methods should be incorprated when designing experiments. Shadish (2010) compared Campbell's and Rubin's causal models and concluded that Campbell's model is broad while Rubin's model is narrow. Little and Yau (1998) successfully applied statistical techniques to estimate missing data in Rubin's causal model whereas Gutman and Rubin (2013) successfully estimated causal effects of binary data.

Tam Cho *et al.* (2013) successfully applied an optimization method in causal inferences based on Rubin's model by identifying the minimum discrepancy between the distributions of these covariates in the control and treatment groups. Turner *et al.* (2013) applied Rubin's causal model to identity conditions necessary to assign causal status to headache triggers. Other successful applications of Rubin's causal model include to model surrogate endpoints with semi-competing risks data (Ghosh, 2012) as well as Li *et al.* (2012) in evaluating the effect of early versus late antiretriviral regimen change for treatment of AIDS.

To give an example of a Neyman-Rubin causal model, suppose we want to establish whether certain tree leaves from a tree called *Muvhale* is able to reduce sugar level when ingested. Then we have 100 participants to test this and from each participant we measure the sugar level obtained when the participant has not ingested the leaves (y_c) and the sugar level when the participant has ingested the leaves (y_t) and these results can be represented as in Table 6.1. In order to complete this causal identification process, the missing data in Table 6.1 needs to be estimated and thus the causality identification process using the Neyman-Rubin causality model is essentially a missing data estimation problem and this is a subject of the next sub-section.

On implementing the Rubin Causal Model, it is desirable that a subject treatment and control occur simultaneously. However, this is physically impossible.

Table 6.1 Results from a study on the impact of administering leaves of Muvhale tree on subjects

Subject	y_c	y_t	$\sigma = y_t - y_c$
Denga	3.5	?	?
John	?	5.3	?
Khathu	4.2	?	?
Mary	?	5.5	?
Mashudu	?	38	?
Thendo	5.9	?	?

Consequently, a technique called matching was proposed to ensure that each control case and its corresponding treatment are matched and this procedure was proposed by Rubin (1973). Further applications of matching can be found in Anderson *et al.* (1980) as well as Kupper *et al.* (1981). Section 6.2.1 describes missing data estimation methods which is core to the Rubin Causal Model.

6.2.1 Missing data mechanism

In missing data imputation, it is important to identify the reason why data are missing and this is called a mechanism and more details on this can be found in Marwala (2009). A variable is considered a mechanism, if it explains why other variables are missing or not missing. For instance, in a household survey, it is found that people with low-income are sometimes ashamed to reveal their income because it is too low and therefore income in this case is a mechanism (Little and Rubin, 1987). There are different types of missing data mechanisms and these include Missing at Random (MAR), Missing Completely at Random (MCAR) and Missing Not at Random (MNAR).

MAR is a mechanism or reason why a variable entry is missing is unrelated to the missing variable itself and the reason for this may be related to other observed variables (Little and Rubin, 1987). MAR occurs when the missing data are different from the observed data but the pattern of missing data can be predicted from other observed variables. For MAR, the characteristics of the missing and observed observations have identical statistical behavior with other observations, whether they are observed or not.

MCAR is a mechanism where the probability of data missing is not related to the values of any other variables, whether missing or observed (Little and Rubin, 1987; Acork, 2005). In the MCAR, the complete data are not differentiable from cases with incomplete data.

MNAR is a mechanism where the missing data is related to the missing values themselves. An MNAR example that was explained by Marwala (2009) include a case where two databases from different cities are merged and one database is short of some features that have been measured in the other database. In this situation, the explanation on why some data are missing can be made clear, nonetheless, this reason is merely dependent on the same variables that are missing and cannot be explained in terms of any other variables in the database.

Jamshidian and Yuan (2013) applied sensitivity analysis to detect missing data mechanism in structural equations. Kang *et al.* (2012) successfully used the Expectation Maximization (EM) algorithm and mean estimation for missing data estimation of different missing data mechanisms. The results obtained demonstrated that the EM algorithm performed better than mean imputation for MAR and MCAR but performed worse for MNAR. Other studies of missing data mechanisms include MCAR by Raykov *et al.* (2012), using Bayesian statistics to model MAR by Mason *et al.* (2012), in dose-finding adaptive trial (Liu and Entsuah, 2012) and to estimate missing data in longitudinal ordinal data in MCAR and MAR (Tuan *et al.*, 2011).

6.2.2 Missing data imputation methods

There are many techniques that have been applied for missing data imputation and these include list deletion, pair-wise deletion, mean substitution, regression-based methods, and stochastic imputation (Marwala, 2009).

Case deletion is a missing data estimation technique that eliminates objects with missing data and uses the data that remains (Velilla, 1993; Zhu *et al.*, 2001). Examples of this include list-wise deletion and pair-wise deletion. In the list-wise deletion only the cases which are complete are retained (Tsikriktsis, 2005) and this may result in large amount of information that is lost in the process and thereby losing substantial information. In the pair-wise deletion method incomplete record is used only if the missing variable is not required in the analysis being performed. It has been observed that unless the missing data mechanism is a MCAR then pair-wise deletion gives biased results.

Another way of dealing with missing data is to estimate it with the mean of the record and this gives biased variances which increase with the increase in the number of missing data records. If the missing data in Table 6.1 are estimated using the mean of the record the updated record is shown in Table 6.2. Other missing data estimation methods are the hot/cold deck imputation where missing data are substituted with data from similar cases that has been observed from the same data set, methods based on neural networks, support vector machines, principal component analysis, rough sets and auto-associative networks. More details on this can be found in the review done by Marwala (2009).

Table 6.2 Results from a study on the impact of administering leaves of Muvhale tree on subjects with missing data estimated

Subject	y_c	y_t	$\sigma = y_t - y_c$
Denga	3.5	4.9	1.4
John	4.5	5.3	1.8
Khathu	4.2	4.9	0.7
Mary	4.5	5.5	1
Mashudu	4.5	3.8	−0.7
Thendo	5.9	4.9	−1

6.3 Pearl Causality

This section introduces Pearl causal model which is a model concerned with primarily inferring interventional probabilities $p(y|do(x))$ from conditional probabilities $p(y|x)$ using DAGs (Pearl and Verma, 1991; Pearl, 1995; Pearl and Dechter, 1996). Conditional probabilities relate the probability that one variable happens given the fact that another variable(s) has/have happened. Conditional probabilities indicate correlation. Pearl causal approach is intended to structure the problem so that it becomes easier to distinguish between causality and correlation in relations defined by conditional probabilities.

Chalak and White (2012) studied the relationship between causality and conditional independence using the principles of d-separation and DAGs whereas Lee (2012) successfully applied Pearl causality to study causal relationship in behavioral traits. Muñoz and van der Laan (2012) successfully introduced a new causal parameter to account for the event that intervention policies can lead to stochastically assigned exposures.

Daniel *et al.* (2012) successfully applied causal diagrams to expedite missing data estimation whereas Zheng and van Der Laan (2012) applied targeted maximum likelihood estimation method to study natural direct causal effects. Other successful application of Pearl causality is on explaining counter-examples by Beer *et al.* (2012).

6.3.1 Directed acyclic graph

Pearl causality model uses what is called directed acyclic model which is directed in the sense that it is pointing at a direction, and if we assume the transmission theory of causality which was described in Chapter 1, indicates the direction in which information flows from the cause to the effect (Castelo and Siebes, 2003; Steinsky, 2003; Czumaj *et al.*, 2007; Xie *et al.*, 2006; Luciani and Stefanini, 2012).

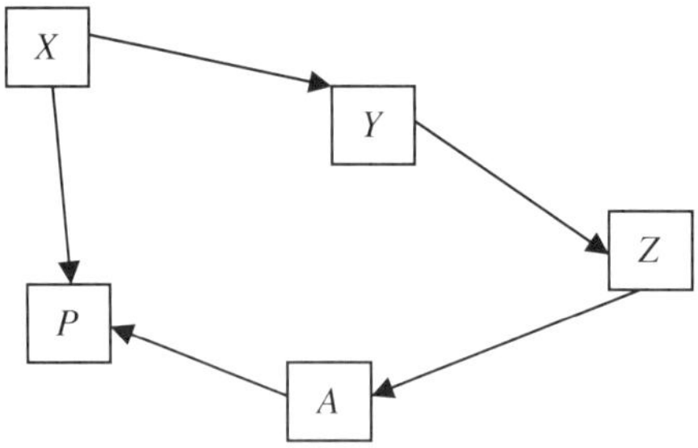

Figure 6.1 An illustration of the DAG

Furthermore, it is thought to be acyclic because it goes from one variable to another rather that from one variable to itself. An illustration of a graph is shown in Figure 6.1. This graph has few objects and these include variables which are X, Y, Z, A, and P. It also has arcs that are directed by the arrows. In this book, we view these arcs as causal models which was described in Chapter 3 and can be modeled parametrically as a function $y = f(x)$ where x happens before y, x and y are connected, and here by an arc, and there is a flow of information from x to y as represented by the direction of the arc. Each variable may have a parent and in this regard the parent of Y is X. Furthermore, each variable can have a child and as an example the child of Y is Z. Each variable may have ancestor, for example the ancestors of Z are X and Y. Furthermore, each variable may have descendants and as an example the descendants of Z are A and P. The general idea of the Pearl causality is to estimate the interventional probability from the conditional probabilities which can be derived from the joint probabilities. In Figure 6.1, the interventional probability may be the $p(Y|do(X))$ from the conditional probability $p(X, Y, Z, A, P)$.

Now that we have described what DAG is, the next task is to describe how two variables can be related to one another. The mathematical relations that describe the data in a DAG can be expressed as a joint probability function as follows:

$$p(X_1, X_2, \ldots, X_n) = \prod_{i}^{n} p(X_i|parX_i). \tag{6.1}$$

Here $\prod$ stands for the product and *par* stands for the parent. From Equation 6.1, the joint probability in Figure 6.1 is $p(X)p(Y|X)p(Z|Y)p(A|Z)p(P|A,X)$.

6.3.2 Associations between variables

There are three causal substructures that define causal relationships between variables and these were identified by Wright (1921) and these are direct and indirect causation (Figure 6.2), common cause confounding (Figure 6.3) and a collider (Figure 6.4). In Figure 6.2, X and Y are conditionally dependent. Furthermore, X

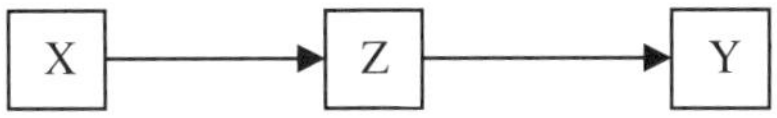

Figure 6.2 Direct and indirect causation

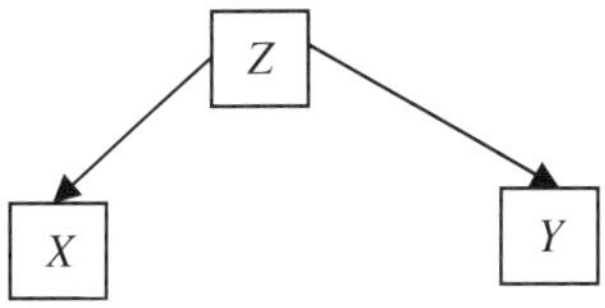

Figure 6.3 Common cause confounding

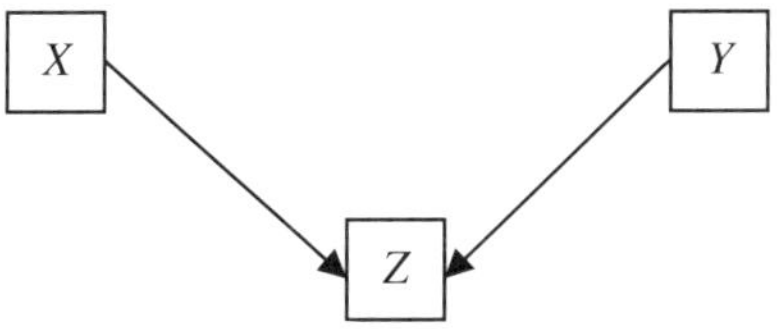

Figure 6.4 The collider

and *Y* are conditionally independent given *Z*. The effect of this on causal model is that it intercepts the causal pathway (Elwert, 2013). Examples of direct and indirect causation include Grassi *et al.* (2007) who studied direct, reverse or reciprocal causation in the relation of homocysteine and ischemic heart disease as well as Hoover (2012) who studied direct and indirect causation within the context of economics.

In Figure 6.3, *X* and *Y* are conditionally dependent. Furthermore, *X* and *Y* are conditionally independent given *Z*. To avoid confounding bias, it is important to condition a common cause (Elwert, 2013). Shpitser (2013) proposed a counterfactual method based on the DAG for longitudinal mediation analysis with unobserved confounding whereas Fraga *et al.* (2013) applied observed that the effect of an interviewer investigating abuse were not matched with effect alteration but in its place with confounding. Toh *et al.* (2013) considered the advantages and disadvantages of different confounding modification methods that can be used in observational comparative effectiveness research studies whereas Sjölander and Bellocco (2013) applied front-door blocking to adjust confounding in longitudinal studies. Greystoke *et al.* (2013) evaluated diurnal variations and confounding elements that affect circulating cell death biomarker levels whereas Henríquez-Hernández *et al.* (2013) used heterogeneity between populations as a confounding aspect on studying polymorphisms in DNA-repair genes in a group of prostate cancer patients.

To explain Figure 6.4, suppose X represents the fact that it has rained and Y represents the fact that the sprinkler was on and Z represents the fact that the grass is wet.

The fact that it has rained is independent from the fact that the sprinkler is on. Mathematically this can be expressed as follows:

$$p(X|Y) = p(X) \quad \text{and} \quad p(Y|X) = p(Y). \tag{6.2}$$

However, if we know that the grass is wet and that it has rained then this reduces the probability that the sprinkler was on. Therefore, the knowledge of X and Z gives us some information about Z. Therefore, for a collider X and Y are conditionally independent. Furthermore, X and Y are conditionally dependent given Z. The effect of this on a causal model is termed endogenous selection bias which is a mistaken conditioning on a common effect (Elwert, 2013). Vanderweele and Robins (2007) integrated adequate component causes into the DAG causal structure to identify properties of conditioning on a common effect to detect conditional independencies within layers of the conditioning variable not obvious on DAGs without the expression of sufficient causes.

In Figures 6.2 and 6.3, X and Y are dependent and are independent given Z and, therefore, are statistically indistinguishable from cross-sectional data. Figure 6.4 is uniquely identifiable because X and Y are independent and are dependent given Z and, therefore, can be identified from cross-sectional data.

6.3.3 *d*-separation

This section describes the concept of d-separation, which is the concept that defines conditions in which DAG transmits causal information (Spirtes, 1996; Geiger *et al.*, 2013). Geiger *et al.* (2013) applied probability theory to develop efficient algorithms to identify dependencies in the structure of Bayesian networks and thus identify d-separation. Geiger and Pearl (2013) studied the function of DAGs as an illustration of conditional independence relationships and observed that they are viable inference technique for identifying causal relationships from conditional independence relationships. Verma and Pearl (2013) demonstrated that the d-separation technique is able to identify independencies from any DAG based on a causal input list.

According to Pearl a path, p, is considered d-separated by a set of nodes Z if and only if:

1. p comprises a chain $x \rightarrow n \rightarrow y$ or a fork $x \leftarrow n \rightarrow y$ in such a way that the middle node n is in Z or
2. p comprises a collider $x \leftarrow n \rightarrow y$ $x \rightarrow n \leftarrow y$ in such a way that the middle node n is not in Z and such that no descendent of n is in Z.

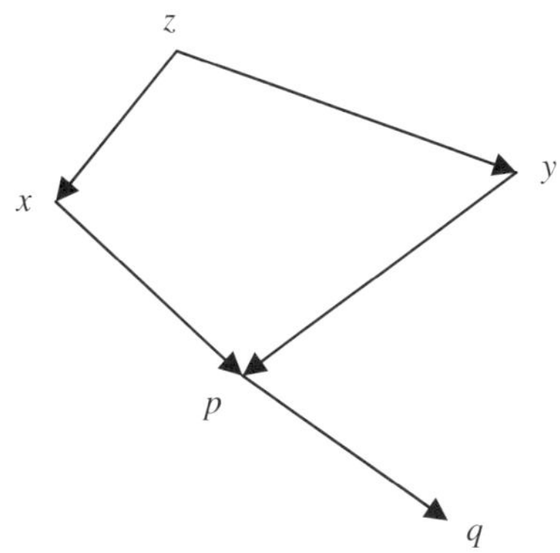

Figure 6.5 Illustration of d-separation

3. A set Z is considered to d-separate X from Y if and only if Z blocks all paths from X to Y.

Using these rules in Figure 6.5, y and x are d-separated by z or x and y are d-separated by a collider while y, p and q are d-connected.

6.3.4 Back-door adjustment

A back-door adjustment is a procedure for estimating the probability of observing one variable y given the fact that another variable x has happened by using conditional probabilities that relate variables x, y, and z where z influences directly x and y (Pearl, 2000; Zhang, 2006). Maathuis and Colombo (2013) generalized Pearl's back-door criterion to other kinds of graphs that describe Markov equivalence classes with or without hidden variables. The back-door criterion is shown in Figure 6.6.

A variable set z meets the back-door criterion with respect to variables x_i and x_j in a DAG if none of the variables in z descend from x_i and z d-separates or blocks all paths between x_i and x_j which include arrows leading to x_i. In Figure 6.5 if x d-separates all paths from p to y and x does not descend from p.

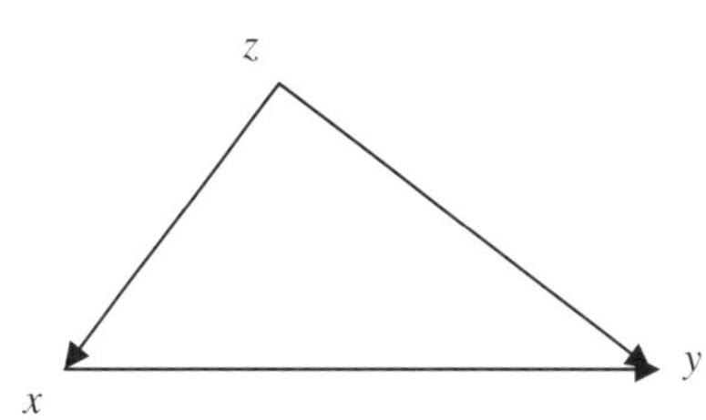

Figure 6.6 Illustration of the back-door criterion

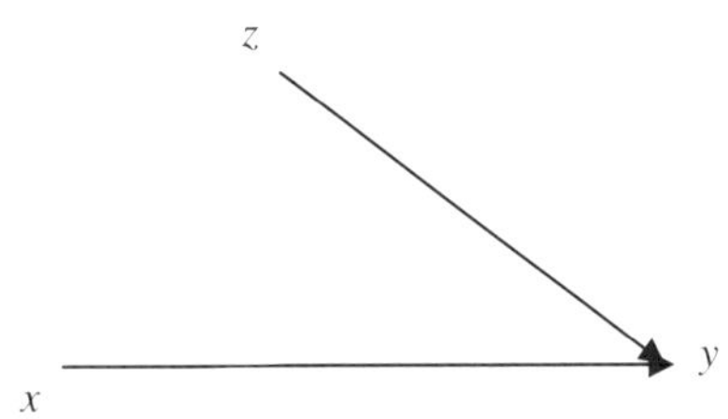

Figure 6.7 Illustration of the back-door criterion with an edge eliminated because x is forced to happen

In order to derive the back-door criterion, firstly, the joint probability $p(x, y, z)$ is calculated (Doob, 1953; Prohorov and Rozanov, 1969; Billingsley, 1979):

$$p(x, y, z) = p(z)p(x|z)p(y|x, z). \tag{6.3}$$

Figure 6.6 is modified as shown in Figure 6.7 by removing the edge between x and z in order to calculate the causal probability $p(y|do(x))$.

By so doing Equation 6.3 is thus modified to become:

$$p(do(x), y, z) = p(z)p(y|x, z). \tag{6.4}$$

Rearranging Equation 6.4 thus forms:

$$p(do(x)|y, z) = p(z)p(y|x, z). \tag{6.5}$$

In Equation 6.5, z can be integrated out to form the following equation (Pearl, 2000):

$$p(y|do(x)) = \sum_z p(y|x, z)p(z). \tag{6.6}$$

The back-door adjustment satisfies the back-door criterion with respect to (x, y) and the causal relationship between x and y can be expressed using Equation 6.6.

6.3.5 Front-door adjustment

According to Pearl (2000), a variable set z fulfills the front-door criterion with respect to variables x_i and x_j in a DAG if and only if every directed path from x_i to x_j contains variable z and there is no back-door route from x_i to z and x_i blocks all back-door paths to x_j. Glynn and Kashin (2013) developed bias formulas for front-door approximations and front-door/back-door hybrid approximations of average treatment effects for measured and unmeasured confounding. In order to describe the causal relations, Figure 6.8 is used.

In order to derive the front-door criterion, firstly, the joint probability $p(x, y, z, u)$ in Figure 6.8 is calculated as follows (Doob, 1953; Prohorov and Rozanov, 1969; Billingsley, 1979):

$$p(x, y, z, u) = p(u)p(x|u)p(z|x)p(y|z, u). \tag{6.7}$$

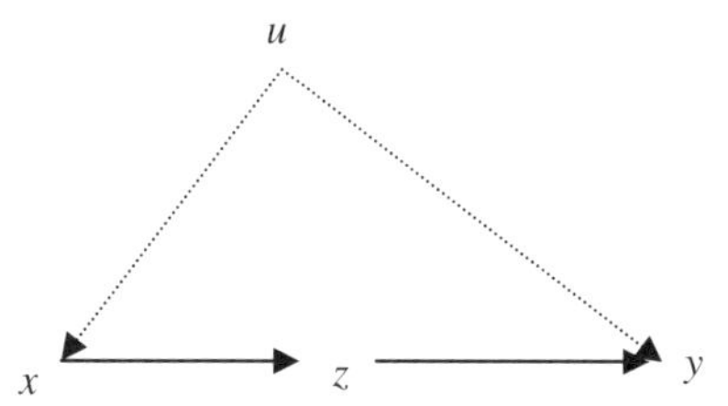

Figure 6.8 Illustration of the front-door criterion

Post intervention $x = x'$ and then eliminating the edge between u and x to accommodate intervention at x gives the following mathematical expression:

$$p(do(x), y, z, u) = p(u)p(z|x)p(y|z, u). \tag{6.8}$$

By integrating out z and x' the front-door adjustment that satisfies the front-door criterion with respect to (x, y) gives the causal relationship between x and y that can be identified as follows (Pearl, 2000):

$$p(y|do(x)) = \sum_z p(z|x) \sum_{x'} p(y|x', z)p(x'). \tag{6.9}$$

6.3.6 Rules for do-calculus

This section presents the three sets of rules that are essential in transforming conditional probabilities into interventional calculus which were proposed by Pearl (1994). Huang and Valtorta (2012) verified that the three basic do-calculus rules that Pearl presented are complete and were identifiable whereas Zhang (2007) successfully generalized do-calculus with testable causal assumptions. Kalisch *et al.* (2012) successfully applied the R package for causal structure learning and estimation of causal effects from observational data. Ceballos and Cantu (2009) proposed causal artificial intelligence design to model intelligent agents. Zhang (2008) studied causal reasoning given an equivalent class of causal diagrams, represented by an ancestral graph and extended the do-calculus framework to ancestral graphs.

Of the three do-calculus rules that were identified by Pearl (1994), the first one is insertion or deletion of observation and it is based on the concept of d-separation. Insertion or deletion of observation (d-separation) does not have any consequences if the variables are conditionally independent. It can thus be expressed mathematically as follows (Pearl, 1994):

$$p(y|do(x), z, w) = p(y|do(x), z) \tag{6.10}$$

where $(y \coprod z|x, w)_{G_{\bar{x}}}$ which means that Equation 6.10 is only valid when y and z are conditionally independent given x and z and $G_{\overline{X}}$ is the graph obtained from G

when the arrows pointing into x are removed. This rule allows the user to ignore irrelevant information.

The second of do-calculus as identified by Pearl (1994) states that actions and observations can be interchanged if all the back-doors are blocked. It can thus be expressed as follows (Pearl, 1994):

$$p(y|do(x), do(z), w) = p(y|do(x), z, w) \tag{6.11}$$

where $(y \coprod z|x, w)_{G_{\bar{x}\underline{z}}}$ meaning that y and z are conditionally independent given x and w where $G_{\overline{X}\underline{Y}}$ is a graph obtained when all arrows pointing into X and pointing out of Y are removed.

The third do-calculus rule proposed by Pearl (1994) is that inserting or deleting of actions after the action does not change anything and this can be expressed mathematically as follows:

$$p(y|do(x), do(z), w) = p(y|do(x), w) \tag{6.12}$$

where $(y \coprod z|x, w)_{G_{\overline{XZ(W)}}}$ and here $z(w)$ is the set of z-nodes that are not ancestors of any w-node in $G_{\overline{X}}$.

6.3.7 Pearl inferred causation algorithm

This section describes what is called the inductive causation (IC) algorithm which was proposed by Rebane and Pearl (1987). Valente *et al.* (2011) successfully applied the IC algorithm to the joint distribution of phenotypes conditional to unobservable genetic effects and observed that coupling prior knowledge with the output using the IC algorithm permitted deeper learning of the phenotypic causal structures when compared to using structural equation modeling. Furthermore, Valente *et al.* (2010) successfully applied the IC algorithm to identify recursive causal structures in multivariate quantitative genetics mixed models. Mazanec (2006) successfully applied the IC algorithm and structural equation modeling to study tourist satisfaction. Lemeire and Janzing (2013) compared independent conditionality to causal faithfulness.

The IC algorithm can be summarized as follows as explained by Rebane and Pearl (1987) as well as Pearl and Verma (1995):

1. Given a set of variables, produce a complete undirected graph connecting every variable with all other variables.
2. Test for correlation and then eliminate edges through tests of no or partial correlation.
3. Identify the direction of the edges that remain after all the possible correlations tests have eliminated edges with no associations.

To illustrate the algorithm above, we implemented the algorithm written by Li and more details can be found in Bielza *et al.* (2011). In this example, 20 variables

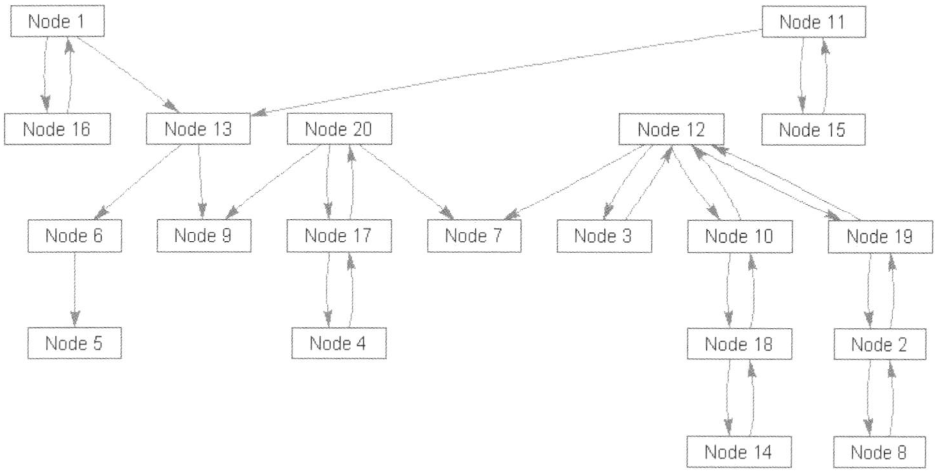

Figure 6.9 Results from the implementation of the IC model developed by Li

are considered and each variable is connected to all other variables. For each edge, the linkages between pairs of variables are established using correlation analysis. Thereafter, where correlation relationships exist, the directions of the connections are established. The results obtained from this exercise can be viewed in Figure 6.9.

6.3.8 Examples of using do-calculus

In South Africa in the 1800, there was a powerful King called Shaka who ruled over a nation called Zulus. He was a military general who was pre-occupied with conquest of other nations. There are many innovations that this great King introduced and he was successful in his endeavors. The Zulus that this great King ruled are the same people as the Xhosas and their language as well as cultures and customs are practically identical. One of these customs that were shared by these groups was circumcision. In these groups, circumcision is usually done at the age of 18 and normally requires these young men to spend a month in the forest healing from the circumcision operation. King Shaka realized that this was a waste of time for young men who according to him should be in the army conquering other nations and decided that the Zulus will no longer undergo circumcision. This basically left the Zulus still very similar to Xhosas except that the Zulus do not circumcise while the Xhosas circumcise. Another difference between Xhosas and Zulus that emerged later was that the Zulus seemed to have a higher incidence of HIV infection than the Xhosas even though the two groups remain virtually identical in all other respect. The only other explanatory variable for this difference in HIV infection rate was circumcision. Rosario *et al.* (2013) studied and observed that circumcision can be used to minimize HIV transmission. Davis *et al.* (2013) studied the relationship

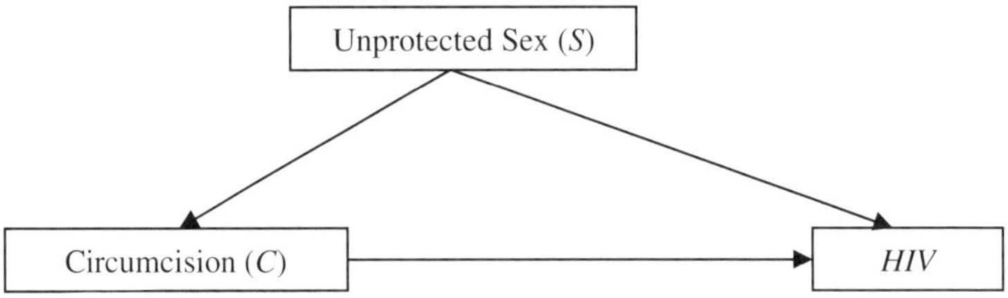

Figure 6.10 The DAG illustrating the relationship of unprotected sex, circumcision and HIV

between male circumcision and high-risk human papillomavirus viral (HR-HPV) load in female partners and observed that females with circumcised partners have low HPV viral load.

Given the evidence that circumcision reduces the incidence of HIV the current king of the Zulus, King Goodwill Zwelithini reintroduced circumcision in the Zulus in 2010. In order to study this causal relationship of HIV and circumcision, Figure 6.10 is used.

From Figure 6.10, the joint distribution is expressed mathematically as follows (Prohorov and Rozanov, 1969; Billingsley, 1979):

$$p(S, C, HIV) = p(S)P(C|S)p(HIV|C, S). \tag{6.13}$$

From Equation 6.13, we can transform C into $do(C)$ and by so doing the conditional probability of C given S is eliminated and therefore Equation 6.13 becomes

$$p(S, do(C), HIV) = p(S)p(HIV|C, S). \tag{6.14}$$

The variable S in Equation 6.14 can be eliminated by integrating it out and Equation 6.14 thus becomes:

$$p(HIV|do(C)) = \sum_{S} p(S)p(HIV|C, S). \tag{6.15}$$

Equation 6.15 demonstrates that to calculate or estimate the interventional probability of a person being *HIV* positive given the fact the person is circumcised depends on the probability that the person is sexually active S and the conditional probability that a person is HIV positive given the fact that the person is sexually active and is circumcised integrated over the fact that a person is sexually active.

6.4 Granger Causality

The other model that is considered in this chapter is the Granger causality which was proposed by Granger and was described in Chapter 8 (Granger, 1969; Hacker and Hatemi, 2006). Granger causality technique is a procedure which is based on the hypothesis that given a time series of y then a vector autoregressive model can be built as follows (Granger, 1969):

$$y_{later} = f(y_{early}) + E_1. \tag{6.16}$$

Here f is the mapping function and $y_{earlier}$ is a vector showing the earlier time history of y and y_{later} is a vector indicating the later time history of y. By introducing variable x which also has a time history available, is stationary and to predict future values of y, then Equation 6.16 is expressed as follows (Granger, 1969):

$$y_{later} = f(y_{early}, x_{earlier}) + E_2 \tag{6.17}$$

here $x_{earlier}$ is a vector showing the earlier time history of x. Granger causality states that given Equations 6.16 and 6.17, then variable x Granger causes variable y if the introduction of variable x to Equation 6.16 to form Equation 6.17 results in Equation 6.17 being better at predicting variable y than Equation 6.16. Variables x and y can be switched around and, therefore, Equations 6.16 and 6.17 then become:

$$x_{later} = f(x_{early}) + E_3 \tag{6.18}$$

$$x_{later} = f(x_{early}, y_{earlier}) + E_4. \tag{6.19}$$

The relative values of E_1 and E_2 compared to E_3 and E_4 gives the direction of causality. The problem with Granger causality is that it cannot be able to discern common cause confounding in Figure 6.3 and therefore can make one infer causality when the reason is that the two variables just happen to have common cause.

6.5 Comparison: Neyman-Rubin, Pearl and Granger Causality

This chapter has introduced Newman-Rubin, Pearl and Granger causality models. This section looks at these models and studies their connectivity. Newman-Rubin model for causality is a procedure that uses experimental observations to establish causality between two variables. Pearl causal model uses DAGs to derive interventional probabilities from conditional probabilities whereas Granger causality is a method that establishes relationships between variables based on time series data. The generalized casual model is the one which consists of variables that are connected by lines with the direction of the line indicating the flow of information from one variable to another and this can be represented by a causal model. The Neyman-Rubin is used to establish the direction of the line (confirming the transmission of information from one variable to another) while the Granger models can be used to establish whether two variables are connected at all.

6.6 Conclusions

This chapter studies the Neyman-Rubin, Pearl and Granger causality models. The Neyman-Rubin causal model is described within the context of missing data estimation whereas Pearl causal model is described within the context of directed acyclic graphs (DAGs) while Granger causality is described within the context of the identification of the causal relations. Examples are used to illustrate these techniques.

References

Acork, A.C. "Working with missing values", *Journal of Marriage and Family*, Vol. 67, pp. 1012–1028, 2005.

Anderson, D.W., Kish, L., Cornell, R.G. "On stratification, grouping and matching", *Scandinavian Journal of Statistics, JSTOR* 4615774, Vol. 7, No. 2, pp. 61–66, 1980.

Beer, I., Ben-David, S., Chockler, H., Orni, A., Trefler, R. "Explaining counterexamples using causality", *Formal Methods in System Design*, Vol. 40, No. 1, pp. 20–40, 2012.

Bielza, C., Li, G., Larrañaga, P. "Multi-dimensional *classification* with Bayesian networks", *International Journal of Approximate Reasoning*, Vol. 52, pp. 705–727, 2011.

Billingsley, P. "Probability and measure", Wiley, 1979.

Ceballos, H.G., Cantu, F.J. "Towards a causal framework for intelligent agents development", *8th Mexican International Conference on Artificial Intelligence — Proceedings of the Special Session*, MICAI 2009, art. no. 5372714, pp. 67–72, 2009.

Castelo, R., Siebes, A. "A characterization of moral transitive acyclic directed graph Markov models as labeled trees", *Journal of Statistical Planning and Inference*, Vol. 115, No. 1, pp. 235–259, 2003.

Chalak, K., White, H. "Causality, conditional independence, and graphical separation in settable systems", *Neural Computation*, Vol. 24, No. 7, pp. 1611–1668, 2012.

Czumaj, A., Kowaluk, M., Lingas, A. "Faster algorithms for finding lowest common ancestors in directed acyclic graphs", *Theoretical Computer Science*, Vol. 380, Nos. 1–2, pp. 37–46, 2004.

Daniel, R.M., Kenward, M.G., Cousens, S.N., De Stavola, B.L. "Using causal diagrams to guide analysis in missing data problems", *Statistical Methods in Medical Research*, Vol. 21, No. 3, pp. 243–256, 2012.

Davis, M.-A., Gray, R.H., Grabowski, M.K., Serwadda, D., Kigozi, G., Gravitt, P.E., Nalugoda, F., Watya, S., Wawer, M.J., Quinn, T.C., Tobian, A.A.R. "Male circumcision decreases high-risk human papillomavirus viral load in female partners: A randomized trial in Rakai, Uganda", *International Journal of Cancer*, Vol. 133, No. 5, pp. 1247–1252, 2013.

Doob, J.L. "Stochastic processes", Wiley, 1953.

Elwert, F. "Graphical Causal Models", In S. Morgan (ed.), Handbook of Causal Analysis for Social Research, New York: Sage Publications, pp. 245–273, 2013.

Fraga, S., Lucas, R., Costa, D., Barros, H. "Interviewer effects when investigating abuse were not compatible with effect modification but instead with confounding", *Journal of Clinical Epidemiology*, Vol. 66, No. 8, pp. 911–918, 2013.

Geiger, D., Pearl, J. "On the logic of causal models", *Proceedings of the Fourth Conference on Uncertainty in Artificial Intelligence* (UAI1988), arXiv:1304.2355, 2013.

Geiger, D., Verma, T.S., Pearl, J. "*d*-Separation: From Theorems to Algorithms", *Proceedings of the Fifth Conference on Uncertainty in Artificial Intelligence* (UAI1989), arXiv:1304.1505, 2013.

Ghosh, D. "A causal framework for surrogate endpoints with semi-competing risks data", *Statistics and Probability Letters*, Vol. 82, No. 11, pp. 1898–1902, 2012.

Glynn, A.N., Kashin, K. "Front-door Versus Back-door Adjustment with Unmeasured Confounding: Bias Formulas for Front-door and Hybrid Adjustments", *2013 Meeting of the Midwest Political Science Association*, 2013.

Granger, C.W.J. "Investigating causal relations by econometric models and cross-spectral methods", *Econometrica*, Vol. 37, No. 3, pp. 424–438, 1969.

Grassi, M., Assanelli, D., Pezzini, A. "Direct, reverse or reciprocal causation in the relation between homocysteine and ischemic heart disease", *Thrombosis Research*, Vol. 120, No. 1, pp. 61–69, 2007.

Greystoke, A., Harris, G., Jenkins, M., Goonetilleke, D., Moore, D., Lancashire, M., Ranson, M., Hughes, A., Clack, G., Dive, C. "Assessment of diurnal changes and confounding factors that affect circulating cell death biomarker levels: A short communication", *Journal of Pharmaceutical and Biomedical Analysis*, Vol. 84, pp. 184–188, 2013.

Gutman, R., Rubin, D.B. "Robust estimation of causal effects of binary treatments in unconfounded studies with dichotomous outcomes", *Statistics in Medicine*, Vol. 32, No. 11, pp. 1795–1814, 2013.

Hacker, R.S., Hatemi, J.A. "Tests for causality between integrated variables using asymptotic and bootstrap distributions: Theory and application", *Applied Economics*, Vol. 38, No. 13, pp. 1489–1500, 2006.

Heckman, J.J. "The scientific model of causality", *Sociological Methodology*, Vol. 35, pp. 1–97, 2005.

Heckman, J.J. "Econometric causality", *International Statistical Review*, Vol. 76, pp. 1–27, 2008.

Henríquez-Hernández, L.A., Valenciano, A., Foro-Arnalot, P., Álvarez-Cubero, M.J., Cozar, J.M., Suárez-Novo, J.F., Castells-Esteve, M., Ayala-Gil, A., Fernández-Gonzalo, P., Ferrer, M., Guedea, F., Sancho-Pardo, G., Craven-Bartle, J., Ortiz-Gordillo, M.J., Cabrera-Roldán, P., Herrera-Ramos, E., Lara, P.C. "Polymorphisms in DNA-repair genes in a cohort of prostate cancer patients from different areas in Spain: Heterogeneity between populations as a confounding factor in association studies", *PLoS ONE*, art. no. e69735, Vol. 8, No. 7, 2013.

Hoover, K.D. "Causal structure and hierarchies of models", *Studies in History and Philosophy of Science Part C: Studies in History and Philosophy of Biological and Biomedical Sciences*, Vol. 43, No. 4, pp. 778–786, December 2012.

Huang, Y., Valtorta, M. "Pearl's Calculus of Intervention Is Complete", *Proceedings of the Twenty-Second Conference on Uncertainty in Artificial Intelligence*, 2012.

Jamshidian, M., Yuan, K.-H. "Data-driven sensitivity analysis to detect missing data mechanism with applications to structural equation modelling", *Journal of Statistical Computation and Simulation*, Vol. 83, No. 7, pp. 1344–1362, 2013.

Kalisch, M., Mächler, M., Colombo, D., Maathuis, M.H., Bühlmann, P. "Causal inference using graphical models with the R package pcalg", *Journal of Statistical Software*, Vol. 47, 2012.

Kang, H.M., Yusof, F., Mohamad, I. "Imputation of missing data with different missingness mechanism", *Jurnal Teknologi (Sciences and Engineering)*, Vol. 57 (Suppl. 1), pp. 57–67, 2012.

Kupper, L.L., Karon, J.M., Kleinbaum, D.G., Morgenstern, H., Lewis, D.K. "Matching in epidemiologic studies: Validity and efficiency considerations", *Biometrics*, Vol. 37, No. 2, pp. 271–291, 1981.

Lee, J.J. "Correlation and causation in the study of personality", *European Journal of Personality*, Vol. 26, No. 4, pp. 372–390, 2012.

Lemeire, J., Janzing, D. "Replacing causal faithfulness with algorithmic independence of conditionals", *Minds and Machines*, Vol. 23, No. 2, pp. 227–249, 2013.

Li, L., Eron, J.J., Ribaudo, H., Gulick, R.M., Johnson, B.A. "Evaluating the effect of early versus late ARV regimen change if failure on an initial regimen: Results from the AIDS clinical trials group study A5095", *Journal of the American Statistical Association*, Vol. 107, No. 498, pp. 542–554, 2012.

Little, R.J.A., Rubin, D.B. "Statistical Analysis with Missing Data", New York: Wiley, 1987.

Little, R.J., Yau, L.H.Y. "Statistical techniques for analyzing data from prevention trials: Treatment of no-shows using Rubin's causal model", *Psychological Methods*, Vol. 3, No. 2, pp. 147–159, 1998.

Liu, K., Entsuah, R. "Missing data mechanisms in a dose-finding adaptive trial", *Journal of Biopharmaceutical Statistics*, Vol. 22, No. 2, pp. 329–337, 2012.

Luciani, D., Stefanini, F.M. "Automated interviews on clinical case reports to elicit directed acyclic graphs", *Artificial Intelligence in Medicine*, Vol. 55, No. 1, pp. 1–11, 2012.

Maathuis, M.H., Colombo, D. "A generalized backdoor criterion", arXiv:1307.5636, 2013.

Marwala, T. "Computational Intelligence for Missing Data Imputation, Estimation and Management: Knowledge Optimization Techniques", *IGI Global Publications*, New York, 2009.

Mason, A., Richardson, S., Plewis, I., Best, N. "Strategy for modelling nonrandom missing data mechanisms in observational studies using Bayesian methods", *Journal of Official Statistics*, Vol. 28, No. 2, pp. 279–302, 2012.

Mazanec, J.A. "Exploring tourist satisfaction with nonlinear structural equation modeling and inferred causation analysis", *Journal of Travel and Tourism Marketing*, Vol. 21, No. 4, pp. 73–90, 2006.

Muñoz, I.D., van der Laan, M. "Population intervention causal effects based on stochastic interventions", *Biometrics*, Vol. 68, No. 2, pp. 541–549, 2012.

Neyman, J. "Sur les applications de la theorie des probabilites aux experiences agricoles: Essai des principes", Master's Thesis (D.M. Dabrowska, T.P. Speed, Translators.), Excerpts reprinted in English, *Statistical Science*, Vol. 5, pp. 463–472, 1923.

Pearl, J. "Probabilistic Reasoning in Intelligent Systems", San Mateo, California: Morgan Kaufmann, 1988.

Pearl, J. "A probabilistic calculus of actions", *Proceedings of the Tenth international conference on Uncertainty in Artificial intelligence*, pp. 454–462, 1994.

Pearl, J. "Causal diagrams for empirical research", *Biometrika*, Vol. 82, No. 4, pp. 669–710, 1995.

Pearl, J. "Graphs, causality and structural equation models", *Sociological Methods and Research*, Vol. 27, Nos. 226–284, 1998.

Pearl, J. "Causality: Models, Reasoning, and Inference", Cambridge, UK: Cambridge University Press, 2000.

Pearl, J. "The Foundations of Causal Inference", *Sociological Methodology*, Vol. 40, pp. 75–150, 2010.

Pearl, J., Dechter, R. "Identifying Independencies in Causal Graphs with Feedback", *Proceedings of the Twelfth Annual Conference on Uncertainty in Artificial Intelligence*, San Francisco: Morgan Kaufmann, pp. 420–426, 1996.

Pearl, J., Verma, T. "A Theory of Inferred Causation Verma", *Proceedings of the Second International Conference of Representation and Reasoning*, San Francisco: Morgan Kaufmann, 1991.

Pearl, J., Verma, T.S. "A theory of inferred causation", *Studies in Logic and the Foundations of Mathematics*, Vol. 134, pp. 789–811, 1995.

Prohorov, Y.V., Rozanov, Yu.A. "Probability Theory, Basic Concepts. Limit Theorems, Random Processes", Springer, 1969.

Raykov, T., Lichtenberg, P.A., Paulson, D. "Examining the missing completely at random mechanism in incomplete data sets: A multiple testing approach", *Structural Equation Modeling*, Vol. 19, No. 3, pp. 399–408, 2012.

Rebane, G., Pearl, J. "The Recovery of Causal Poly-trees from Statistical Data", *Proceedings, 3rd Workshop on Uncertainty in AI* (Seattle, WA), pp. 222–228, 1987.

Rosario, I.J., Kasabwala, K., Sadeghi-Nejad, H. "Circumcision as a strategy to minimize HIV transmission", *Current Urology Reports*, Vol. 14, No. 4, pp. 285–290, 2013.

Rubin, D.B. "Matching to remove bias in observational studies", *Biometrics*, Vol. 29, No. 1, pp. 159–183, 1973.

Rubin, D. "Estimating causal effects of treatments in randomized and nonrandomized studies", *Journal of Educational Psychology*, Vol. 66, No. 5, pp. 688–701, 1974.

Rubin, D. "Assignment to treatment group on the basis of a covariate", *Journal of Educational Statistics*, Vol. 2, pp. 1–26, 1977.

Rubin, D. "Bayesian inference for causal effects: The role of randomization", *The Annals of Statistics*, Vol. 6, pp. 34–58, 1978.

Rubin, D. "Causal inference using potential outcomes", *Journal of the American Statistical Association*, Vol. 100, No. 469, 2005.

Shadish, A. "W.R. Campbell and Rubin: Primer and Comparison of Their Approaches to Causal Inference in Field Settings", *Psychological Methods*, Vol. 15, No. 1, pp. 3–17, 2010.

Shpitser, I. "Counterfactual graphical models for longitudinal mediation analysis with unobserved confounding", *Cognitive Science*, Vol. 37, No. 6, pp. 1011–1035, 2013.

Sjölander, A., Bellocco, R. "Confounding adjustment through front-door blocking in longitudinal studies", *Epidemiology Biostatistics and Public Health*, Vol. 10, No. 1, pp. 1–10, 2013.

Spirtes, P. "Using *d*-separation to calculate zero partial correlations in linear models with correlated errors", Carnegie Mellon University Technical Report, 1996.

Steinsky, B. "Enumeration of labelled chain graphs and labelled essential directed acyclic graphs", *Discrete Mathematics*, Vol. 270, Nos. 1–3, pp. 267–278, 2003.

Tam Cho, W.K., Sauppe, J.J., Nikolaev, A.G., Jacobson, S.H., Sewell, E.C. "An optimization approach for making causal inferences", *Statistica Neerlandica*, Vol. 67, No. 2, pp. 211–226, 2013.

Toh, S., Gagne, J.J., Rassen, J.A., Fireman, B.H., Kulldorff, M., Brown, J.S. "Confounding adjustment in comparative effectiveness research conducted within distributed research networks", *Medical Care*, Vol. 51, No. 8 (Suppl. 3), pp. S4–S10, 2013.

Tsikriktsis, N. "A review of techniques for treating missing data in OM survey research", *Journal of Operations Management*, Vol. 24, No. 1, pp. 53–62, 2005.

Tuan, L.-W., Chen, Y.-J., Li, P.-L., Lin, K.-C. "Evaluation of multiple imputation for longitudinal ordinal data under MCAR and MAR missing-data mechanisms", *ICIC Express Letters*, Vol. 5, No. 6, pp. 1833–1838, 2011.

Turner, D.P., Smitherman, T.A., Martin, V.T., Penzien, D.B., Houle, T.T. "Causality and headache triggers", *Headache*, Vol. 53, No. 4, pp. 628–635, 2013.

Valente, B.D., Rosa, G.J.M., De Los Campos, G., Gianola, D., Silva, M.A. "Searching for recursive causal structures in multivariate quantitative genetics mixed models", *Genetics*, Vol. 185, No. 2, pp. 633–644, 2010.

Valente, B.D., Rosa, G.J.M., Silva, M.A., Teixeira, R.B., Torres, R.A. "Searching for phenotypic causal networks involving complex traits: An application to European quail", *Genetics Selection Evolution*, art. no. 37, Vol. 43, No. 1, 2011.

Vanderweele, T.J., Robins, J.M. "Directed acyclic graphs, sufficient causes, and the properties of conditioning on a common effect", *American Journal of Epidemiology*, Vol. 166, No. 9, pp. 1096–1104, 2007.

Velilla, S. "On eigenvalues, case deletion and extremes in regression", *Computational Statistics & Data Analysis*, Vol. 16, No. 3, pp. 299–309, 1993.

Verma, T.S., Pearl, J. "Causal Networks: Semantics and Expressiveness", *Proceedings of the Fourth Conference on Uncertainty in Artificial Intelligence* (UAI1988), arXiv:1304.2379, 2013.

West, S.G., Thoemmes, F. "Campbell's and Rubin's Perspectives on Causal Inference", *Psychological Methods*, Vol. 15, No. 1, pp. 18–37, 2010.

Wright, S. "Correlation and causation", *Journal of Agricultural Research*, Vol. 7, No. 3, pp. 557–585, 1921.

Xie, X., Geng, Z., Zhao, Q. "Decomposition of structural learning about directed acyclic graphs", *Artificial Intelligence*, Vol. 170, Nos. 4–5, pp. 422–439, 2006.

Zhang, J. "Causal Inference and Reasoning in Causally Insufficient Systems", Ph.D. thesis, Carnegie Mellon University, 2006.

Zhang, J. "Generalized do-calculus with testable causal assumptions", *Journal of Machine Learning Research*, Vol. 2, pp. 667–674, 2007.

Zhang, J. "Causal reasoning with ancestral graphs", *Journal of Machine Learning Research*, Vol. 9, pp. 1437–1474, 2008.

Zheng, W., Van Der Laan, M.J. "Targeted maximum likelihood estimation of natural direct effects", *International Journal of Biostatistics*, art. no. 3, Vol. 8, No. 1, 2012.

Zhu, H., Lee, S.-Y., Wei, B.-C., Zhou, J. "Case-deletion measures for models with incomplete data", *Biometrika*, Vol. 88, No. 3, pp. 727–737, 2001.

Chapter 7

Causal, Correlation and Automatic Relevance Determination Machines for Granger Causality

Abstract. In this chapter, the causal, correlation and automatic relevance determination (ARD) machines are built to model non-linear Granger causality and are compared. The multi-layer perceptron (MLP) neural network trained using the scaled gradient method is used to build both the causal, correlation and ARD machines. The causal machine is a feed-forward MLP with past data being used as inputs to predict future values of a chaotic time series. The correlation machine is the auto-associative model which maps the past and present values to predict itself and a Nelder-Mead optimization method is used to predict future values. The ARD machine is an MLP which models the input–output relationship via Bayesian approach by penalizing the prior coefficient associated with each input variable. When these methods were tested, it was found that the correlation machine models Granger causality better than the causal machine while the ARD performs well. The complex nature of the correlation machine (inference using auto-associative neural networks) compared to the MLP causal machine renders the correlation machine more sensitive to Granger causality than the causal machine.

7.1 Introduction

This chapter introduces and compares the causal, correlation and automatic relevance determination (ARD) machines for modeling Granger causality. Granger causality model is based on the proposition that for an input–output model that maps the cause to the effect, if the inclusion of additional inputs improves the accuracy of the input–output model then the additional inputs Granger causes the output. Granger causality was proposed by the Nobel Laureate Clive Granger and has been used successfully in many different applications (Granger, 1969). As indicated by Barrett and Barnett (2013), the objective of Granger causality is to estimate the effect of a variable or variables on another variable or variables and it does not fully deconstruct the mechanism of causality. Tang (2013) applied Granger causality to analyze the causal relationship among tourism receipts, income and exchange rates in Malaysia and could not observe Granger causality between tourism receipt and income in the short-term but detected bidirectional causality in the long-run. Hsueh *et al.* (2013) applied Granger causality successfully to model the relationship between economic growth and financial development in Asian countries. They observed that there was a causal relationship between financial development and economic growth which was dependent on the financial development variables. Liang *et al.* (2013) applied Granger causality successfully to analyze the causal relationship between stock prices and exchange rates. The results showed that monetary establishments must permit currency to be determined by economic fundamentals instead. Other successful applications of Granger causality include detecting and estimating connectivity in neural networks (Friston *et al.*, 2013) as well as analyzing multiple blocks of interacting time series data (Faes and Nollo, 2013).

The application of Granger causality requires the construction of a model that relates the input data to the output data. To articulate this more generally, the application of Granger causality model requires a relationship between the cause and the effect to be identifiable. In this chapter, we investigate three paradigms and these are the causal, correlation, and ARD machines for modeling causal relations. For an example, the concept of causality can be mathematically expressed by writing an equation y as a function of x to represent the fact that x causes y provided that x happens before y, x and y are connected and that there is a flow of information from x to y. However, the concept of a correlation machine is based on the premise that after one has captured the correlation relationships that define the data then the effect can be estimated by identifying the effect that will result from the cause such that the correlation relationships are maintained. The ARD assesses the relevance of each input by evaluating the variance of the weights associated with various inputs.

In this chapter, causal, correlations, and ARD machines are all built using the multi-layered perceptron (MLP) neural network. The correlation machine is, however, convoluted in that it estimates the cause and effect through the auto-associative neural network which captures the inter-correlations amongst variables. The correlation machine is built using the auto-associative neural network which is a network which is built such that the input data are recalled as inputs and this was explained in earlier chapters. Section 7.2 describes causal machine for Granger causality, Section 7.3 describes the correlation machine for Granger causality and Section 7.4 describes the ARD technique for Granger causality while the Section 7.5 describes an experimental investigation to compare the causal, correlation, and ARD machines.

7.2 Causal Machine to Granger Causality

As explained in earlier chapters, Granger causality method is a technique which is used to detect the so-called Granger causality and has been applied in many fields. It is premised on the assumption that given a time series y then an autoregressive linear model can be constructed using the following mathematical equation (Granger, 1969; Hacker and Hatemi, 2006):

$$y(t) = \sum_{j=1}^{p} B_j y(t-j) + E_1(t). \tag{7.1}$$

Here p is the maximum number of past data points while E is the error of this model and B_j is the jth coefficient. If we introduce variable x which also has a time history available, is stationary and can also be modeled using linear assumptions to predict future values of y, then Equation 7.1 may then be re-written as follows (Granger, 1969; Hacker and Hatemi, 2006):

$$y(t) = \sum_{j=1}^{q} A_j x(t-j) + \sum_{j=1}^{p} B_j y(t-j) + E_2(t). \tag{7.2}$$

A_j is the jth coefficient while q is the past time points to be included. Granger observed that given Equations 7.1 and 7.2, then variable x Granger causes variable y if the introduction of variable x to Equation 7.1 to form Equation 7.2 results in Equation 7.2 being better at predicting variable y than Equation 7.2. Generalizing Equations 7.1 and 7.2 forms:

$$y_{later} = f(y_{early}) + E_1 \tag{7.3}$$

$$y_{later} = f(y_{early}, x_{earlier}) + E_2. \tag{7.4}$$

Here f is the mapping function and $y_{earlier}$ is a vector showing the earlier time history of y while $x_{earlier}$ is a vector showing the earlier time history of x and y_{later} is a vector indicating the later time history of y.

The multi-layer perceptron (MLP) equation is applied in this chapter to transform Equations 7.3 and 7.4 to the non-linear domain resulting in the following equations (Rosenblatt, 1961; Rumelhart *et al.*, 1986; Bishop, 1995; Haykin, 1998; Bishop, 2006):

$$y_{later} = f_{outer}\left(\sum_{j=1}^{M} w_{kj}^{(2)} f_{inner}\left(\sum_{i=1}^{d} w_{ji}^{(1)} x_i^{earlier} + w_{j0}^{(1)}\right) + w_{k0}^{(2)}\right) + E_1, \tag{7.5}$$

$$y_{later} = f_{outer}\left(\sum_{j=1}^{M} w_{kj}^{(2)} f_{inner}\left(\sum_{i=1}^{d} w_{ji}^{(1)} x_i^{earlier} + \sum_{i=d}^{e} w_{ji}^{(1)} y_i^{earlier} + w_{j0}^{(1)}\right) + w_{k0}^{(2)}\right) + E_2. \tag{7.6}$$

Here, $w_{ji}^{(1)}$ and $w_{kj}^{(2)}$ are the weights in the first and second layers, respectively, moving from input i to hidden unit j, M is the number of hidden units, d is the number of time units for the previous time history of x while e is the number of time units for the previous time history of y, whereas $w_{j0}^{(1)}$ is the bias for the hidden unit j and $w_{k0}^{(2)}$ designates the bias for the output unit k.

Babanouri *et al.* (2013) successfully applied the MLP algorithm to estimate rock fractures roughness using fractal analysis whereas Golzan *et al.* (2012) applied the MLP network to estimate successfully cerebrospinal fluid pressure. Sulistiyo *et al.* (2012) applied the MLP successfully for optical character recognition and Aghayan *et al.* (2012) successfully applied the MLP to model extended traffic crash y. Other successful applications of the MLP include classifying electroencephalography (EEG) signal (Zabidi *et al.*, 2012), for face detection (Cavalcanti *et al.*, 2012) and for Arabic speech recognition (Ben Nasr *et al.*, 2012).

Given the availability of historical values of x and y then the next step is to apply system identification techniques to identify the weights that will map the input–output relationship and in this chapter, we apply the maximum likelihood approach to achieve this task (Bishop, 1995). The example of the causal machine is in Figure 7.1 for Equation 7.5 and Figure 7.2 for Equation 7.6.

7.2.1 Multi-layer perceptron

In order to identify the network weights in Equations 7.5 and 7.6, the objective function that represents the difference between the model prediction and the target data need to be identified. The objective function is a function that represents the objective that ought to be achieved when optimizing a function (Avriel, 2003; Bonnans *et al.*, 2006). In this chapter, we apply the least square error to identify the network weights in the optimization process which can be written as follows (Björck, 1996; Rao *et al.*, 1999; Wolberg, 2005):

$$E = \sum_{m=1}^{M}\sum_{k=1}^{K}\{y_{mk} - t_{mk}\}^2. \tag{7.7}$$

Here E is the error, t is the target output, y is the output predicted by the MLP, M is the number of output values and K is the number of training examples. The weight update feature uses the output delta and input activation to obtain the gradient of the weight. Then the weight in the opposite direction of the gradient is used by subtracting a ratio of it from the weight and then this ratio impacts on the performance of the learning process. The sign of the gradient of a weight describes the direction where the error increases and this is the reason the weight is updated in the opposite direction (Bishop, 1995) and this process is repeated until convergence.

To identify the network weights given the training data using an optimization technique, the following iterative method is applied (Werbos, 1974):

$$\{w\}_{i+1} = \{w\}_i - \eta\frac{\partial E}{\partial\{w\}}(\{w\}_i). \tag{7.8}$$

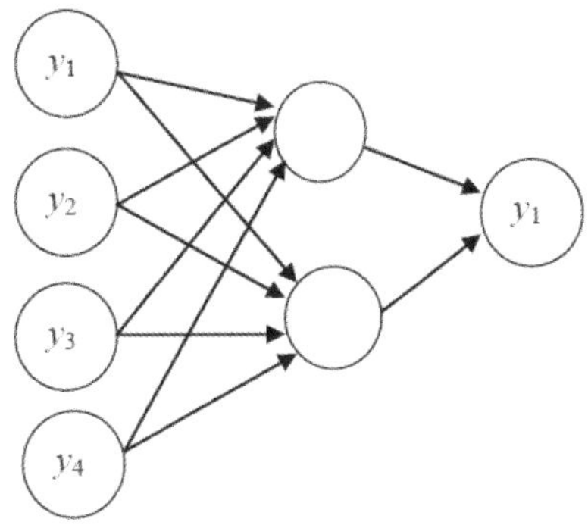

Figure 7.1 Estimation of future value of y from 4 previous values of y

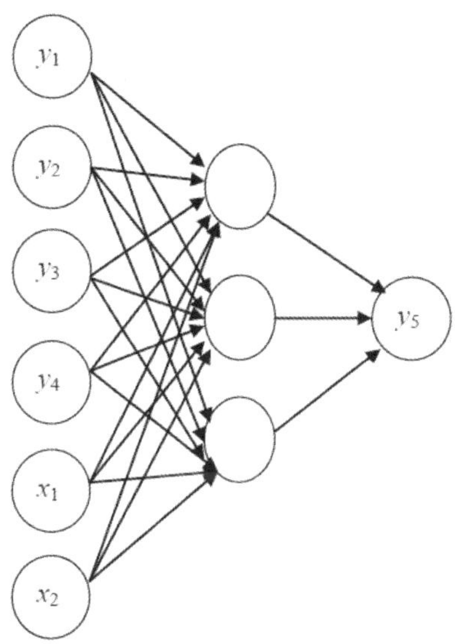

Figure 7.2 Estimation of future value of y from 4 previous values of y and 2 past values of x

In Equation 7.8, the parameter η is the learning rate while { } represents a vector. To optimize the objective function, E, the derivative of the errors, in Equation 7.8, with respect to the network weight is calculated and, in this chapter, we apply the scaled conjugate gradient (SCG) method which is the subject of Section 7.2.2.

7.2.2 Scaled conjugate gradient method

The method in which the network weights are approximated from the data in this chapter is the SCG method (Møller, 1993). The SCG has been applied successfully in many areas such as in inverse natural convention modeling (Wong and Protas,

2013), handwritten text identification (Chel *et al.*, 2011), fault location in high voltage transmission lines (Gayathri and Kumarappan, 2010), solving unconstrained optimization problems (Al-Bayati and Muhammad, 2010) and estimating radar pulse modulation (Lundén and Koivunen, 2007).

The basis of the SCG is the gradient descent and the conjugate gradient methods (Hestenes and Stiefel, 1952). In the gradient descent technique, the step size is $-\eta\partial E/\partial w$ and the parameter η is the learning rate. When the learning rate is adequately small, the value of the error decreases at each sequential step until a minimum value for the error between the model prediction and training target data is reached. This method is, however, computationally expensive when compared to other methods. In the conjugate gradient technique, the quadratic function of error is minimized at each step over an increasingly expanding linear vector space (Luenberger, 1984; Fletcher, 1987; Bertsekas, 1995). In the conjugate gradient method, the following steps are followed as described by Haykin (1999), Marwala (2009) and Babaie-Kafaki *et al.* (2010):

1. Select the initial weight vector $\{w\}_0$.
2. Compute the gradient vector $\frac{\partial E}{\partial\{w\}}(\{w\}_0)$.
3. At each iteration, n, use the line search to identify $\eta(n)$ that minimizes $E(\eta)$ indicating the cost function expressed in terms of η for fixed values of w and $-\frac{\partial E}{\partial\{w\}}(\{w_n\})$.
4. Evaluate whether the Euclidean norm of the vector $-\frac{\partial E}{\partial w}(\{w_n\})$ is adequately less than $-\frac{\partial E}{\partial w}(\{w_0\})$.
5. Use Equation 7.8 to update the weight vector.
6. Calculate the updated gradient $\frac{\partial E}{\partial\{w\}}(\{w\}_{n+1})$.
7. Apply Polak–Ribiére technique to compute:
$$\beta(n+1) = \frac{\nabla E(\{w\}_{n+1})^T(\nabla E(\{w\}_{n+1}) - \nabla E(\{w\}_n)))}{\nabla E(\{w\}_n)^T \nabla E(\{w\}_n)}.$$
8. Update the direction vector
$$\frac{\partial E}{\partial\{w\}}(\{w\}_{n+2}) = \frac{\partial E}{\partial\{w\}}(\{w\}_{n+1}) - \beta(n+1)\frac{\partial E}{\partial\{w\}}(\{w\}_n).$$
9. Fix $n = n + 1$ and go back to Step 3.
10. Stop when the following condition is reached:
$$\frac{\partial E}{\partial\{w\}}(\{w\}_{n+2}) = \varepsilon\frac{\partial E}{\partial\{w\}}(\{w\}_{n+1})$$
where ε is a small number.

The SCG technique is different from the conjugate gradient process in that it does not include the line search, as described in Step 3 and the step-size is thus computed using the following formula as proposed by Møller (1993):

$$\eta(n) = 2\left(\eta(n) - \left(\frac{\partial E(n)}{\partial\{w\}}(n)\right)^T H(n)\left(\frac{\partial E(n)}{\partial\{w\}}(n)\right) + \eta(n)\left\|\left(\frac{\partial E(n)}{\partial\{w\}}(n)\right)\right\|^2 \Big/ \left\|\left(\frac{\partial E(n)}{\partial\{w\}}(n)\right)\right\|\right)^2. \quad (7.9)$$

where H is the Hessian of the gradient.

7.3 Correlation Machine to Granger Causality

This section describes the correlation approach to Granger causality. In earlier chapters, we indicated that to build the correlation machine we use an auto-associative neural network which is a network trained to recall its inputs as outputs.

González and Villanueva (2013) applied the auto-associative network to fault diagnose vehicle lateral dynamics whereas Masuda *et al.* (2012) applied auto-associative network to store information which was represented as binary patterns. Valle and Vicente (2012) applied the auto-associative network to successfully reconstruct color images whereas Hayworth (2012) successfully applied auto-associative networks to bind properties of objects with the correct objects. Masuda *et al.* (2012) applied auto-associative networks to increase memorization accuracy.

Sub-section 7.3.1 describes the auto-associative network and how it can be applied to model Granger causality. Sub-section 7.3.2 describes the Nelder-Mead optimization method and how it can be used to estimate missing data from the auto-associative network and Sub-section 7.3.3 describes Granger causality and how it is applied using the auto-associative missing data estimation framework.

7.3.1 Auto-associative network for missing data estimation

As it was described earlier, the auto-associative model is a model that is intended to predict or recall its own inputs. A model that describes the estimation of the output $\{y\}$ given the input $\{x\}$ and free parameters $\{w\}$ can be mathematically written as follows:

$$\{y\} = f(\{x\}, \{w\}). \quad (7.10)$$

For the reason that in this framework, a model is created to recall its own input vector, the input vector $\{x\}$ is almost equal to output vector $\{y\}$ and thus $\{x\} \approx \{y\}$.

Always, the input vector $\{x\}$ and output vector $\{y\}$ will not always be exactly the same and consequently, there will be an error function represented as the difference between the input and output vector. Therefore, the error can be written as follows as stated by Marwala (2009):

$$\{e\} = \{x\} - \{y\}. \tag{7.11}$$

Substituting the value of $\{y\}$ from Equation 7.10 into Equation 7.11 the following expression is obtained:

$$\{e\} = \{x\} - f(\{x\}, \{w\}). \tag{7.12}$$

The aim is for the error to be minimized and to be non-negative and consequently, the error function can be expressed as a square of Equation 7.12:

$$\{e\} = (\{x\} - f(\{x\}, \{w\}))^2. \tag{7.13}$$

Suppose some of the values for the input vector $\{x\}$ are available, then we can split the input vector elements into $\{x\}$ known vector represented by $\{x_k\}$ and $\{x\}$ unknown vector represented by $\{x_u\}$. By re-organizing Equation 7.13, in terms of $\{x_k\}$ and $\{x_u\}$ we have:

$$\{e\} = \left(\left\{\begin{matrix}\{x_k\}\\ \{x_u\}\end{matrix}\right\} - f\left(\left\{\begin{matrix}\{x_k\}\\ \{x_u\}\end{matrix}\right\}, \{w\}\right)\right)^2. \tag{7.14}$$

The error vector in Equation 7.14 can be expressed in a scalar format by integrating over the size of the input vector and the number of training examples as follows:

$$E = \left\|\left(\left\{\begin{matrix}\{x_k\}\\ \{x_u\}\end{matrix}\right\} - f\left(\left\{\begin{matrix}\{x_k\}\\ \{x_u\}\end{matrix}\right\}, \{w\}\right)\right)\right\|. \tag{7.15}$$

Equation 7.15 is known as the missing data estimation equation and to estimate the missing input values, Equation 7.15 is minimized. There are many types of optimization techniques, and some of these were described in Chapter 5, that can be applied to achieve this objective and in this chapter, the Nelder-Mead optimization method which is the subject of Chapter 8 is used because of its simplicity.

7.3.2 Nelder-Mead simplex optimization method

In this chapter, the Nelder-Mead simplex method is used to optimize for the estimation of the missing value in Equation 7.15. Abedi *et al.* (2013) applied the Nelder-Mead algorithm successfully to optimize a process in an atmospheric pressure vertical rotating disk reactor whereas Osgood and Huang (2013) successfully used the Nelder-Mead optimization to calibrate laser scanner and camera fusion system for intelligent vehicles. Corominas *et al.* (2013) applied successfully the Nelder-Mead algorithm to optimize meta-heuristics whereas Choudhury and Ghose (2013) successfully used the Nelder-Mead algorithm to predict the propagation parameters of graded-index fibers while Cheng and Shi (2012) successfully applied the Nelder-Mead algorithm for multiple parameter optimization in a plasma application.

The Nelder-Mead simplex technique is a direct optimization routine which builds a simplex with $N + 1$ vertices (x_{i}) in an N dimensional space. A simplex of a prescribed dimension (p) is generated around x_0 using the following equation with e representing the unit base vectors (Luersen and Riche, 2004; Ransome, 2006; Marwala, 2010):

$$x_i = x_0 + \frac{p}{n\sqrt{2}}\left(\sqrt{n+1} + n - 1\right)e_i + \sum_{k=1 \neq i}^{n} \left[\frac{p}{n\sqrt{2}}\left(\sqrt{n+1} - 1\right)\right] e_k, \; i = 1, n. \tag{7.16}$$

The simplex vertices coordinates are altered using reflection, expansion and contraction operators and this technique was explained in detail by Ransome (2006) and Ransome *et al.* (2005) as follows:

- At a particular iteration in the optimization process, the vertex with the least fitness according to Equation 7.15 is replaced by a new vertex;
- Coordinates of the new vertex are identified by reflecting the old vertex's point about the outstanding vertices as shown in Figure 7.3 (Ransome, 2006; Ransome *et al.*, 2005);
- If the fitness of the current vertices is lower than the fitness of the past removed vertex, the dimension of the simplex is minimized and if not, it is enlarged;
- Proceed until the functional evaluation values of the vertices converge.

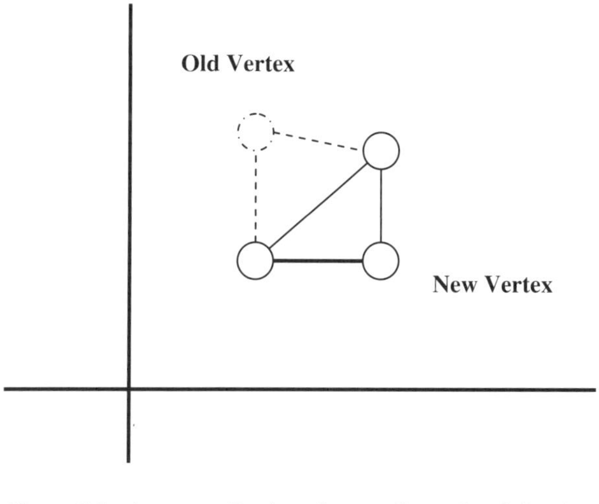

Figure 7.3 An easy reflection of a two-dimensional simplex

The convergence process can be measured using the following inequality (Luersen and Riche, 2004; Ransome, 2006; Marwala, 2010):

$$\sqrt{\sum_{i=1}^{n+1}\frac{(f_i-\bar{f})^2}{n}} < \tau \tag{7.17}$$

here τ is a small positive scalar and is calculated by using the following equation (Luersen and Riche, 2004; Ransome, 2006; Marwala, 2010):

$$\bar{f} = \frac{1}{n+1}\sum_{i=1}^{n+1} f_i. \tag{7.18}$$

The advantages of the Nelder-Mead simplex technique are as follows (Bürmen *et al.*, 2006; Luersen and Riche, 2004; Ransome, 2006; Marwala, 2010):

- It converges fast;
- A single or double functional calculation is normally required per iteration if one excludes a shrink transformation;
- It is computationally efficient; and
- It is easy to understand or use.

The disadvantages of the Nelder-Mead simplex are (McKinnon, 1998; Marwala, 2010):

- No clear theory of convergence;
- Numerical failures encountered even for smooth functions;
- Premature convergence.

The process described which entails using the auto-associative network and the Nelder-Mead optimization method to identify a relationship mapping some piece of data to another is illustrated in Figure 7.4.

This relationship in Figure 7.4 can be mathematically represented as follows:

$$x_{\text{unknown}} = F(x_{\text{known}}, AT). \tag{7.19}$$

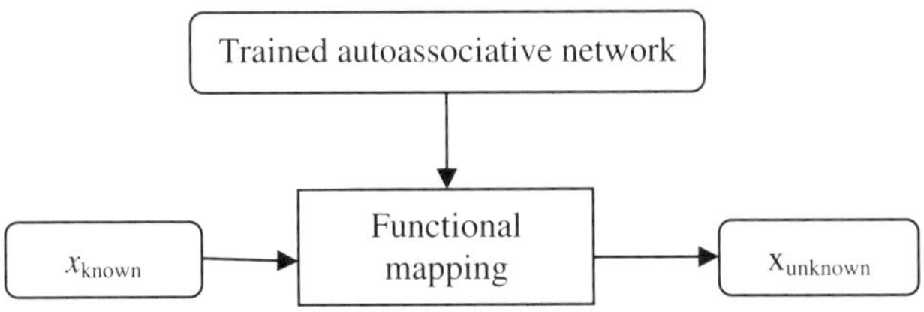

Figure 7.4 Conceptual illustration of the estimation of the unknown components of the input variables from the known components of the input variables and a trained auto-associative network

Here *AT* is a trained auto-associative neural network and this relationship states that you can estimate an unobserved piece of data from a trained auto-associative network by optimizing Equation 7.15. Of course, this is a convoluted way of inference but it makes perfect sense for Granger causality analysis as it will be observed in Section 7.3.3.

7.3.3 Granger causality

Granger causality model basically says that if you have two sets of time series (variables x and y) then Granger causality relations exist between these two variables if by estimating the future values of one variable (y_{t+1}) from its previous values ($y_t, \ldots, y_{t-p}$) when compared to predicting the future values of the same variable (y_{t+1}) from the combined previous values of both variables ($y_t, \ldots, y_{t-p}$ and $x_t, \ldots, x_{t-p}$), it is observed that the latter case gives more accurate results than the former case.

To build Granger causality analysis using this figure, one builds two different auto-associative networks (Figures 7.5 and 7.6). The first network maps a window of a time series to itself (e.g. vector $\{y_1, y_2, y_3, y_4, y_5\}$ and the components of each vector means an observation at time $1, 2, \ldots, 5$). Then for an independent time windows which were not used to train the auto-associative network one assumes that observations at time 5 have not been observed and estimates these values by treating the problem as a missing data estimation problem with y_5 to be estimated and solving Equation 7.15 using the framework in Figure 7.5 and storing the accuracy obtained.

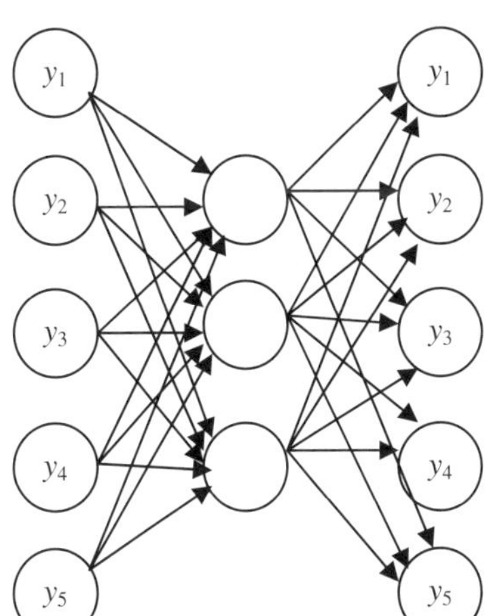

Figure 7.5 Granger causality modeling using auto-associative network: one set of variable

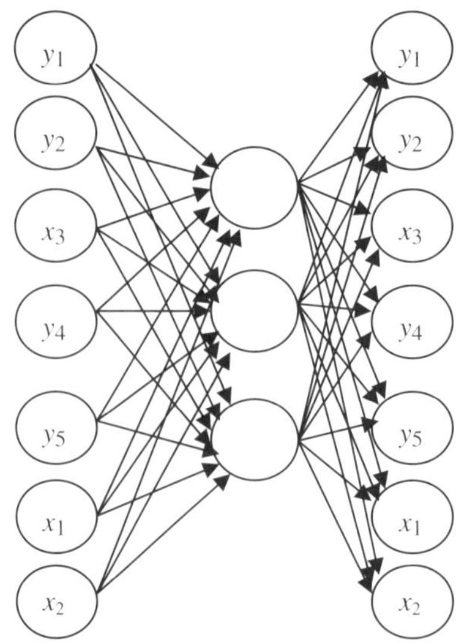

Figure 7.6 Granger causality modeling using auto-associative network: two sets of variables

Then the second network is trained with input values being the combined values of $y(\{y_1, y_2, y_3, y_4, y_5\})$ and $x(\{x_1, x_2\})$. The dimension of the input is flexible and can include as many previous values of both x and y as it is necessary. Similarly, for an independent time windows which were not used to train the auto-associative network one assumes that observations at time 5 have not been observed and estimates these values by treating the problem as a missing data estimation problem with y_5 to be estimated and solving Equation 7.15 using the framework in Figure 7.5 and storing accuracy obtained.

The accuracies of the model in Figures 7.5 and 7.6 are then compared and if model in Figure 7.6 is not higher than that from model in Figure 7.5 then there is no Granger causality relation and the reverse is also the case. The comparison between the two models of course requires rigorous statistical analysis.

The model proposed is sensitive to the dependency between two sets of variables because the auto-associative model captures the character of the causal dynamics of the two sets of variables through the cross correlation analysis.

7.4 Automatic Relevance Determination for Granger Causality

This section proposes ARD to construct a non-linear Granger causality model. The ARD has been applied successfully in many areas including trading (Shutin and Buchgraber, 2012), in missing data estimation (Duma *et al.*, 2012), in virtual sensors in diesel soot (Johri *et al.*, 2012), in image classification (Zhang *et al.*, 2012), in

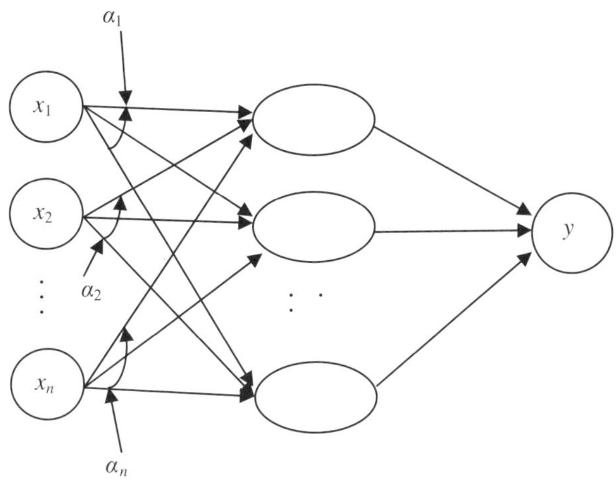

Figure 7.7 Illustration of the ARD with the hyper-parameters of the prior associated to each input

compressing sensing (Huang *et al.*, 2012) and to model antenna input characteristics (Jacobs, 2012).

ARD is a method where in a predictive model the causal variable is ranked in order of the significance of its effect on the output variable. If there is no causal relationship between variables a and b then variable a will be assigned a value that indicates irrelevance. The application of the ARD within the context of causality studies has been performed by Marwala (2013). The schematic illustration of the ARD is shown in Figure 7.7 (Marwala, 2013).

To build the ARD, Bayesian statistics is necessary. Bayesian statistics has been applied to many complex problems, including in finite element model updating (Marwala and Sibisi, 2005), missing data estimation (Marwala, 2009), safety control (Zhang *et al.*, 2013), estimation of the abundance of salmon (Sethi and Tanner, 2013), prediction of entrepreneurial activity (Sohn and Lee, 2013), in satellite application (Li *et al.*, 2013) and risk analysis of offshore drilling activities (Khakzad *et al.*, 2013). The problem of identifying the weights (w_i) and biases in Equations 7.5 and 7.6 can be framed in the Bayesian form as follows (Box and Tiao, 1973; Marwala, 2013):

$$P(\{w\}|[D]) = \frac{P([D]|\{w\})P(\{w\})}{P([D])} \tag{7.20}$$

here $P(w)$ is the probability distribution function of the weight-space in the absence of any data, also known as the prior distribution and $D \equiv (y_1, \ldots, y_N)$ is a matrix containing the data. $P(w|D)$ is the posterior probability distribution after the data have been seen and $P(D|w)$ is the likelihood function.

The ARD technique is built by associating hyper-parameters of the prior with each input variable and the prior distribution in Equation 7.19 can be generalized as follows (MacKay, 1991; 1992):

$$E_W = \frac{1}{2}\sum_k \alpha_k \{w\}^T [I_k]\{w\} \tag{7.21}$$

where superscript T is the transpose, k is the weight group and $[I]$ is the identity matrix. Thus the posterior probability in Equation 7.20 can be written as follows using the error in Equation 7.7 (Bishop, 1995):

$$P(\{w\}|[D], H_i) = \frac{1}{Z_s}\exp\left(\sum_{m=1}^{M}\sum_{k=1}^{K}\{t_{mk} - y_{mk}\}^2 - \frac{1}{2}\sum_k \alpha_k \{w\}^T [I_k]\{w\}\right) \tag{7.22}$$

here

$$Z_E(\alpha, \beta) = \left(\frac{2\pi}{\beta}\right)^{N/2} + \prod_k \left(\frac{2\pi}{\alpha_k}\right)^{W_k/2} \tag{7.23}$$

here W_k is the number of weights in group k. The evidence can be written as follows as was done by Bishop (1995):

$$\begin{aligned} p([D]|\alpha, \beta) &= \frac{1}{Z_D Z_W}\int \exp(-E(\{w\}))d\{w\} \\ &= \frac{Z_E}{Z_D Z_W} \\ &= \frac{\left(\frac{2\pi}{\beta}\right)^{N/2} + \prod_k \left(\frac{2\pi}{\alpha_k}\right)^{W_k/2}}{\left(\frac{2\pi}{\beta}\right)^{N/2} \prod_k \left(\frac{2\pi}{\alpha_k}\right)^{W_k/2}}. \end{aligned} \tag{7.24}$$

The log evidence can be maximized giving the following estimations for the hyper-parameters (Bishop, 1995):

$$\beta^{MP} = \frac{N - \gamma}{2E_D(\{w\}^{MP})} \tag{7.25}$$

$$\alpha_k^{MP} = \frac{\gamma_k}{2E_{W_k}(\{w\}^{MP})} \tag{7.26}$$

here $\gamma = \sum_k \gamma_k$, $2E_{W_k} = \{w\}^T [I_k]\{w\}$ and

$$\gamma_k = \sum_j \left(\frac{\pi_j - \alpha_k}{\eta_j}([V]^T [I_k][V])_{jj}\right) \tag{7.27}$$

and $\{w\}^{MP}$ is the weight vector at the maximum point and this is identified in this chapter using the SCG technique which was discussed earlier, η_j are the eigenvalues of $[A]$, and $[V]$ is the eigenvector such that $[V]^T[V] = [I]$. The relevance of each input variable (α_k^{MP}) and β^{MP} are estimated by choosing the initial values for the hyper-parameters randomly, training the network using SCG method to identify $\{w\}^{MP}$ and using Equations 7.26 and 7.27 to estimate the hyper parameters and repeating the procedure until convergence without further initialization of the hyper-parameters as explained by MacKay (1991). Small α represents high relevance of a variable in predicting the outcome and vice-versa.

7.5 Experimental Investigation: Mackey–Glass Time-Delay Differential Equation

In this chapter, we apply the Mackey–Glass equation which is a differential equation to test the three methods proposed to model Granger causality. As described in earlier chapters, the Mackey–Glass equation models periodic and chaotic phenomena. As was done in earlier chapters, in this chapter, we generate a time series from the Mackey–Glass equation. The Mackey–Glass equation can be expressed as follows (Mackey and Glass, 1977; Glass and Mackey; 1979):

$$\frac{dx(t)}{dt} = \beta\frac{x(t-\tau)}{1+x(t-\tau)^n} - \gamma x(t), \beta, \gamma, n > 0. \tag{7.28}$$

The data is generated using the following parameters: $\beta = 0.2$, $\gamma = 0.1$, $n = 10$, $x(0) = 1.2$ and $\tau = 17$. In this chapter, as it was done in earlier chapters, we built a model that ultimately predicts $x(t+6)$ from previous values at $x(t-18)$, $x(t-12)$, $x(t-6)$, and $x(t)$. Additional two sets of randomly generated data were also included in the modeling exercise. A total of 1000 data were collected and 500 were used to train the MLP and 500 to test the models. The causal, correlation and ARD machines which were built using the MLP network were used to model Granger causality as indicated in Table 7.1.

Table 7.1 The characteristics of neural networks

Method	Causal machine	Correlation machine	ARD machine
Number of Inputs	3, 4, 6	7	6
Number of Hidden Units	4	6	6
Number of Outputs	1	7	1
α	0.001	0.001	Identified as relevance
β	50	50	50
Number of steps in each trajectory	100	100	—
Number of retained samples	500	500	—
Step size	0.002	0.002	—
Number of optimization cycles	—	—	300

Table 7.2 Results obtained from modeling the Mackey–Glass equation using causal network (Figures 7.1 and 7.2)

Aspect	3 Inputs (%)	4 Inputs (%)	6 Inputs (%)
Mean (Error)	1.9%	1.6%	1.7%
Variance (Error)	5.7	3.8	4.6

Table 7.3 Results obtained from modeling the Mackey–Glass equation using auto-associative network

Aspect	4 Inputs (%)	5 Inputs (%)	7 Inputs (%)
Mean (Error)	10.2	7.4	29
Variance (Error)	82	66	683

Table 7.4 Results obtained from modeling the Mackey–Glass equation using ARD machine

Variable	1	2	3	4	5	6
α	2.0245	0.7412	2.3208	3.6531	22.7026	202.7054

When the data set generated from the Mackey–Glass equation is used to evaluate the MLP-based Granger causality model the results in Table 7.2 are obtained.

These results indicate that the addition of the fourth relevant variable increases the accuracy of the causal model while the addition of two random irrelevant variables does not statistically significantly change the accuracy.

The correlation machine was also built and the results show that the addition of one relevant variable from 4 to 5 inputs results in the increase in accuracy while the addition of two irrelevant variables results in a sharp decrease of accuracy. Tables 7.2 and 7.3 indicate that the correlation machine picks up relevance better than the causal machine. The complex nature of the correlation machine (inference using auto-associative networks) compared to the MLP causal machine renders the correlation machine more sensitive to Granger causality than the causal machine.

When the ARD was used to implement Granger causality and the relevance factors obtained are shown in Table 7.4. The table shows that the two last variables are not as relevant and this is indicated by the inverse of the alpha where the higher the alpha the lower is the relevance. The summary of the comparison of the 3 methods are shown in Table 7.5.

Table 7.5 Comparing causal, correlation and ARD machines

Method	Complexity	Number of networks	Accuracy
Causal Machine	Simple	2	Fair
Correlation Machine	Complex	2	Good
ARD	Complex	1	Good

7.6 Conclusions

In this chapter, the causal, correlation, and ARD machines were built to model non-linear Granger causality and were compared. The MLP neural network trained using the scaled gradient method was used to build the causal, correlation, and ARD machines. When these methods were tested, it was found that the correlation machine and the ARD model Granger causality better than the causal machine.

References

Abedi, S., Farhadi, F., Boozarjomehry, R.B. "Integration of CFD and Nelder-Mead algorithm for optimization of MOCVD process in an atmospheric pressure vertical rotating disk reactor", *International Communications in Heat and Mass Transfer*, Vol. 43, pp. 138–145, 2013.

Aghayan, I., Noii, N., Kunt, M.M. "Extended traffic crash modeling through precision and response time using fuzzy clustering algorithms compared with multi-layer perceptron", *Promet–Traffic–Traffico*, Vol. 24, No. 6, pp. 455–467, 2012.

Al-Bayati, A.Y., Muhammad, R.S. "New scaled sufficient descent conjugate gradient algorithm for solving unconstraint optimization problems", *Journal of Computer Science*, Vol. 6, No. 5, pp. 511–518, 2010.

Avriel, M. "Nonlinear Programming: Analysis and Methods", Dover Publishing, 2003.

Babaie-Kafaki, S., Ghanbari, R., Mahdavi-Amiri, N. "Two new conjugate gradient methods based on modified secant equations", *Journal of Computational and Applied Mathematics*, Vol. 234, pp. 1374–1386, 2010.

Babanouri, N., Karimi Nasab, S., Sarafrazi, S. "A hybrid particle swarm optimization and multi-layer perceptron algorithm for bivariate fractal analysis of rock fractures roughness", *International Journal of Rock Mechanics and Mining Sciences*, Vol. 60, pp. 66–74, 2013.

Barrett, A.B., Barnett, L. "Granger causality is designed to measure effect, not mechanism", *Frontiers in Neuroinformatics*, Vol. 7, No. 2, pp. 6–7, 2013.

Ben Nasr, M., Talbi, M., Cherif, A. "Arabic Speech Recognition by Bionic Wavelet Transform and MFCC using a Multi Layer Perceptron", *2012 6th International Conference on Sciences of Electronics, Technologies of Information and Telecommunications*, SETIT 2012, art. no. 6482017, pp. 803–808, 2012.

Bertsekas, D.P. "Non-linear Programming", Athenas Scientific, Massachusetts, 1995.

Bishop, C. "Neural networks for pattern recognition", Oxford: Clarendon Press, 1995.

Bishop, C. "Pattern recognition and machine learning", Berlin: Springer, ISBN 0-387-31073-8, 2006.

Björck, Å. "Numerical Methods for Least Squares Problems", SIAM, 1996.

Bonnans J.F., Gilbert, J. Charles, Lemaréchal, Claude, Sagastizábal, Claudia A. "Numerical optimization: Theoretical and practical aspects", Berlin: Springer-Verlag, 2006.

Box, G.E.P., Tiao, G.C. "Bayesian Inference in Statistical Analysis", Wiley & Sons, New Jersey, 1973.

Bürmen, A., Puhan, J., Tuma, T. "Grid restrained Nelder-Mead algorithm, *Computational Optimization and Applications*, Vol. 34, pp. 359–375, 2006.

Cavalcanti, G.D.C., Magalhaes, J.P., Barreto, R.M., Tsang, I.R. "MLPBoost: A combined AdaBoost/multi-layer perceptron network approach for face detection, *Conference Proceedings — IEEE International Conference on Systems, Man and Cybernetics*, art. no. 6378093, pp. 2350–2353, 2012.

Chel, H., Majumder, A., Nandi, D. "Scaled conjugate gradient algorithm in neural network based approach for handwritten text recognition", *Communications in Computer and Information Science*, 204 CCIS, pp. 196–210, 2011.

Cheng, L., Shi, J.-M. "Nelder-Mead algorithm for inversion analysis of plasma parameters in stealth application", *Hejubian Yu Dengliziti Wuli/Nuclear Fusion and Plasma Physics*, Vol. 32, No. 4, pp. 362–365, 2012.

Choudhury, A.R., Ghose, M.K. "Petermann I and II spot size: Accurate semi analytical description involving Nelder-Mead method of nonlinear unconstrained optimization and three parameter fundamental modal field", *Optics Communications*, Vol. 287, pp. 117–121, 2013.

Corominas, A., García-Villoria, A., Pastor, R. "Technical note: A systematic procedure based on CALIBRA and the Nelder & Mead algorithm for fine-tuning metaheuristics", *Journal of the Operational Research Society*, Vol. 64, No. 2, pp. 276–282, 2013.

Duma, M., Twala, B., Nelwamondo, F., Marwala, T. "Predictive modeling with missing data using an automatic relevance determination ensemble: A comparative study", *Applied Artificial Intelligence*, Vol. 26, No. 10, pp. 967–984, 2012.

Faes, L., Nollo, G. "Measuring frequency domain Granger causality for multiple blocks of interacting time series", *Biological Cybernetics*, Vol. 107, No. 2, pp. 217–232, 2013.

Fletcher, R. "Practical Methods of Optimization", Wiley, New York, 1987.

Friston, K., Moran, R., Seth, A.K. "Analysing connectivity with Granger causality and dynamic causal modelling", *Current Opinion in Neurobiology*, Vol. 23, No. 2, pp. 172–178, 2013.

Gayathri, K., Kumarappan, N. "Comparison of fault location on extra high voltage lines using support vector machine and scaled conjugate gradient with ANN", *Modelling, Measurement and Control A*, Vol. 83, Nos. 1–2, pp. 1–19, 2010.

Glass, L., Mackey, M.C. "Pathological physiological conditions resulting from instabilities in physiological control systems", *Annals of the New York Academy of Sciences*, Vol. 316, pp. 214–235, 1979.

Golzan, S.M., Avolio, A., Graham, S.L. "Non-invasive cerebrospinal fluid pressure estimation using multi-layer perceptron neural networks", *Proceedings of the Annual International Conference of the IEEE Engineering in Medicine and Biology Society*, EMBS, art. no. 6347185, pp. 5278–5281, 2012.

González, J.P.N., Villanueva, P.P. "Vehicle lateral dynamics fault diagnosis using an autoassociative neural network and a fuzzy system", *Lecture Notes in Computer Science (including subseries Lecture Notes in Artificial Intelligence and Lecture Notes in Bioinformatics)*, 7630 LNAI (PART 2), pp. 236–246, 2013.

Granger, C.W.J. "Investigating causal relations by econometric models and cross-spectral methods", *Econometrica*, Vol. 37, No. 3, pp. 424–438, 1969.

Hacker, R.S., Hatemi, J.A. "Tests for causality between integrated variables using asymptotic and bootstrap distributions: Theory and application", *Applied Economics*, Vol. 38, No. 13, pp. 1489–1500, 2006.

Haykin, S. "Neural Networks: A Comprehensive Foundation", 2nd Edition, Prentice Hall, 1998.

Haykin, S. "Neural Networks", 2nd Edition, New Jersey: Prentice-Hall, 1999.

Hayworth, K.J. "Dynamically partitionable auto-associative networks as a solution to the neural binding problem", *Frontiers in Computational Neuroscience*, (September), pp. 1–22, 2012.

Hestenes, M.R., Stiefel, E. "Methods of conjugate gradients for solving linear systems", *Journal of Research of the National Bureau of Standards*, Vol. 6, pp. 409–436, 1952.

Hsueh, S.-J., Hu, Y.-H., Tu, C.-H. "Economic growth and financial development in Asian countries: A bootstrap panel Granger causality analysis", *Economic Modelling*, Vol. 32, No. 1, pp. 294–301, 2013.

Huang, Y., Beck, J.L., Wu, S., Li, H. "Stochastic optimization using automatic relevance determination prior model for Bayesian compressive sensing", *Proceedings of SPIE — The International Society for Optical Engineering*, 8348, art. no. 834837, 2012.

Jacobs, J.P. "Bayesian support vector regression with automatic relevance determination kernel for modeling of antenna input characteristics", *IEEE Transactions on Antennas and Propagation*, Vol. 60, No. 4, art. no. 6143986, pp. 2114–2118, 2012.

Johri, R., Salvi, A., Filipi, Z. "Virtual sensors for transient diesel soot and NOx emissions: Neuro-fuzzy model tree with automatic relevance determination", *Proceedings of the American Control Conference*, art. no. 6315229, pp. 5737–5744, 2012.

Khakzad, N., Khan, F., Amyotte, P. "Quantitative risk analysis of offshore drilling operations: A Bayesian approach", *Safety Science*, Vol. 57, pp. 108–117, 2013.

Li, A., Bo, Y., Zhu, Y., Guo, P., Bi, J., He, Y. "Blending multi-resolution satellite sea surface temperature (SST) products using Bayesian maximum entropy method", *Remote Sensing of Environment*, Vol. 135, pp. 52–63, 2013.

Liang, C.-C., Lin, J.-B., Hsu, H.-C. "Reexamining the relationships between stock prices and exchange rates in ASEAN-5 using panel Granger causality approach", *Economic Modelling*, Vol. 32, No. 1, pp. 560–563, 2013.

Luenberger, D.G. "Linear and Non-linear Programming", Addison Wesley, Massachusetts, 1984.

Luersen, M., Riche, R.L. "Globalized Nelder-Mead method for engineering optimization", *Computers & Structures*, Vol. 82, pp. 2251–2260, 2004.

Lundén, J., Koivunen, V. "Scaled conjugate gradient method for radar pulse modulation estimation", ICASSP, *IEEE International Conference on Acoustics, Speech and Signal Processing — Proceedings*, 2, art. no. 4217404, pp. II297–II300, 2007.

MacKay, D.J.C. "Bayesian Methods for Adaptive Models", Ph.D. Thesis, California Institute of Technology, 1991.

MacKay, D.J.C. "A practical Bayesian framework for back propagation networks", *Neural Computation*, Vol. 4, pp. 448–472, 1992.

Mackey, M.C., Glass, L. "Oscillation and chaos in physiological control systems", *Science*, Vol. 197, No. 4300, pp. 287–289, 1977.

Marwala, T. "Computational intelligence for missing data imputation, estimation and management: Knowledge optimization techniques", Information Science Reference Imprint, IGI Global Publications, New York, USA, 2009.

Marwala, T. "Finite Element Model Updating Using Computational Intelligence Techniques", Springer-Verlag, London, UK, 2010.

Marwala, T. "Economic Modelling Using Artificial Intelligence Methods", Springer-Verlag, London, UK, 2013.

Marwala, T., Sibisi, S. "Finite Element Model updating using Bayesian framework and modal properties", *Journal of Aircraft*, Vol. 42, pp. 275–278, 2005.

Masuda, K., Fukui, B., Kurihara, K. "A weighting approach for autoassociative memories to maximize the number of correctly stored patterns", *Proceedings of the SICE Annual Conference*, art. no. 6318692, pp. 1520–1524, 2012.

McKinnon, K.I.M. "Convergence of the Nelder-Mead Simplex Method to a Nonstationary Point", *SIAM Journal of Optimization*, Vol. 9, pp. 148–158, 1998.

Møller, A.F. "A Scaled Conjugate Gradient Algorithm for Fast Supervised Learning", *Neural Nets*, Vol. 6, pp. 525–533, 1993.

Osgood, T.J., Huang, Y. "Calibration of laser scanner and camera fusion system for intelligent vehicles using Nelder-Mead optimization", *Measurement Science and Technology*, Vol. 24, No. 3, art. no. 035101, 2013.

Ransome, T.M. "Automatic Minimisation of Patient Setup Errors in Proton Beam Therapy", Master's Thesis, University of the Witwatersrand, 2006.

Ransome, T.M., Rubin, D.M., Marwala, T., de Kok, E.A. "Optimising the verification of patient positioning in proton beam therapy", *In Proceedings of the IEEE 3rd International Conference on Computational Cybernetics*, Mauritius, pp. 279–284, 2005.

Rao, C.R., Toutenburg, H., Fieger, A., Heumann, C., Nittner, T., Scheid, S. Linear Models: Least Squares and Alternatives, Springer Series in Statistics, 1999.

Rosenblatt, F. "Principles of Neurodynamics: Perceptrons and the Theory of Brain Mechanisms", Spartan Books, Washington DC, 1961.

Rumelhart David E., James L. McClelland and the PDP research group (eds.). "Parallel distributed processing: Explorations in the microstructure of cognition", Volume 1: Foundations, MIT Press, 1986.

Sethi, S.A., Tanner, T.L. "Bayesian implementation of a time stratified Lincoln–Petersen estimator for salmon abundance in the upper Matanuska River, Alaska, USA", *Fisheries Research*, Vol. 145, pp. 90–99, 2013.

Shutin, D., Buchgraber, T. "Trading approximation quality versus sparsity within incremental automatic relevance determination frameworks", *IEEE International Workshop on Machine Learning for Signal Processing*, MLSP, art. no. 6349805, 2012.

Sohn, S.Y., Lee, A.S. "Bayesian network analysis for the dynamic prediction of early stage entrepreneurial activity index", *Expert Systems with Applications*, Vol. 40, No. 10, pp. 4003–4009, 2013.

Sulistiyo, M.D., Saepudin, D., Adiwijaya "Optical character recognition using modified direction feature and nested multi layer perceptrons network, *Proceeding — 2012 IEEE International Conference on Computational Intelligence and Cybernetics*, CyberneticsCom 2012, art. no. 6381611, pp. 30–34, 2012.

Tang, C.F. "Temporal Granger causality and the dynamics relationship between real tourism receipts, real income and real exchange rates in Malaysia", *International Journal of Tourism Research*, Vol. 15, No. 3, pp. 272–284, 2013.

Valle, M.E., Vicente, D.M.G. "Sparsely connected autoassociative lattice memories with an application for the reconstruction of color images", *Journal of Mathematical Imaging and Vision*, Vol. 44, No. 3, pp. 195–222, 2012.

Werbos, P.J. "Beyond Regression: New Tool for Prediction and Analysis in the Behavioral Sciences", Ph.D. Thesis, Harvard University, 1974.

Wolberg, J. "Data Analysis Using the Method of Least Squares: Extracting the Most Information from Experiments", Springer, 2005.

Wong, J.C.-F., Protas, B. "Application of scaled nonlinear conjugate-gradient algorithms to the inverse natural convection problem", *Optimization Methods and Software*, Vol. 28, No. 1, pp. 159–185, 2013.

Zabidi, A., Mansor, W., Lee, K.Y., Che Wan Fadzal, C.W.N.F. "Classification of EEG signal from imagined writing using a combined Autoregressive model and multi-layer perceptron", *2012 IEEE-EMBS Conference on Biomedical Engineering and Sciences*, IECBES 2012, art. no. 6498209, pp. 964–968, 2012.

Zhang, X., Wang, W., Li, Y., Jiao, L.C. "PSO-based automatic relevance determination and feature selection system for hyperspectral image classification", *Electronics Letters*, Vol. 48, No. 20, pp. 1263–1265, 2012.

Zhang, L., Wu, X., Ding, L., Skibniewski, M.J., Yan, Y. "Decision support analysis for safety control in complex project environments based on Bayesian Networks", *Expert Systems with Applications*, Vol. 40, No. 11, pp. 4273–4282, 2013.

Chapter 8

Flexibly-bounded Rationality

Abstract. This chapter describes the theory of flexibly-bounded rationality which extends the theory of bounded rationality. Specifically, it is viewed that a decision making process which encompasses three components, information collection and analysis, the correlation, and the causal machines. Rational decision making entails utilizing information which is imperfect and incomplete jointly with human brain which is erratic on making decisions. The theory of bounded rationality prescribes making this decision despite the fact that the information is incomplete and imperfect and that the human brain is inconsistent and the decision is made within the bounds of these limitations. The theory of flexibly-bounded rationality entails using signal processing to filter noise and outliers in the data and using the correlation machine to complete missing information and artificial intelligence to make more reliable decisions. Flexibly-bounded rationality is applied to condition monitoring and HIV diagnosis problems and it is found to enlarge the bounds within which rational decision making process is employed and, thus, rises the probability of making accurate decisions than the theory of bounded rationality.

8.1 Introduction

Decision making is a complicated process and has puzzled philosophers for a very long time. In primeval society making decisions was cluttered with superstitions (Vyse, 2000; Foster and Kokko, 2009). There has been even conjecture that superstition also transpires in other animals such as pigeons (Skinner, 1948). In quintessence, superstition can be viewed as supernatural causality where something is caused by another without them linked to one another. The idea of one event causing another without any connection between them whatsoever is characterized as irrational thinking.

This chapter advances that the three essentials of a decision making process are information, correlation machine which approximates missing data, and causal machine which connects the inputs to outputs. As societies evolves away from irrational concepts such as superstition, the notion of rational decision making comes to attention. The notion of rationality has fascinated various philosophers from diverse fields. Max Weber investigated the function of rationality in social action (Weber, 1922) although Mosterin (2008) specified reason as a psychological facility and rationality as the optimizing strategy. In artificial intelligence approach, a rational agent maximizes utility in making its decision. A utility here is defined as the usefulness of its decisions. Various researchers have stretched the meaning of rationality not only to embrace the use of logic and reason to make this decision but to state that such decisions should be optimized.

Essentially rational decision making is a process of attaining decisions through logic and reason (Nozick, 1993; Spohn, 2002). Decision making can be defined as a process through which a decision is obtained. It ordinarily includes various possible decision outcomes and is thought to be rational and optimal if it maximizes the good that results from its consequences and at the same time minimizes the bad that is also derived from its consequences. The philosophical idea that the best policy is that which maximizes utility is branded as utilitarianism and was promoted by theorists such as Jeremy Bentham and John Stuart Mill (Adams, 1976; Anscombe, 1958; Bentham, 2009; Mill, 2011).

There is a theory that has been proposed to realize this desired outcome of maximizing utility and this is the theory of rational choice in decision making. The theory of rational choice states that an optimal decision is constructed based on the product of the effect of the decision and its probability of incidence (Allingham, 2002; Bicchieri, 2003). Nevertheless, this theory was observed to be insufficient for the reason that it does not take into consideration where the person will be compared to where they originally were before making a decision. Kahneman and Tversky (1979) improved the theory of rational choice by introducing the prospect theory which includes the reference situation to assess the decision (Kahneman, 2011).

This chapter, describes a comprehensive decision making process with two sets of input information which form the foundation for decision making and choices that are accessible for making such decisions as well as the output which is the decision being made. It additionally proposes that this general decision making structure consists of the statistical analysis device, correlation machine, and a causal machine. As a result, the model proposed in this chapter for decision making can be briefly described in this way: Optimization Device: e.g. maximizing utility (maximizing the good and minimizing the bad) which is what Prospect Theory proposes; and Decision making Device: This component has statistical analysis scheme, correlation and causal machines.

Section 8.2 explains the notion of rational decision making, then the theory of bounded rationality, then the theory of flexibly-bounded rationality and a generalized model for decision making (Marwala, 2013).

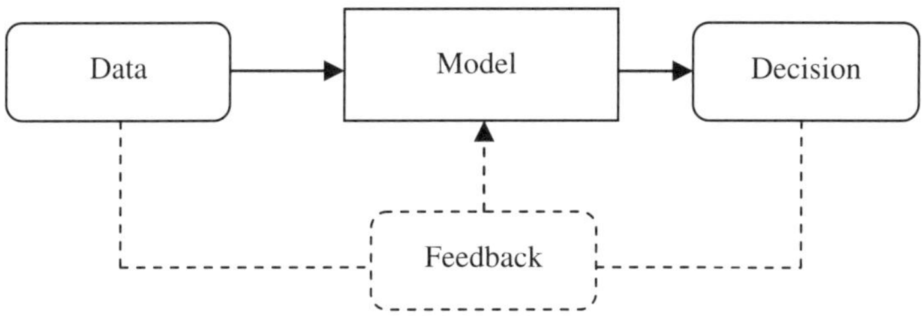

Figure 8.1 A diagram of a rational decision making system

8.2 Rational Decision Making: A Causal Approach

Rational decision making is a process by which a decision is arrived at using some collected information and intelligence to make an optimized decision. It is considered to be rational for the reason that it uses evidence in the form of relevant information. Making decisions in the absence of some information is considered irrational. Rational decision making as illustrated in Figure 8.1 entails using data and a model (e.g. human brain) to make a decision (Marwala, 2013). The association between data and the influence of the decision is used to improve or strengthen the model.

Serrano González *et al.* (2013) successfully used rational decision making to identify the optimal structure of transmissions systems for offshore wind farms. Salem *et al.* (2013) applied successfully rational multi-criteria decision making to select an operational plan for bridge rehabilitation. Multi-criteria optimization is an optimization of problem with more than one objective (Steuer, 1986; Köksalan and Sagala 1995; Zionts and Wallenius, 1976). Baker (2013) studied a case on rational decision making in a hybrid organization for a Southwestern Drug Court treatment program. For instance, one is given an option to buy a certain number of Microsoft stocks and General Electric stocks and the decision to be made is how one combines these two stocks.

Chai *et al.* (2013) studied how rational decision making has been used successfully to select a supplier, however, Badri *et al.* (2013) used rational decision making successfully to identify fireproofing requirements against jet fires. Other studies on rational decision making include studying the relationship between subjective memory and rational decision making (Hembacher and Ghetti, 2013) as well as rational decision making in economics (Gu *et al.*, 2013).

8.3 Rational Decision Making Process

A decision making process comprises of decision making actions. Decision making action is a basic unit of a decision making process. A decision making action can be either rational or irrational and it is rational if it is logical and optimized, it is irrational if it is illogical and/or not optimized. A decision making process can possess numerous decision making actions. A decision making process can either be rational or irrational and if at the minimum one of the decision making actions that produce a decision making process is irrational then a decision making process is irrational for the reason that it cannot feasibly be completely logical nor optimized. Decisions can be complete under rational or irrational conditions. Nobel Prize Laureate Hebert Simon's theory of bounded rationality simply suggests the bounds within which rationality is practiced and does not cut or divide rationality.

The context that a rational process does not accommodate irrationality and that it cannot be divided is a contentious proposal. To demonstrate this position, assuming a young lady named Vele who was diagnosed with breast cancer chooses to consult an astrologer who throws down some stones and proposes that Vele needs to drink salty sea water from Cape Town to be healed. If Vele accepts this advice we will declare her to be thinking irrationally. Suppose Vele decides to go and consult an oncologist to deal with her breast cancer, then we will declare her to be rational. If Vele chooses to consult both the astrologer and an oncologist, then is she acting rationally, irrationally or half rationally? Obviously, Vele is acting irrationally. This indicates that if a person is making a decision even a minor measure of irrationality makes the entire decision making process irrational. Rationality is indivisible. Vele either acts rationally or irrationally and not in between the two.

The definition of rationality proposed in this chapter comprises three key concepts: Logic (based on scientific principles), information (it should be based on relevant information) and optimization (it should be optimized and thus not waste effort). The perception that for a decision to be rational it has to be optimized has extensive consequence on human decision making. It fundamentally implies that the entire human beings are basically irrational beings. An optimized decision fundamentally implies that such a decision results in the maximization of utility (DeGroot, 1970; Berger, 1980). If for instance, if one desired to go from London to Vancouver then he chooses to go to Johannesburg then to New York and then to Vancouver for no other reason except to attempt to reach Vancouver then these actions are deemed irrational. The rationale why this will be deemed irrational is for the reason that it is not an optimized decision and, consequently, wastes sources. Wasting resources is not rational. As we change from human decision making into decision making by artificial intelligent machines, it is important that we enable these machines with the capability to make logical and optimized decisions.

8.4 Bounded-Rational Decision Making

Rationality embraces the notion of making an optimized decision and this is not practically possible for the reason that information necessary to make decisions and the limitation of the infrastructure to make sense of such incomplete decision (Simon, 1990). This is what is known as the theory of bounded rationality which was proposed by Nobel Laureate Herbert Simon (Simon, 1957; Tisdell, 1996). The consequence of this thought on many economic systems is pretty considerable (Simon, 1991). It interrogates the reliability of the theory of the efficient market hypothesis particularly given the fact that players in the market are at best only rational within the bounds of limited information and limited model to make sense of the information.

Gama (2013) effectively used the notion of bounded rationality to examine the performance of stream mining processes and suggested ubiquitous stream mining and self-adaption models. Jin *et al.* (2013) positively used the theory of bounded rationality and game theory to build a computer virus propagation model and found that the proposed model was capable of forecasting the propagation of computer virus. Lee (2013) built a model to investigate an economy using bounded rational agents and observed that rational agents increase the price bubble cooperation amongst rational agents. Jiang *et al.* (2013a) effectively used bounded rationality in evolution game analysis of water saving and pollution prevention.

Stanciu-Viziteu (2012) replicated the behavior of sharks to model financial markets where investors are personified by hungry sharks. The results obtained showed that sharks approximating investors synchronize and yield equilibrium under rational expectations.

Yao and Li (2013) inferred that the notion of bounded rationality can be regarded as a basis of loss aversion and optimism and in this respect studied psychological adaptation within the background of incomplete information. They found that loss aversion and optimism come about when the degree of data incompleteness surpasses a specific threshold. Additionally, they detected that loss aversion and optimism were more obvious when information was sparser. They then concluded that psychological biases benefit from apparent information incompleteness when value creation is considered.

Aviad and Roy (2012) used bounded rationality to build a decision support system and used this to identify feature saliency in clustering problems. Bounded rationality was used to manage the availability of target characteristic by using an S-shaped function as a saliency measure to describe the end user's logic to identify traits that define each prospective set.

Murata *et al.* (2012) applied bounded rationality to analyze the relationship between group heuristics and cooperative behavior and observed that group consciousness stimulate actively mutual cooperation.

The literature evidently shows that the theory of bounded rationality is a potent instrument that has found usage in many diverse fields. The theory of bounded rationality has not replaced the theory of rationality which was described in earlier sections but places limitations or constraints on the applicability of the theory

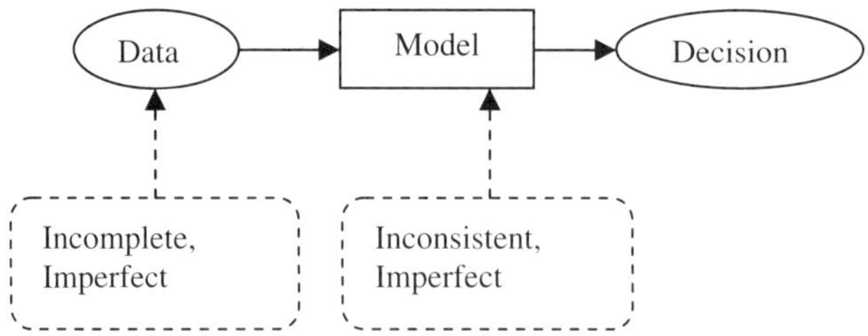

Figure 8.2 Illustration of the theory of bounded rationality

of rationality. The theory of rationality which was described in Figure 8.1 can thus be updated to construct the theory of bounded rationality as described in Figure 8.2.

Figure 8.2 illustrates that on making decisions rationally, certain considerations must be taken into account and these are the data that is used to make such decisions are never complete and are subject to measurement errors and are thus imperfect and incomplete. The second aspect that should be observed is that the model which takes data and translates these into decisions is also imperfect. If for example, this model is a human brain then it is inconsistent in the sense that it may be influenced by other factors such as whether the individual concerned is hungry, or angry. Herbert Simon coined a term *satisficing*, thereby hybridizing the terms satisfying and sufficing, which is the concept of making optimized decision under the limitations that the data used in making such decisions are imperfect and incomplete while the model used to make such decisions is inconsistent and imperfect.

Now that we have described the theory of bounded rationality, which resulted in the limitations of the applicability of the theory of rational decision making, Section 8.5 describes the theory of flexibly-bounded rationality which is the theory proposed in this book.

8.5 Flexibly-bounded Rational Decision Making

This section proposes the theory of flexibly-bounded rationality which is shown in Figure 8.3. In order to understand the theory of flexibly-bounded rationality, it is important to state few propositions and these are:

1. Rational decision making is a process of making optimized decisions based on logic and scientific thought. The issue of optimized decision becomes even necessary given the migration of decision making toward using machines.
2. Rationality whether as in a decision process or decision action is indivisible. In other words, you cannot be half rational and half irrational. If you are half rational

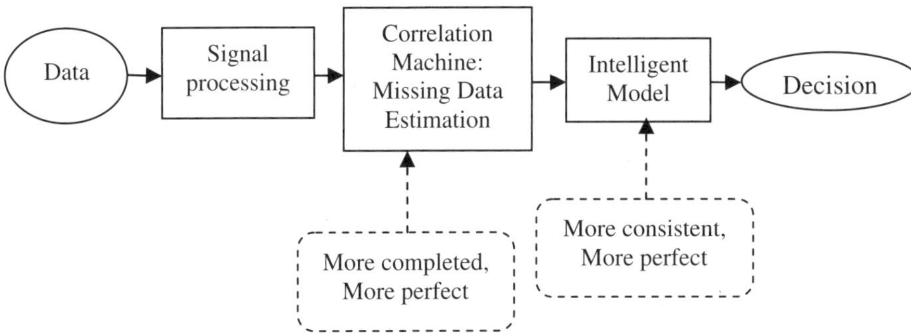

Figure 8.3 Illustration of the theory of flexibly-bounded rationality

and half irrational you are being irrational. The concept of the indivisibility of rationality and the impact of this on many facets of life is a powerful concept that requires further investigation.

3. The principle of bounded rationality does not truncate the theory of rationality but merely specifies the bounds within which the principle of rationality is applied.

With advances in information processing techniques, enhanced theories of auto-associative machines and advances in artificial intelligence methods, it has become necessary to revise the theory of bounded rationality. The fact that information which is used to make decisions is imperfect because of factors such as measurement errors can be partially corrected by using advanced information analysis methods and the fact that some of the data that are missing and, thereby, incomplete can be partially completed using missing data estimation methods. The fact that a human brain which is influenced by other social and physiological factors can be substituted by recently developed artificial intelligence machines implies that the bounds under which rationality is exercised can be shifted and thus bounded rationality can now be transformed into the theory of flexibly-bounded rationality.

Tsang (2008) proposed that computational intelligence determines effective rationality. What Tsang implies is that there is a degree of rationality, a situation which is not true. Rationality cannot be divided, it is either there or absent. The model of flexibly-bounded rationality can thus be expressed as shown in Figure 8.3.

The implications of the model in Figure 8.3 to many disciplines such as economics, political science and social science are extensive. It goes to the heart of the relationship between rationality and technology. Basically, modern technology now allows us to update the limiting concept of bounded rationality to a less limited concept of flexibly-bounded rationality. The implication of the concept of the notion of indivisibility of rationality and the application of this profound notion to many areas such as economics, sociology and political science is far reaching and requires

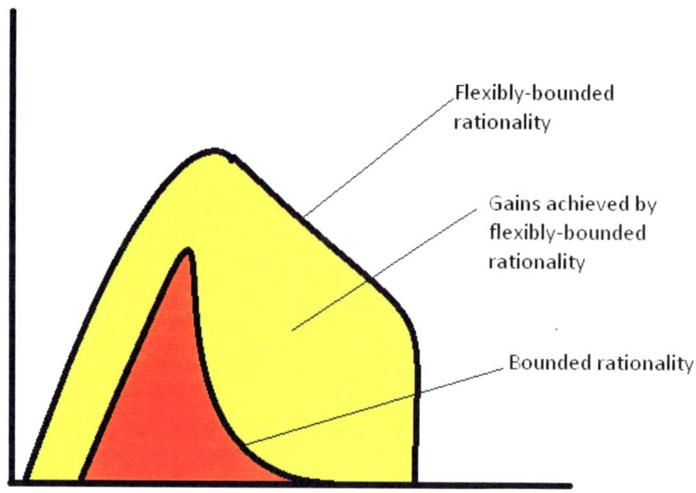

Figure 8.4 Comparison between flexibly-bounded rationality and bounded rationality

further investigation. The schematic illustration of flexibly-bounded rationality as compared to bounded rationality is shown in Figure 8.4.

Figure 8.4 demonstrates that the theory of flexibly-bounded rationality only expands the bounds within which the principle of rationality is applied. It also shows that the theory of bounded rationality only prescribes the bounds within which the principle of rationality is applied.

This section investigates whether rationality is divisible while the subsequent subsections describe advanced information processing, missing data estimation methods and artificial intelligence techniques which are elements that are proposed in this chapter to take the theory of bounded rationality into a theory of flexibly-bounded rationality.

8.5.1 Advanced information processing

This section describes advanced information processing techniques that are required in order to use data to make decisions within the context of flexibly-bounded rationality possible. These techniques are the time domain, frequency domain and time–frequency domain frameworks.

A. *Time Domain Data*

When decisions are made, data can be used in the time domain to make decisions. In simple terms, data in the time domain means that the data set is used exactly as it was sampled at a given time. For example, if one wants to use the data of temperature per unit time today to predict the average temperature tomorrow one can observe a series of data today to make tomorrow's predictions.

Coillet *et al.* (2013) successfully applied the time domain methods to analyze optoelectronic oscillators based on whispering-gallery mode resonators. Szurley *et al.* (2013) successfully applied the time domain technique to enhance binaural speech. Pereira *et al.* (2013) applied the time domain data from nuclear magnetic resonance and chemometrics to classify fresh plums according to sweetness. Herckenrath *et al.* (2013) successfully applied electromagnetic data in the time domain methods to calibrate salt water intrusion model. Paulraj *et al.* (2013) successfully applied the time domain data to classify moving vehicle.

B. *Frequency Domain*

The basis of frequency domain method is the Fourier series and it fundamentally states that every periodic function can be approximated by a Fourier series which is a combination of series of cosines and sine functions of various frequencies (Fourier, 1822; Boashash, 2003; Bochner and Chandrasekharan, 1949; Bracewell, 2000). This means that a signal can be characterized by a series of cycles with different amplitudes and frequencies.

Qu *et al.* (2013) successfully applied frequency domain methods to filter gradient image for contour detection whereas Oh *et al.* (2013) applied hydrodynamic load in the frequency domain to analyze offshore wind turbine. Mohapatra *et al.* (2013) successfully applied electromechanical disturbances in the frequency domain to study electric power systems whereas Zhang *et al.* (2013a) successfully applied optical coherence tomography in the frequency domain to detect glaucoma.

C. *Time–Frequency Domain*

Time–frequency methods are approaches where it is possible to view data in both the time and frequency domains simultaneously. There are different types of time–frequency methods and these comprise short-time Fourier transform (Jont, 1977; Jacobsen and Lyons, 2003), wavelet transform (Chui, 1992; Akansu and Haddad, 1992), Wigner distribution function (Wigner, 1932; Qian and Chen, 1996) and Gabor distribution (Daugman, 1980; Jones and Palmer, 1987).

Ma *et al.* (2013) successfully applied time–frequency analysis for blind source separation whereas Le and Paultre (2013) successfully applied time–frequency analysis for modal identification. Zhang *et al.* (2013b) successfully applied time–frequency analysis for real world source separation whereas Jiang *et al.* (2013b) successfully applied time–frequency analysis for fault diagnosis. Finally, Heideklang and Ivanova (2013) successfully applied time–frequency analysis to extract features from brain signals.

8.5.2 Missing data estimation

One aspect of the theory of flexibly-bounded rationality is that it uses missing data estimation techniques to reduce information that is not observed or known. In this section, we describe missing data estimation method as discussed by Marwala (2009). Missing data estimation method is technique that is used to estimate data and thus information that is missing. It necessitates mathematical models that describe interrelationships that exist amongst the variables. There are many methods that have been proposed to approximate missing data. One of these is one which successfully applied auto-associative neural networks to capture variables' interrelationships and genetic algorithms to identify missing values (Abdella and Marwala, 2006).

The other technique that has been used is the one that uses a hybrid of the principal component analysis and neural networks to capture the interrelationships that exist amongst the data and genetic algorithm to estimate missing values (Mistry *et al.*, 2009). Nelwamondo *et al.* (2007) successfully applied two missing data estimation techniques which were the Gaussian Mixture Models trained using the Expectation Maximization (EM) algorithm and auto-associative neural networks which used particle swarm optimization to estimate missing values. Nelwamondo and Marwala (2007) proposed the use of rough set theory to estimate missing values. Nelwamondo *et al.* (2013) successfully applied dynamic programming and auto-associative neural network method to estimate missing data whereas Shi *et al.* (2013) successfully applied Bayesian principal component analysis and iterative local least squares to estimate missing values in microarray data. Pati and Das (2012) successfully applied similarity measurement for missing value estimation in microarray data whereas Luy and Saray (2012) successfully applied back-propagation algorithms to estimate missing wind speed data. Garnier *et al.* (2012) successfully estimated missing data for energy resources management in tertiary buildings whereas Bose *et al.* (2012) successfully applied a unique interpolation based missing value estimation method to predict missing values in microarray gene expression data.

This chapter estimates missing data using auto-associative multi-layer perceptron (MLP) neural networks to capture the model that describes the data and genetic algorithms to estimate the missing values. This technique is described in detail by Marwala (2009).

8.5.3 Intelligent machines

The core of the theory of flexibly-bounded rationality is that it assumes that an artificial intelligent machine is used for decision making process because it is deemed to be better than the human brain. There are many different types of artificial intelligence methods that can be used to make decisions and one of these is neural network which is used in this chapter. Neural network is an artificial intelligence technique which is inspired by how a human brain in structured which is used to learn patterns from data (Patel and Marwala, 2006). There are many types of neural networks and these include the radial basis function and the MLP neural network which is used in this chapter. Ensemble of neural networks and also called a committee of networks have been used to relate two sets of data (Marwala, 2001; Marwala *et al.*, 2001). Other types of artificial intelligence techniques that can be used include the Gaussian mixture models (Marwala *et al.*, 2006; Bishop, 2006), hidden Markov model (Baum and Petrie, 1966), fuzzy logic (Zadeh, 1996), fuzzy ARTMAP (Carpenter and Grossberg, 2003; Vilakazi and Marwala, 2006), rough sets (Tettey *et al.*, 2007), and support vector machine (Vapnik, 1995; Schölkopf and Smola, 2002).

8.6 Experimental Investigations

This section employs two examples to illustrate this theory of flexibly-bounded rationality and these are condition monitoring and HIV modeling problems.

8.6.1 Condition monitoring

Condition monitoring is a process of assessing the condition of an object. In villages somewhere in Africa, there are clay pot makers who after making these clay pots put them in the furnace. After this process, they tap each pot and listen to how it rings and based on this ring they decide whether the pot is fit for purpose. This is condition monitoring in its nascent form and the process followed is rational. The process is actually rationally bounded because tapping a clay pot and listening to how it rings, without any modern listening device and sophisticated signal processing technology, makes the data being used to be less accurate for reliable diagnosis. Secondly, the fact that these clay pot makers use their brains, under all forms of variation of circumstances such as fatigue, makes this diagnosis less optimal, and erratic. Therefore, this process is governed by the theory of bounded rationality.

If you fast forward the same process as performed by a modern industrial company the listening device becomes a machine and the brain becomes a computer. This modern approach is more accurate and is governed by the theory of flexibly-bounded rationality.

Condition monitoring has been applied successfully in many diverse areas. Hung *et al.* (2013) successfully applied condition monitoring technique to monitor greenhouse environment whereas Zimroz and Bartkowiak (2013) applied multivariate methods based condition monitoring technique to successfully monitor planetary gearboxes in non-stationary operating conditions. Other successful applications of condition monitoring include in wind and marine turbines (Yang *et al.*, 2013), in

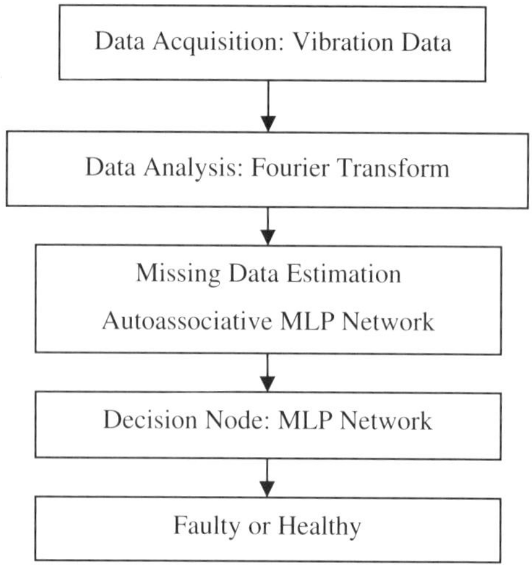

Figure 8.6 A process for using vibration data to diagnose the condition of cylindrical shells

railway vehicles (Dybała and Radkowski, 2013), and in hydrostatic self-levitating bearings (Garcia *et al.*, 2013).

In this chapter, we propose the uses of vibration data, Fourier transform and neural networks to diagnose a population of cylindrical shells in the manufacturing plant settings. More information on this condition monitoring process can be found in a book by Marwala (2012) and is illustrated in Figure 8.6. The process in this figure illustrates that this condition monitoring process includes the acquisition of vibration data which is done by tapping the cylinders and measuring their responses by using sophisticated data acquisition devices such as accelerometers which measure the acceleration of the surfaces of cylinders.

The second aspect is data analysis and, in this chapter, we use the Fourier transform which is an old technique of identifying the frequency content of a signal (Bochner and Chandrasekharan, 1949) to deconstruct the data. The third aspect, which is introduced to assess the missing data estimation capacity of the proposed method, is the application of the auto-associative neural networks to estimate missing data. The fourth component of this framework is the application of the MLP neural networks, which is deemed a causal device, to take the completed input data and predict whether a cylindrical shell is healthy or faulty.

This procedure is tested as it was done in Marwala (2012). Here the missing data estimation method is conducted using the MLP neural network and the missing data are estimated using genetic algorithm (Marwala, 2002; Mohamed *et al.*, 2008). Genetic algorithm is an optimization technique which is inspired by the mechanism of evolution.

When this method was implemented on a population of cylindrical shells as was done in Marwala (2012) the accuracy of 91% was observed when two variables were missing and then estimated, and an accuracy 94% was observed when one variable was missing and, therefore, estimated and an accuracy of 96% was achieved when the full input data set was used. It could be philosophically argued that the 96% which was achieved instead of 100% because of all the missing information such as additional variables to be included in the modeling exercise and requisite infrastructure which could be a more optimized and perfect MLP. It is clear that the more the information which is available as inputs to the neural network the more accurate is the process of condition diagnosis.

This demonstrates that the bounds within which rational process of decision making is exercised expands as a result of the introduction of the principle of flexibly-bounded decision making and, thereby, increasing the probability of making accurate decisions. The main conclusion that can be drawn from this investigation is that flexibly-bounded rationality increases the probability of making accurate decisions when compared to the theory of bounded rationality.

8.6.2 HIV modeling

The second example used in this chapter to evaluate the theory of flexibly-bounded rationality is the problem of modeling HIV. Marivate and Marwala (2008) applied relational networks to successfully build a causal model that related the demographic characteristics to HIV status whereas Marwala and Crossingham (2008) successfully applied Neuro-rough technique to build a causal model that related demographic data to HIV status. Mistry *et al.* (2008) successfully applied ensemble techniques to build a causal model that related demographic data to HIV status. Successful implementations of neural networks to model HIV included by Arab-Chamjangali (2009), Fernández and Caballero (2006) as well as Atencia *et al.* (2003).

The method followed in this section is shown in Figure 8.7. In this figure, measurements of demographic characteristics are conducted. These demographic characteristics are race, age of mother, education, parity which is the number of times a person has given birth, gravidity which is a number of pregnancy, age of the father, and income and these are discussed in detail by Tim (2007), Tim and Marwala (2006) and Leke *et al.* (2006). The measured data are put through an auto-associative MLP neural networks that estimate whatever variable is missing and a MLP causal machine which makes the HIV diagnostics. This framework is rational because it uses data, logic and is optimized to make a decision and will be classified as operating under flexibly-bounded rationality because it estimates missing data and uses neural network which is more consistent than a human being.

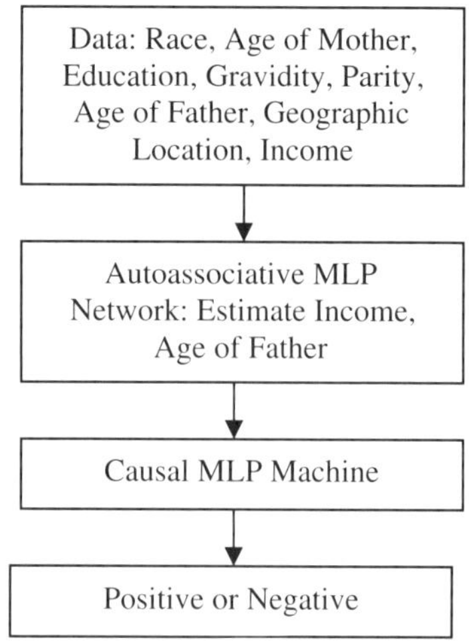

Figure 8.7 A process for using demographic data to diagnose HIV

When this framework was implemented to estimate the HIV status from demographic data an accuracy of 57% was obtained when two variables income and age of the father were missing, and an accuracy of 60% was obtained when only the income was missing and an accuracy of 62% when the missing values were estimated as well as when none of these variables were missing.

As in the previous example, the reason than the best results obtained was 62% and not 100% is because of other missing information and that the MLP is not sufficiently perfect to sufficiently capture the data. Again the results show that the more the information which is available the more accurate is the process of HIV diagnosis. This validates that the bounds within which the rational process of decision making is implemented is expanding and, thereby, increasing the scope of making accurate decisions. Again the conclusion is that flexibly-bounded rationality increases the probability of making accurate decisions when compared to the theory of bounded rationality.

8.7 Conclusions

In this chapter, the concept of flexibly-bounded rationality is introduced as an extension to the notion of bounded rationality. It is based on the principle of rationality but is realized by using advanced signal processing, missing data estimation methods and artificial intelligence techniques. Flexibly-bounded rationality expands the bounds within which rational decision making process is exercised and, thereby, increases the probability of making accurate decisions when compared to the theory of bounded rationality. This chapter also proposes that rational non-trivial decision making uses correlation and/or causality.

References

Abdella, M., Marwala, T. "The use of genetic algorithms and neural networks to approximate missing data in database", *Computing and Informatics*, Vol. 24, pp. 1001–1013, 2006.

Adams, R.M. "Motive Utilitarianism", *The Journal of Philosophy*, Vol. 73, No. 14, 1976.

Akansu, A.N., Haddad, R.A. "Multiresolution Signal Decomposition: Transforms, Subbands, Wavelets", San Diego: Academic Press, ISBN 978-0-12-047141-6, 1992.

Allingham, M. "Choice Theory: A Very Short Introduction", Oxford, 2002.

Anscombe, G.E.M. "Modern Moral Philosophy", *Philosophy*, Vol. 33, No. 124, January 1958.

Arab-Chamjangali, M. "Modelling of cytotoxicity data (CC50) of anti-HIV 1-[5-chlorophenyl) sulfonyl]-1H-pyrrole derivatives using calculated molecular descriptors and Levenberg-Marquardt artificial neural network", *Chemical Biology and Drug Design*, Vol. 73, No. 4, pp. 456–465, 2009.

Atencia, M., Joya, G., Sandoval, F. "Modelling the HIV-AIDS Cuban epidemics with Hopfield neural networks", *Lecture Notes in Computer Science (including subseries Lecture Notes in Artificial Intelligence and Lecture Notes in Bioinformatics)*, Vol. 2687, pp. 449–456, 2003.

Aviad, B., Roy, G. "A decision support method, based on bounded rationality concepts, to reveal feature saliency in clustering problems", *Decision Support Systems*, Vol. 54, No. 1, pp. 292–303, 2012.

Badri, N., Rad, A., Kareshki, H., Abdolhamidzadeh, B., Parvizsedghy, R., Rashtchian, D. "A risk-based decision making approach to determine fireproofing requirements against jet fires", *Journal of Loss Prevention in the Process Industries*, Vol. 26, No. 4, pp. 771–781, 2013.

Baker, K.M. "Decision making in a hybrid organization: A case study of a Southwestern drug court treatment program", *Law and Social Inquiry*, Vol. 38, No. 1, pp. 27–54, 2013.

Baum, L.E., Petrie, T. "Statistical inference for probabilistic functions of finite state Markov chains", *The Annals of Mathematical Statistics*, Vol. 37, No. 6, pp. 1554–1563, 1966.

Bentham, J. "An Introduction to the Principles of Morals and Legislation (Dover Philosophical Classics)", Dover Publications Inc., 2009.

Berger, J.O. "Statistical Decision Theory and Bayesian Analysis", Springer-Verlag, Heidelberg, 1980.

Bicchieri, C. "Rationality and Game Theory", In *The Handbook of Rationality*, The Oxford Reference Library of Philosophy, Oxford University Press, 2003.

Bishop, C. "Pattern recognition and machine learning", New York: Springer, 2006.

Boashash, B. (ed.). "Time–Frequency Signal Analysis and Processing: A Comprehensive Reference", Oxford: Elsevier Science, 2003.

Bochner, S., Chandrasekharan, K. "Fourier Transforms", Princeton University Press, 1949.

Bose, S., Das, C., Dutta, S., Chattopadhyay, S. "A novel interpolation based missing value estimation method to predict missing values in microarray gene expression data", *Proceedings of the 2012 International Conference on Communications, Devices and Intelligent Systems*, CODIS 2012, art. no. 6422202, pp. 318–321, 2012.

Bracewell, R.N. "The Fourier Transform and Its Applications", 3rd Edition, Boston: McGraw-Hill, 2000.

Carpenter, G.A., Grossberg, S. "Adaptive Resonance Theory", In Michael A. Arbib (ed.), The Handbook of Brain Theory and Neural Networks, Second Edition, Cambridge, MA: MIT Press, pp. 87–90, 2003.

Chai, J., Liu, J.N.K., Ngai, E.W.T. "Application of decision-making techniques in supplier selection: A systematic review of literature", *Expert Systems with Applications*, Vol. 40, No. 10, pp. 3872–3885, 2013.

Chui, C.K. "An Introduction to Wavelets. San Diego", Academic Press, 1992.

Coillet, A., Henriet, R., Salzenstein, P., Huy, K.P., Larger, L., Chembo, Y.K. "Time-domain dynamics and stability analysis of optoelectronic oscillators based on whispering-gallery mode resonators", *IEEE Journal on Selected Topics in Quantum Electronics* art. no. 6477074, Vol. 19, No. 5, 2013.

Daugman, J.G. "Two-dimensional spectral analysis of cortical receptive field profiles", *Vision Research*, PMID: 7467139, Vol. 20, No. 10, pp. 847–856, 1980.

DeGroot, M. "Optimal Statistical Decision", McGraw-Hill, New York, 1970.

Dybała, J., Radkowski, S. "Reduction of Doppler effect for the needs of wayside condition monitoring system of railway vehicles", *Mechanical Systems and Signal Processing*, Vol. 38, No. 1, pp. 125–136, 2013.

Fernández, M., Caballero, J. "Modeling of activity of cyclic urea HIV-1 protease inhibitors using regularized-artificial neural networks", *Bioorganic and Medicinal Chemistry*, Vol. 14, No. 1, pp. 280–294, 2006.

Foster, K.R., Kokko, H. "The evolution of superstitious and superstition-like behaviour", *Proceedings of the Royal Society B: Biological Sciences*, Vol. 276, No. 1654, pp. 31–7, 2009.

Fourier, J.-B. "Théorie Analytique de la Chaleur", Paris: Chez Firmin Didot, père et fils, 1822.

Gama, J. "Data stream mining: The bounded rationality", *Informatica (Slovenia)*, Vol. 37, No. 1, pp. 21–25, 2013.

Garcia, R.F., Rolle, J.L.C., Gomez, M.R., Catoira, A.D. "Expert condition monitoring on hydrostatic self-levitating bearings", *Expert Systems with Applications*, Vol. 40, No. 8, pp. 2975–2984, 2013.

Garnier, A., Eynard, J., Caussanel, M., Grieu, S. "Missing data estimation for energy resources management in tertiary buildings", *2nd International Conference on Communications Computing and Control Applications*, CCCA 2012, art. no. 6417902, 2012.

Gu, J., Bohns, V.K., Leonardelli, G.J. "Regulatory focus and interdependent economic decision-making", *Journal of Experimental Social Psychology*, Vol. 49, No. 4, pp. 692–698, 2013.

Heideklang, R., Ivanova, G. "A novel flexible model for the extraction of features from brain signals in the time-frequency domain", *International Journal of Biomedical Imaging*, Vol. 2013, art. no. 759421, 2013.

Hembacher, E., Ghetti, S. "How to bet on a memory: Developmental linkages between subjective recollection and decision making", *Journal of Experimental Child Psychology*, Vol. 115, No. 3, pp. 436–452, 2013.

Herckenrath, D., Odlum, N., Nenna, V., Knight, R., Auken, E., Bauer-Gottwein, P. "Calibrating a salt water intrusion model with time-domain electromagnetic data", *Ground Water*, Vol. 51, No. 3, pp. 385–397, 2013.

Hung, S.-S., Chang, H.-C., Kao, P.-T., Lin, S.-L. "Automatic monitoring and control for green house environment based on optimal plant growing condition", *Advanced Science Letters*, Vol. 19, No. 10, pp. 2895–2900, 2013.

Jacobsen, E., Lyons, R. "The sliding DFT", *Signal Processing Magazine*, Vol. 20, No. 2, pp. 74–80, 2003.

Jiang, R., Xie, J., Wang, N., Li, J. "Evolution game analysis of water saving and pollution prevention for city user groups based on bounded rationality", *Shuili Fadian Xuebao/Journal of Hydroelectric Engineering*, Vol. 32, No. 1, pp. 31–36, 2013a.

Jiang, Z., Jiao, W., Meng, S. "Fault diagnosis method of time domain and time-frequency domain based on information fusion", *Applied Mechanics and Materials*, Vols. 300–301, pp. 635–639, 2013b.

Jin, C., Jin, S.-W., Tan, H.-Y. "Computer virus propagation model based on bounded rationality evolutionary game theory", *Security and Communication Networks*, Vol. 6, No. 2, pp. 210–218, 2013.

Jones, J.P., Palmer, L.A. "An evaluation of the two-dimensional Gabor filter model of simple receptive fields in cat striate cortex", *Journal of Neurophysiology*, Vol. 58, No. 6, pp. 1233–1258, 1987.

Jont, B.A. "Short Time Spectral Analysis, Synthesis, and Modification by Discrete Fourier Transform", *IEEE Transactions on Acoustics, Speech, and Signal Processing*. ASSP-25, No. 3, pp. 235–238, 1977.

Kahneman, D. "Thinking, Fast and Slow" Macmillan, New York, 2011.

Kahneman, D., Tversky, A. "Prospect Theory: An analysis of decision under risk", *Econometrica*, Vol. 47, No. 2, pp. 263–291, 1979.

Köksalan, M.M., Sagala, P.N.S. "Interactive approaches for discrete alternative multiple criteria decision making with monotone utility functions", *Management Science*, Vol. 41, No. 7, pp. 1158–1171, 1995.

Le, T.-P., Paultre, P. "Modal identification based on the time-frequency domain decomposition of unknown-input dynamic tests", *International Journal of Mechanical Sciences*, Vol. 71, pp. 41–50, 2013.

Lee, I.H. "Speculation under bounded rationality", *Journal of Economic Theory and Econometrics*, Vol. 24, No. 1, pp. 37–53, 2013.

Leke, B.B., Marwala, T., Tim, T., Lagazio, M. "Prediction of HIV Status from Demographic Data Using Neural Networks", *Proceedings of the IEEE International Conference on Systems, Man and Cybernetics*, Taiwan, pp. 2339–2344, 2006.

Luy, M., Saray, U. "Wind speed estimation for missing wind data with three different backpropagation algorithms", *Energy Education Science and Technology Part A: Energy Science and Research*, Vol. 30, No. 1, pp. 45–54, 2012.

Ma, X., Ding, S., Wei, L., Yang, J. "Blind identification of underdetermined mixing matrix and source separation by finding and solving a row echelon-like form of system in the time-frequency domain", *ICIC Express Letters, Part B: Applications*, Vol. 4, No. 3, pp. 739–746, 2013.

Marivate, V., Marwala, T. "Relational networks for HIV classification", *In* F.J. Ogwu (ed.), *Proceedings of the IASTED Africa Conference on Modelling and Simulation*, pp. 275–279, 2008.

Marwala, T., Crossingham, B. "Neuro-rough models for modelling HIV", *Proceedings of the IEEE International Conference on Man, Systems and Cybernetics*, pp. 3089–3095, 2008.

Marwala, T. "Probabilistic fault identification using a committee of neural networks and vibration data", American Institute of Aeronautics and Astronautics, *Journal of Aircraft*, Vol. 38, pp. 138–146, 2001.

Marwala, T. "Finite element updating using wavelet data and genetic algorithm", American Institute of Aeronautics and Astronautics, *Journal of Aircraft*, Vol. 39, pp. 709–711, 2002.

Marwala, T. "Computational Intelligence for Missing Data Imputation, Estimation and Management: Knowledge Optimization Techniques", Information Science Reference Imprint, IGI Global Publications, New York, 2009.

Marwala, T. "Condition Monitoring Using Computational Intelligence Methods", Springer-Verlag, Heidelberg, 2012.

Marwala, T. "Flexibly-bounded Rationality and Marginalization of Irrationality Theories for Decision Making". arXiv: 1306.2025, 2013.

Marwala, T., de Wilde, P., Correia, L., Mariano, P., Ribeiro, R., Abramov, V., Szirbik, N., Goossenaerts, J. "Scalability and optimisation of a committee of agents using genetic algorithm", *In Proceedings of the International Symposia on Soft Computing and Intelligent Systems for Industry*, Scotland, 2001.

Marwala, T., Mahola, U., Nelwamondo, F. "Hidden Markov models and Gaussian mixture models for bearing fault detection using fractals", *In the Proceedings of the IEEE International Joint Conference on Neural Networks*, BC, Canada, ISBN: 0-7803-9489-5, pp. 5876–5881, 2006.

Mill, J.S. "A System of Logic, Ratiocinative and Inductive (Classic Reprint)", Oxford University Press, 2011.

Mistry, J., Nelwamondo, F.V., Marwala, T. "Investigating a Predictive Certainty measure for Ensemble Based HIV Classification", *IEEE International Conference on Systems, Computational Cybernetics, 2008*, ICCC 2008, pp. 231–236, 27–29 November, 2008.

Mistry, J., Nelwamondo, F.V., Marwala, T. "Missing Data Estimation using Principal Component Analysis and Autoassociative Neural Networks", *Journal of Systemics, Cybernetics and Informatics*, Vol. 7, No. 3, pp. 72–79, 2009.

Mohamed, A.K., Nelwamondo, F.V., Marwala, T. "Estimation of missing data: Neural networks, principal component analysis and genetic algorithms", *Proceedings of the 12th World Multi-Conference on Systemics, Cybernetics and Informatics*: WMSCI 2008, Orlando, Florida, USA, pp. 36–41, 29th June–2nd July, 2008.

Mohapatra, S., Zhu, H., Overbye, T.J. "Frequency-domain analysis of electromechanical disturbances in electric power systems", *2013 IEEE Power and Energy Conference at Illinois*, PECI 2013, art. no. 6506063, pp. 230–237, 2013.

Mosterín, J. "*Lo mejor posible: Racionalidad y acción humana*", Madrid: Alianza Editorial, pp. 318, ISBN: 978-84-206-8206-8, 2013.

Murata, A., Kubo, S., Hata, N. "Study on promotion of cooperative behavior in social dilemma situation by introduction of bounded rationality — Effects of group heuristics on cooperative behavior", *Proceedings of the SICE Annual Conference*, art. no. 6318444, pp. 261–266, 2012.

Nelwamondo, F.V., Marwala, T. "Rough set theory for the treatment of incomplete data", *Proceedings of the IEEE Conference on Fuzzy Systems*, pp. 338–343, 2007.

Nelwamondo, F.V., Mohamed, S., Marwala, T. "Missing Data: A Comparison of Neural Network and Expectation Maximisation Techniques", *Current Science*, Vol. 93, No. 11, pp. 1514–1521, 2007.

Nelwamondo, F.V., Golding, D., Marwala, T. "A dynamic programming approach to missing data estimation using neural networks", *Information Sciences*, Vol. 237, pp. 49–58, 2013.

Nozick, R. "The Nature of Rationality", Princeton: Princeton University Press, 1993.

Oh, K.-Y., Kim, J.-Y., Lee, J.-S. "Preliminary evaluation of monopile foundation dimensions for an offshore wind turbine by analyzing hydrodynamic load in the frequency domain", *Renewable Energy*, Vol. 54, pp. 211–218, 2013.

Patel, P., Marwala, T. "Neural networks, fuzzy inference systems and adaptive-neuro fuzzy inference systems for financial decision making", *Lecture Notes in Computer Science*, Springer-Verlag, Berlin Heidelberg, Vol. 4234, pp. 430–439, 2006.

Pati, S.K., Das, A.K. "Missing value estimation of microarray data using similarity measurement", *Lecture Notes in Computer Science (including subseries Lecture Notes in Artificial Intelligence and Lecture Notes in Bioinformatics)*, 7677 LNCS, pp. 602–610, 2012.

Paulraj, M.P., Adom, A.H., Sundararaj, S. "Classification of moving vehicle using multi-frame time domain features", *7th International Conference on Intelligent Systems and Control*, ISCO 2013, art. no. 6481211, pp. 529–533, 2013.

Pereira, F.M.V., Carvalho, A.D.S., Cabeça, L.F., Colnago, L.A. "Classification of intact fresh plums according to sweetness using time-domain nuclear magnetic resonance and chemometrics", *Microchemical Journal*, 108, pp. 14–17, 2013.

Qian, S., Chen, D. "Joint Time-Frequency Analysis: Methods and Applications", Chap. 5, Prentice Hall, NJ, 1996.

Qu, Z.-G., Wang, P., Gao, Y.-H., Wang, P., Shen, Z.-K. "Frequency domain filtering of gradient image for contour detection", *Optik*, Vol. 124, No. 13, pp. 1398–1401, 2013.

Raol, J.R. "Multi-sensor data fusion: Theory and Practice" CRC Press, 2009.

Salem, O.M., Miller, R.A., Deshpande, A.S., Arurkar, T.P. "Multi-criteria decision-making system for selecting an effective plan for bridge rehabilitation", *Structure and Infrastructure Engineering*, Vol. 9, No. 8, pp. 806–816, 2013.

Schölkopf, B., Smola, A.J. "Learning with Kernels", MIT Press, Cambridge, MA, 2002.

Serrano González, J., Burgos Payán, M., Riquelme Santos, J. "Optimum design of transmissions systems for offshore wind farms including decision making under risk", *Renewable Energy*, Vol. 59, pp. 115–127, 2013.

Shi, F., Zhang, D., Chen, J., Karimi, H.R. "Missing value estimation for microarray data by Bayesian principal component analysis and iterative local least squares", *Mathematical Problems in Engineering*, Vol. 2013, art. no. 162938, 2013.

Simon, H. "A Behavioral Model of Rational Choice", in Models of Man, Social and Rational: Mathematical Essays on Rational Human Behavior in a Social Setting. New York: Wiley, 1957.

Simon, H. "A mechanism for social selection and successful altruism", *Science*, Vol. 250, No. 4988, pp. 1665–1668, 1990.

Simon, H. "Bounded Rationality and Organizational Learning", *Organization Science*, Vol. 2, No. 1, pp. 125–134, 1991.

Skinner, B.F. "Superstition' in the Pigeon", *Journal of Experimental Psychology*, Vol. 38, No. 2, pp. 168–172, 1948.

Spohn, W. "The Many Facets of the Theory of Rationality", *Croatian Journal of Philosophy*, Vol. 2, pp. 247–262, 2002.

Stanciu-Viziteu, L.D. "The shark game: Equilibrium with bounded rationality", *Lecture Notes in Economics and Mathematical Systems*, Vol. 662, pp. 103–111, 2012.

Steuer, R.E. "Multiple Criteria Optimization: Theory, Computation and Application", New York: John Wiley, 1986.

Szurley, J., Bertrand, A., Moonen, M. "On the use of time-domain widely linear filtering for binaural speech enhancement", *IEEE Signal Processing Letters*, art. no. 6511977, Vol. 20, No. 7, pp. 649–652, 2013.

Tettey, T., Nelwamondo, F.V., Marwala, T. "HIV data analysis via rule extraction using rough sets", *In Proceedings of the 11th IEEE International Conference on Intelligent Engineering Systems*, Budapest, Hungary, pp. 105–110, 29 June–1 July 2007.

Tim, T. "Predicting HIV status using neural networks and demographic factors", University of the Witwatersrand, M.Sc. Dissertation, 2007.

Tim, T.N., Marwala, T. "Computational Intelligence Methods for Risk Assessment of HIV", *In Imaging the Future Medicine, Proceedings of the IFMBE*, Vol. 14, Sun I. Kim, Tae Suk Sah (eds.), Springer-Verlag, Berlin Heidelberg, pp. 3581–3585, 2006.

Tisdell, C. "Bounded Rationality and Economic Evolution: A Contribution to Decision Making, Economics, and Management", Cheltenham, UK: Brookfield, 1996.

Tsang, E.P.K. "Computational intelligence determines effective rationality", *International Journal on Automation and Control*, Vol. 5, No. 1, pp. 63–66, 2008.

Vapnik, V. "The Nature of Statistical Learning Theory", Springer, 1995.

Vilakazi, B.C., Marwala, T. "Application of feature selection and fuzzy ARTMAP to intrusion detection", *In Proceedings of the IEEE International Conference on Systems, Man and Cybernetics*, Taiwan, pp. 4880–4885, 2006.

Vyse, S.A. "Believing in Magic: The Psychology of Superstition", Oxford, England: Oxford University Press, 2000.

Weber, M. "Ueber einige Kategorien der verstehenden Soziologie", *In Gesammelte Aufsaetze zur Wissenschaftslehre*, pp. 427–474, 1922.

Wigner, E.-P. "On the quantum correlation for thermodynamic equilibrium", *Physical Review*, Vol. 40, pp. 749–759, 1932.

Yang, W., Tavner, P.J., Court, R. "An online technique for condition monitoring the induction generators used in wind and marine turbines", *Mechanical Systems and Signal Processing*, Vol. 38, No. 1, pp. 103–112, 2013.

Yao, J., Li, D. "Bounded rationality as a source of loss aversion and optimism: A study of psychological adaptation under incomplete information", *Journal of Economic Dynamics and Control*, Vol. 37, No. 1, pp. 18–31, 2013.

Zadeh, L.A. "Fuzzy Sets, Fuzzy Logic, Fuzzy Systems", World Scientific Press, 1996.

Zhang, X., Raza, A.S., Hood, D.C. "Detecting glaucoma with visual fields derived from frequency-domain optical coherence tomography", *Investigative Ophthalmology and Visual Science*, Vol. 54, No. 5, pp. 3289–3296, 2013a.

Zhang, Z., Aoki, Y., Toda, H., Imamura, T., Miyake, T. "Real world source separation by combining ICA and VD-CDWT in time-frequency domain", *International Journal of Innovative Computing, Information and Control*, Vol. 9, No. 4, pp. 1737–1757, 2013b.

Zimroz, R., Bartkowiak, A. "Two simple multivariate procedures for monitoring planetary gearboxes in non-stationary operating conditions", *Mechanical Systems and Signal Processing*, Vol. 38, No. 1, pp. 237–247, 2013.

Zionts, S., Wallenius, J. "An interactive programming method for solving the multiple criteria problem", *Management Science*, Vol. 22, No. 6, pp. 652–663, 1976.

Chapter 9

Marginalization of Irrationality in Decision Making

Abstract. The theory of marginalization of irrationality in decision making is proposed as a way of making satisficing decisions in the presence of irrationality. This is achieved by assuming that decision making process is made of a series of decision making actions which are either rational or irrational. The aggregation of these actions determine whether an irrational decision process will satisfice or not. This method is applied in the diagnosis of breast cancer and it is observed that the more irrational a decision making process the less accurate the results become. It is also observed that indeed it is possible for irrational actions to be marginalized by rational actions and that irrationality also marginalizes rationality.

9.1 Introduction

This chapter studies the concept of making sensible decisions in the presence of irrationality. Chapter 10 defined the concept of making rational decisions as consisting of three core elements which are, that the decision process should be based on relevant information, the process must be logical and that the whole process should be optimized (Yu and Lai, 2011; Chen and Lee, 2003). It was also stated that if any of these elements i.e. logic, based on relevant information and optimization are violated then the decision process is irrational. Based on this fact, it then becomes difficult for human beings to make rational decisions and, therefore, humans are fundamentally irrational beings.

The fact that human beings are irrational beings fundamentally implies that making decisions should on the whole be largely an irrational process and the science of making decisions should in the whole focus on irrationality, its essence, manifestations and its implications (Kaplan, 1987; Samuels and Stich, 2001).

This chapter develops a framework for making decisions in the presence of irrationality which is called the marginalization of irrationality theory of decision making. This theory is based on the premise that making decisions based on rationality is good and that making decisions based on irrationality is bad. In order to develop this theory, two fundamental concepts are discerned and these are decision actions and process.

Švecová *et al.* (2012) studied the impact of irrationality on the quality of decision making whereas Yang and Lester (2008) studied rational choice and irrationality and observed that rationality in economic decision-making is rare. Furthermore, Luo (2002) applied evolutionary approach to study the relationship between irrationality and monopolistic competition.

This chapter describes rational decision making, then irrationality, then the marginalization of irrationality theory and then applied the multi-layer perceptron (MLP) and radial basis function (RBF) to test the marginalization of irrationality for decision making theory. Section 9.1 thus describes what decision making is.

9.2 Rational Decision Making

This section describes the concept of rational decision making and the first task is to define what decision making is. Decision making is a process in which a decision is made (Campanella and Ribeiro, 2011; Wu and Xu, 2012; Polman, 2012). This process can either be rational i.e. logical, based on relevant information and optimized and therefore maximizes the utility while minimizing the loss (Mill, 1998) or it can be irrational which means it is not optimized nor based on relevant information nor logical. The concept of making decisions that are fully rational is viewed in this chapter as falling under the concept of utilitarianism where the aim of the rational agent is to fully or globally maximize utility (Bentham, 2001; Bentham *et al.*, 2005; Brandt, 1979; Mill, 1998; Bredeson, 2011). In this case, the rational agent has all the information to make decisions, has all the cognitive capability to make decisions and can globally optimize this decision making process.

This chapter proposes that on making decisions there is something called a process of making such decisions that can be followed for non-trivial decision making. A process can be rational or irrational and usually contains decisions actions which can be rational or irrational. An illustration of a decision making process is shown in Figure 9.1 with 5 decision actions whereas Figure 9.2 shows a decision making

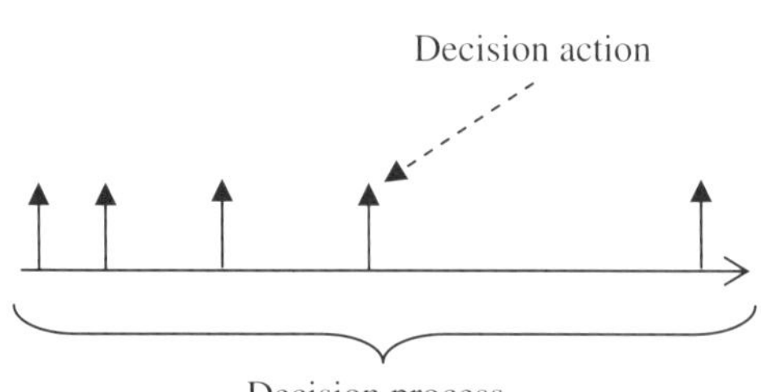

Figure 9.1 An illustration of a decision making process with a set of decision making actions

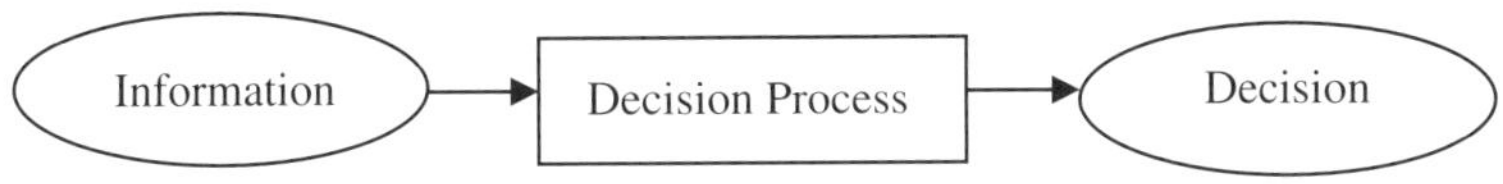

Figure 9.2 An illustration of a decision making framework

framework. The decision process in Figure 9.2 normally contains a correlation device (Aitken, 1957; Rodgers and Nicewander, 1988; Dowdy and Wearden, 1983), a causal device (Gasking, 1955; Simon and Rescher, 1966; Pearl, 2000; Byrne, 2005) as well as a control device (Abdoos *et al.*, 2011; Achili *et al.*, 2009; Al-Faiz and Sabry, 2012; Farouk, 2012; Ghosh and Gude, 2012). A correlation machine, and was discussed in detail in Chapters 2 and 4, has a function of filling the missing information and many routines such as artificial intelligence have been developed to deal with this problem. A causal machine, which was discussed in detail in Chapters 3 and 5, has a function of guiding what sort of action needs to be undertaken and, therefore, has *if then else loops* or its mathematical equivalence. The control device has a function of initiating actions given a set of information and causal rules.

The calculus of rational decision making states that a process is rational if and only if all decision actions in a process are all rational. If one of the decision making actions in a process is irrational then the decision making process is irrational. The rational decision making is rational because it uses relevant information, is logical and is optimized but such decisions are rare if not completely impossible. There is a commonly known classical artificial intelligence problem about a robot that tries to cross the road and on doing so it undertakes to do a series of decision actions which are to look to the right, look to the left and if the road is clear then to cross the road in the shortest distance possible (Russell and Norvig, 2009).

The question is whether the robot acted rationally. Sure, its decision process of crossing the road involved using relevant information whether there was a car coming from the left or the right and optimized the distance to the other side of the road by pursuing the shortest distance and was logical, e.g. it did not dig the road as part of a process of crossing the road.

However, if after having done all these decision actions the robot is struck by a falling aeroplane, did it act rationally? It did locally optimize but it only pursued a local optimum point not a global optimum solution which would involve searching for all possible sources of destruction such as the falling aeroplane which will be suboptimal if the exhaustive search process ends up taking a longer time. Herbert Simon coined this as bounded rationality which is a process of making rational decisions in the knowledge that the information is incomplete, is not globally optimized and is not optimally logical (Simon and Rescher, 1966; Horaguchi, 1996; Foss, 2003; Chao and Jian, 2007; Schwartz, 2008).

The concept of bounded rationality is grounded in the philosophical theory of pragmatism because it says that given the fact that the information available to make decisions is incomplete and imperfect, that there is no perfect cognitive device to make such decisions and that it is usually impossible to globally optimize the decision process, then one accepts the constrains and proceeds to make decisions in the presence of such constrains (Quine, 1951; 1980; Ramsey, 1927; 1990; Rescher, 1977; 2000; Peirce, 1998).

In Chapter 8, this book proposed flexibly-bounded rationality which results from the intense application of information technology into rational decision making which makes the bounds of rational decision making flexible depending on the intensity of technology applied. Section 9.3 describes irrationality.

9.3 What is Irrationality?

This section studies irrationality primarily because in the last section, it was surmised that human beings are essentially irrational beings (Vogt, 2010; Ariely, 2010a; 2010b). The first task is to define what irrationality is and the easiest way of defining irrationality is to define it as an antithesis of rationality. It is an antithesis of rationality because it can be defined as that which rationality is not. For example, in the last section, we defined rationality within the context of decision making as a procedure for making decisions which by using relevant information and sound logic to make optimized decisions. Therefore, taking the antithesis route of defining rationality, irrationality in extreme can be defined as a process of making decisions without the use of information or by using irrelevant information, based on illogical principles in an un-optimized manner. Of course, the process can still be irrational if only one of the three elements information, logic or optimization is absent.

Earle (2013) studied the relationship between rationality and irrationality whereas Rose (2013) studied decision making within the context of irrationality. Manapat *et al.* (2013) studied information, irrationality and how trust evolves whereas Brahmana *et al.* (2012) applied herd behavior to understand irrationality of investors on *Monday irrationality*.

Within the context of causality which is the subject of this book, irrationality can be defined as a process of inferring causal link between two sets of variables where causality does not exist. There is an old superstitious belief that if one sees a black cat passing the road in front then one will encounter bad luck. In this irrational superstition, a causal link between crossing the road by the black cat and the person who sees it crossing the road encountering bad luck. The other irrational superstition is the old superstition between an owl crowing in one's family house and death in that family. Here again, an irrational causal link is drawn between the owl crowing and the death in the family.

The theory of bounded rationality states that even though one can be constrained by lack of complete relevant information, and robust logic also appropriately called cognitive limitation as well as optimization, one can still be able to derive solutions that are satisfactory and sufficient (satisficing) (Ballester and Hernández, 2012; Radicchi *et al.*, 2012). One issue that ought to be clarified is whether these constrains on relevant information, logic and optimization necessarily lead to irrationality and in this book we propose that it does not but merely leads to bounded rationality. When we are operating under the realms of the more common irrationality, we can no longer talk about satisficing but arriving at a workable solution. It is workable because it allows one to move forward with a decision. This chapter describes the theory of the marginalization of irrationality which is a decision making theory where the advantages (rationality) overwhelm the disadvantages (irrationality). In summary, one cannot be irrational and still satisfices but can be irrational and identifies a workable solution.

The concept of optimization and irrationality deserves study. For example, if one intends to fly from Johannesburg to Cape Town and decides to fly from Johannesburg to Windhoek and then from Windhoek to Cape Town instead of flying from Johannesburg to Cape Town directly, then this trip will be puzzling. If it is discovered that the person used the route Johannesburg–Windhoek–Cape Town because he thought that was the quickest and most convenient route, then this will even be more puzzling because it is clearly not an optimized route. Taking the Johannesburg–Windhoek–Cape Town route instead of Johannesburg–Cape Town route can be classified as irrational because it does not satisfy the classical definition of a rational agent which seeks to maximize utility. Here it is not maximizing utility because it wastes time and consumes more energy to fulfil the goal of reaching Cape Town from Johannesburg. This irrational approach Johannesburg–Windhoek–Cape Town does not prevent the person from attaining the goal of reaching Cape Town (workable solution). Therefore, it is quite possible to be irrational by not pursuing an optimal route in this case and still be able to identify a workable solution.

The question of irrationality and information also deserves further investigation. Information has been defined by many researchers as usually imperfect and incomplete. In fact in economics, there is a theory that is solely based on the theory of imperfect and incomplete information. The fact that information is imperfect and incomplete does not necessarily imply that using such information is irrational. What is irrational is deliberately using irrelevant information or not using information at all to make a decision. As an example, there is classical Russian story of Rasputin where the Russian Royal Family used irrelevant information that Rasputin had mystic powers that allowed him to heal even better than the scientific approaches and this faith in Rasputin ultimately brought down the Russian Royal Family (Fuhrmann, 1990; 2013). It can be observed that in general not optimizing when making a decision is less dangerous than making decisions using irrelevant information. Of course, there are cases where decision are made with information that is relevant and information that is irrelevant and in this case, the goal of the decision can be reached depending on whether relevant information overwhelms or marginalizes irrelevant information.

The question of irrationality and logic is important because for many instances rationality is defined within the context of logic. If an action makes logical sense then it is often assumed that it is rational. The absence of logic in an action or process automatically indicates irrationality. The example of Johannesburg–Windhoek–Cape Town (as opposed to Johannesburg–Cape Town) was deemed irrational because it was not optimized. It can also be deemed irrational because it is illogical because it makes no sense for a person to take a longer route to reach a destination without any other reason except to reach a particular destination. Now that we have studied what irrationality is and some of the factors that cause it, the next section describes the marginalization of irrationality theory for decision making.

9.4 Marginalization of Irrationality Theory

This chapter introduces the theory of the marginalization of irrationality for effective decision making. This theory is based on the principles that in decision making rationality offers advantages over irrationality. It is also as a result of the fact that it is apparent that for a complex decision making process it is not very often that one can eliminate irrationality all together. This theory of the marginalization of irrationality for decision making process essentially states that when making a complex decision which involves rational and irrational decision actions, that decision will be effective or workable if the irrational actions are subdued by the rational actions.

To illustrate this principle of the marginalization of irrationality, we will invoke the principle of signal to noise ratio that has been widely applied in information theory (Schroeder, 1999; Choma *et al.*, 2003; Russ, 2007; González and Woods, 2008; Raol, 2009). The principle of signal to noise ratio is used to assess the degree through which the signal is corrupted or influenced by noise. When the noise overwhelms or marginalizes the signal, then the signal cannot transmit the relevant information effectively while when the signal marginalizes the noise then the signal is able to transmit a significant part of the original information. By the same token, when the rational aspect of a decision making process marginalizes the irrational aspect, then the consequence of the decision is effective or workable while when the irrational aspect of decision making marginalizes the rational aspect, then the decision is ineffective or unworkable.

In line with information theory, the rational (wanted actions) to irrational (unwanted actions) ratio (RIR) can be defined as follows (Schroeder, 1999; Choma *et al.*, 2003; Russ, 2007):

$$RIR = \frac{P_{rational}}{P_{irrational}}. \tag{9.1}$$

Here $P_{rational}$ is the impact of the rational actions whereas $P_{irrational}$ is the impact of the irrational actions. When *RIR* is high then the rational actions marginalize irrational actions and therefore the decision is *satisffective* meaning that the outcome of the decision making process is satisfactory and effective while a low *RIR* simply means an unsatisfactory and/or ineffective decision making. The term satisffective was derived in a similar manner as the word satisficing. Satisficing is obtained when decision making is conducted under rational circumstances where the limitations are incomplete and imperfect information and limited decision making engine. On the other hand, satisffective is obtained when decision making is conducted under irrational circumstances where the rational actions marginalize irrational actions. Of course, the challenge of implementing Equation 9.1 is to estimate the impact of an action.

9.5 Irrational Decision Making and the Theory of Marginalization of Irrationality in Decision Making

In this chapter, we define rational decision making as a process of making decisions based on the process that is logical and is premised on information and is optimized. Given this definition, then what is irrational decision making? A decision making process becomes irrational if it is not based on information (evidence) or it is illogical or it is un-optimized. In the earlier part of this chapter, we did conclude that human beings are essentially irrational beings.

The sobering conclusion that human beings are most often than not irrational poses an additional dilemma on how they do manage to satisfice even when they are acting irrationally. I will go back to the patient Masindi who after being diagnosed with a serious heart problem he consulted an astrologer. On the morning of day 1, he goes to the astrologer to seek help and thereafter goes straight to see a cardiologist who examines him and tells him that he is going for an operation the following day. The following day, before going to the operation room, he consults an astrologer to strengthen the chances of success of the operation. Now, in the process of dealing with his heart problem, is Masindi being rational? The three aspects of rationality discussed in this chapter are logic, relevant information, and optimization. In this example, the decision actions that Masindi takes is to see an astrologer twice and sees a cardiologist twice. Each of these decision making actions is classified as either irrational or rational and in this regard seeing an astrologer is classified as irrational and seeing a cardiologist is classified as rational. Masindi is not being logical and certainly his decision is not optimized and, therefore, is irrational.

Now under these circumstances, how does one make decisions that are not rational but are still satisffective? In this regard, we propose the theory of marginalization of irrationality to make satisffective decisions. If we consider the Masindi example, then we can see that in the process of dealing with the heart problem, he pursued two approaches one which we deem rational (going to the cardiologist twice) and another one that we deem irrational (going to an astrologer twice) but collectively the whole process of dealing with the problem is irrational because it is neither optimal nor logical. In this case, a satisffective decision will only emerge if the irrational aspect of the process that Masindi follows is marginalized in favor of the rational decision of seeing a cardiologist. It may quite be possible that the astrologer could have recommended the ingestion of lithium battery which could have been fatal and, therefore, the irrational aspect of the process could have overwhelmed the rational aspect.

Given this example, how then do we generalize this theory of the marginalization of irrationality for decision making? The steps that ought to be followed to make a decision when the process is not rational are as follows:

1. Collect the information needed to make a decision.
2. Outline a process to be followed to make such as a decision.
3. Divide the decision making process into sets of actions with each action classified into whether it is rational or irrational.
4. Assess whether the irrational actions of the process are marginalizable when compared to the rational actions.
5. If the irrational actions are marginalizable then the solution is satisffective whereas if these actions are not marginalizable then the solution is not satisffective.

Clearly satisffective an irrational decision requires the assessment as to whether the irrational aspect of an irrational process of decision making is marginalizable. How do we achieve this? In this chapter, we borrow from the field of information theory the concept of signal to noise ratio and adapt it to the concept of the ratio of the power of rationality to the power of irrationality (Raol, 2009). One difficult way is to identify the causal loop between the irrational part of the process and a decision and evaluate the impact of this on the decision and compare this to the impact of the rational part of the decision process on the decision to be able to calculate the power of rationality to the power of irrationality ratio.

To illustrate this point, I will invoke the story of Nongqawuse, the Xhosa prophet who advised her community that if they kill their cattle and crops then God will drive the British into the sea (Peires, 1989; Stapleton, 1991; Welsh, 2000). Indeed the overwhelming majority which is estimated to be approximately 95% of community members killed the cattle and crops. From this, the power of rationality to the power of irrationality is approximately 0.05 and, therefore, there was no chance that this decision process could have resulted in a satisficed outcome. The process this community followed had both rational and irrational aspects but was in the whole irrational. The result of this was famine and deaths leading to a population decline from 127,000 to 27,000. Using the theory of marginalization of irrationality, the outcome was not satisffective and the reason for this is because the irrational aspects of this irrational process could not be marginalized.

The theory of marginalization of information is also applicable to any decision making process where the information that is needed to make such a decision is not complete and there is no mechanism of completing either partially or optimistically fully the missing information. In this situation, the decision maker simply ignores or marginalizes the missing information and continues to make a decision. The efficacy of this decision will depend on the ratio of the power of observed information to the power of the missing information just exactly as is the case in information theory where the usefulness of the information depends on the signal to noise ratio. Section 9.6 applies the marginalization of irrationality theory in breast cancer diagnosis.

9.6 Application of the Marginalization of Irrationality Theory for Breast Cancer Diagnosis

The theory of the marginalization of irrationality in decision making is tested on the Wisconsin breast cancer data from the UCI data depository. This data set is a multivariate, with integer attributes and has 699 instances. More details on this data set are found in Wolberg and Mangasarian (1990) as well as Zhang (1992). The data set has 10 attributes that will be used to test the marginalization of irrationality theory. These attributes are the sample code number (A1), clump thickness which varies from 1 to 10 (A2), uniformity of cell size which varies from 1 to 10 (A3), uniformity of cell shape which varies from 1 to 10 (A4), marginal adhesion which varies from 1 to 10 (A5), single epithelial cell size which varies from 1 to 10 (A6), bare nuclei which varies from 1 to 10 (A7), bland chromatin which varies from 1 to 10 (A8), normal nucleoi which varies from 1 to 10 (A9) and mitoses which varies from 1 to 10 (A10). From these attributes, the outcome of the classification process should either be cancerous or not.

Azar and El-Said (2013) successfully applied this data set and probabilistic neural network for breast cancer classification whereas Koyuncu and Ceylan (2013) successfully applied artificial neural network based on rotation forest for breast cancer diagnosis using this data set. Stamoulias and Manolakos (2013) used this data set successfully to test parallel architectures for the k-nearest neighbor classifier whereas Uzer *et al.* (2013) successfully applied this data set, neural network, and the principal component analysis for breast cancer detection.

This next subsections use the MLP and RBF to test the marginalization of irrationality theory for decision making. To do this, the 699 instances are divided into three segments each with 233 instances. The first 233 instances are used to train the MLP and the RBF, the second to validate the models and third to test the models.

9.6.1 MLP

The MLP is an input–output network which can be used to relate two sets of data. It is type of a neural network system. Sarma and Mitra (2013) successfully applied the MLP for multiple-input–multiple-output channel modeling whereas Ikuta *et al.* (2013) successfully applied the MLP in circuit systems. Chung and Rhee (2013) successfully applied the MLP neural network to group XOR-collusion.

The MLP network that is implemented in this section to diagnose breast cancer has 10 input units, one hidden layer with 20 hidden nodes and 1 output unit. The first layer activation function is the logistic activation function and the second layer activation function is the linear activation function. Ten networks were trained using the scaled conjugate gradient method (Babaie-Kafaki, 2012; Chel *et al.*, 2011; Gayathri and Kumarappan, 2010). An appropriate model is chosen using the validation part of the data set. The method is tested using the 233 test data set. The first experiment test the data using the 233 data as is, then the second experiment reconstructs variable A1 in the test set randomly and this is deemed irrational because it might as well been the temperature of a pole outside the hospital, in the third experiment A1 and A2 were randomly generated in the test data set, in the fourth experiment A1, A2, and A3 were randomly generated in the test data set, in the fifth experiment A1, A2, A3, and A4 were randomly generated in the test data set, in the sixth experiment A1, A2, A3, A4, and A5 were randomly generated in the test data set, in the seventh experiment A1, A2, A3, A4, A5, and A6 were randomly generated in the test data set, in the eighth experiment A1, A2, A3, A4, A5, A6, and A7 were randomly generated in the test data set, in the ninth experiment A1, A2, A3, A4, A5, A6, A7, and A8 were randomly generated in the test data set, in the tenth experiment A1, A2, A3, A4, A5, A6, A7, A8, and A9 were randomly generated in the test data set and in the eleventh all variables were randomly generated. The results of these experiments are shown in Figures 9.3 and 9.4.

When no variable was randomly generated in the test data, the MLP gave an accuracy of 100%. When the variable sample code number (A1) was randomly generated the MLP gave an accuracy of 100%. This is largely because this variable

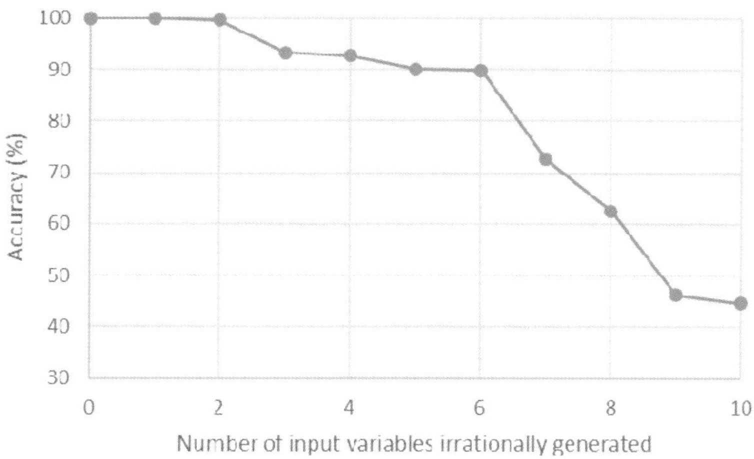

Figure 9.3 The performance of the MLP with a variable number of inputs randomly generated (irrational)

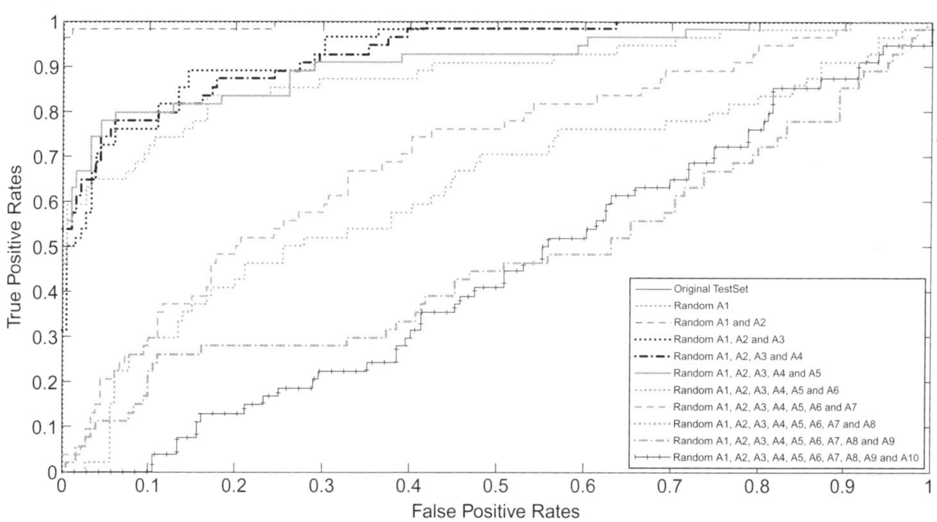

Figure 9.4 The receiver operation characteristics curve of the MLP with a variable number of inputs randomly generated (irrational)

has no impact on the breast cancer diagnosis and the MLP is able to marginalize this information which could confuse the diagnosis process. When two variables were randomly generated (A1 and A2) the diagnosis accuracy dropped to 99.7%. When three variables were randomly generated (A1, A2, and A3) the diagnosis accuracy dropped to 93.3% which means the cost of marginalization of irrationality was a drop of 6.7%. When four variables were randomly generated (A1, A2, A3, and

A4) the diagnosis accuracy dropped to 92.8%. When five variables were randomly generated (A1, A2, A3, A5, and A6), the diagnosis accuracy dropped to 90%. When six variables were randomly generated (A1, A2, A3, A5, A6, and A7) the diagnosis accuracy dropped to 89.9%.

When seven variables were randomly generated (A1, A2, A3, A5, A6, A7, and A8) the diagnosis accuracy dropped to 72.6%. When seven variables were randomly generated (A1, A2, A3, A5, A6, A7, and A8) the diagnosis accuracy dropped to 62.6%. When nine and ten variables were randomly generated the accuracy fell to be below 50%. These experiments illustrate that rationality is good for decision making and that irrationality leads to confusion and suboptimal decision making.

9.6.2 RBF

The RBF is an input–output network which can be used to relate two sets of data. It is type of a neural network system. Riverol and Pilipovik (2014) successfully applied the RBF to assess the failure frequency of potential hazardous incidents in milk pasteurization unit whereas Lian (2014) successfully applied RBF to control a robotic system. Lee and Chen (2013) successfully applied the RBF in molecular dynamics systems whereas Li *et al.* (2013) the RBF to predict gas solubility in polymers.

The RBF network has 10 input units, 8 hidden units in one hidden layer, and 1 output unit. The first layer activation function is the Gaussian activation function and the second layer activation function is the linear activation function. The network was trained using an expectation maximization (EM) algorithm. This chapter applies the EM algorithm to train the RBF network instead of the k-means and pseudo inverse method. The EM algorithm was proposed by Dempster *et al.* (1977) and has been applied to many areas (Wang *et al.*, 2007). Bordes *et al.* (2007) successfully applied the EM algorithm to image reconstruction and observed that the results were within 10% of the experimental data whereas Kauermann *et al.* (2007) successfully applied the EM algorithm to identify polymorphism in pharmacokinetic/pharmacodynamic (PK/PD) phenotypes. Haghbin and Nematollahi (2013) successfully applied the EM algorithms to identify the maximum likelihood approximations of model parameters in general autoregressive models. Mao and Zeng (2013) successfully applied the EM algorithm to reduce the artifacts triggered by data reduction and inadequate angular sampling by decreasing step sizes on image updating the pixels exterior to the field of view.

The set of experiments that were conducted in the previous section using the MLP is applied in this section using the RBF. When no variable was randomly generated in the test data, the RBF gave an accuracy of 99.4%. When the variable sample code number (A1) was randomly generated the RBF gave an accuracy of 99.4%. When two variables were randomly generated (A1 and A2) the diagnosis accuracy dropped to 99.3%. When three variables were randomly generated (A1, A2, and A3) the diagnosis accuracy dropped to 99.1%. When four variables were randomly generated (A1, A2, A3, and A4) the diagnosis accuracy dropped to 99.0%. When five variables were randomly generated (A1, A2, A3, A5, and A6) the diagnosis accuracy dropped to 99%. When six variables were randomly generated (A1, A2, A3, A5, A6, and A7) the diagnosis accuracy dropped to 96.7%. When seven variables were randomly generated (A1, A2, A3, A5, A6, A7, and A8) the diagnosis accuracy dropped to 83.2%. When eight variables were randomly generated (A1, A2, A3, A5, A6, A7, and A8) the diagnosis accuracy dropped to 67.4%. When nine and ten variables were randomly generated the accuracy fell to 54.0% and under 50% when all variables were randomly generated.

The results of these experiments are shown in Figures 9.5 and 9.6. When the MLP and RBF are compared it seems that the RBF has a better capacity to marginalize irrationality than the MLP.

9.6.3 Auto-associative neural network based on the MLP

This section applies the missing data approaches to diagnose breast cancer. As described in Chapters 2, 4, and 7, the missing data approach to inference is based on the auto-associative network. In this section, we use the MLP neural networks to

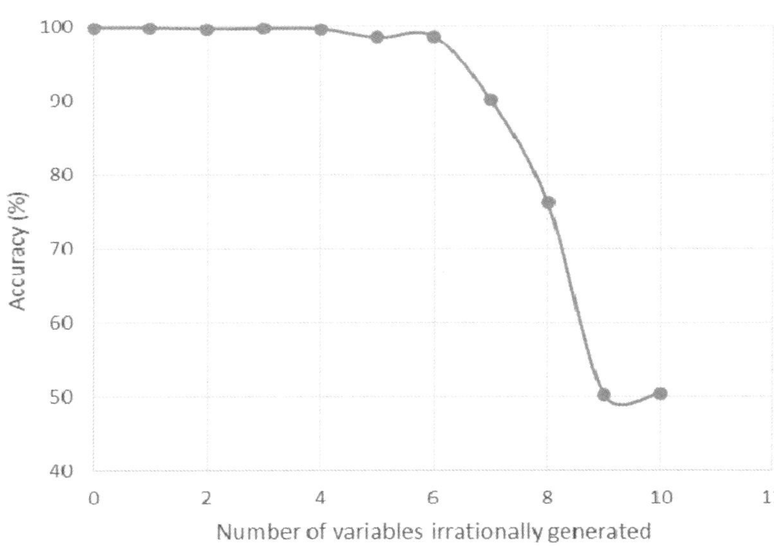

Figure 9.5 The performance of the auto-associative neural network based on the MLP with a variable number of inputs randomly generated (irrational)

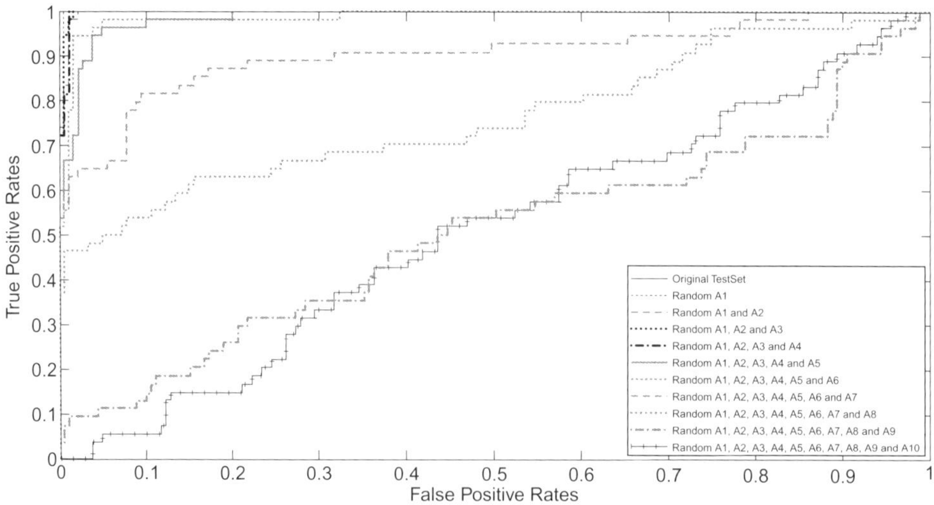

Figure 9.6 The receiver operation characteristics curve of the auto-associative network based on RBF (nor RBF) with a variable number of inputs randomly generated (irrational)

construct the auto-associative network. Reyes *et al.* (2013) successfully used auto-associative network for fault detection and missing data estimation while Valle and Vicente (2012) successfully applied auto-associative network to estimate missing components of an image. Chen (2010) successfully applied auto-associative neural networks to estimate missing values and applied this to classification of business failure.

The auto-associative network based on the MLP used in this section has 11 input units (10 inputs + breast cancer diagnosis), 6 hidden nodes in one hidden layer and 11 output units. The first layer activation function is the logistic activation function and the second layer activation function is the linear activation function. The network was trained using the scaled conjugate gradient method. When the experiments like the ones done in the previous section are conducted, the results obtained are shown in Figures 9.5 and 9.6. The results demonstrate that the auto-associative network based on the MLP marginalizes irrationality.

9.6.4 Auto-associative network based on the RBF

As in the previous section, this section applies the missing data approaches to diagnose breast cancer using the RBF-based auto-associative network. The RBF-based auto-associative AANN has 11 input units, 5 hidden units in 1 hidden layer and 11 output units. The first layer activation function is the Gaussian activation function and the second layer activation function is the linear activation function. The network was trained using an EM algorithm. These were explained in the previous sections.

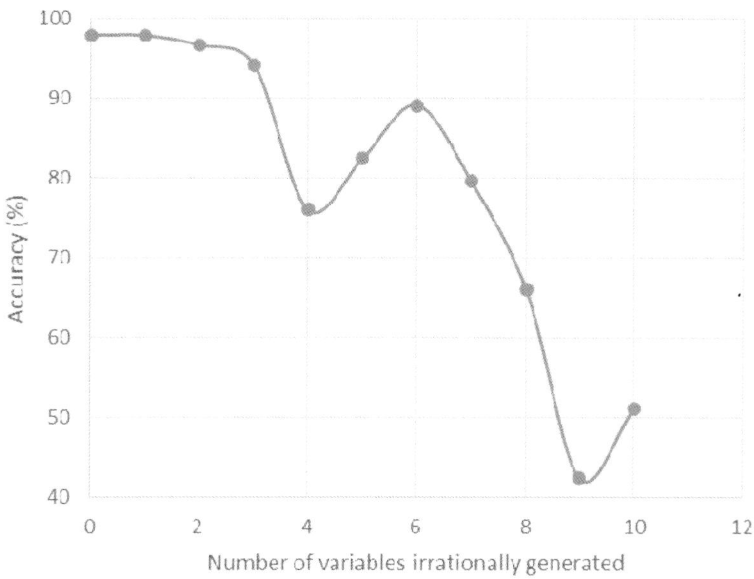

Figure 9.7 The performance of the auto-associative neural network based on the RBF with a variable number of inputs randomly generated (irrational)

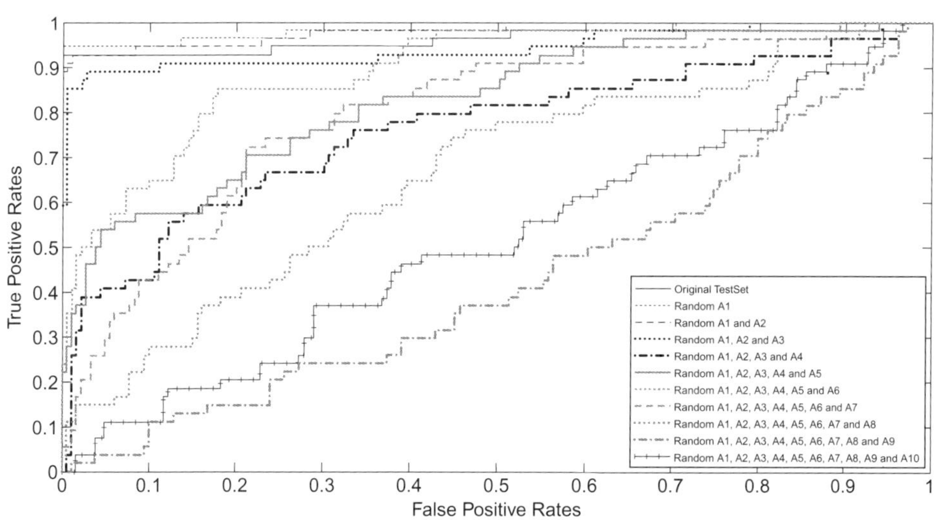

Figure 9.8 The receiver operation characteristics curve of the auto-associative network based on RBF with a variable number of inputs randomly generated (irrational)

When the experiments like the ones done in the previous section are conducted, the results obtained are shown in Figures 9.7 and 9.8. The results demonstrate that the auto-associative network based on the RBF marginalizes irrationality but not as well as the RBF-based auto-associative network.

9.7 Conclusions

This chapter introduced the theory of the marginalization of irrationality for decision making. The theory is tested on breast cancer diagnosis using the MLP and RBF models as well as the MLP and RBF-based auto-associative networks. Irrationality was simulated by randomly generating some of the inputs to a breast cancer diagnostics system. The results obtained indicate that these methods are able to marginalize irrationality because it is possible to make a fairly accurate diagnosis despite the fact that some variables have been irrationally obtained by randomly generating them.

References

Abdoos, M., Mozayani, N. Bazzan, A.L.C. "Traffic Light Control in Non-stationary Environments Based on Multi Agent Q-learning", *In Proceedings of the IEEE Conference on Intelligent Transportation Systems* pp.1580–1585, 2011.

Achili, B., Daachi, B., Ali-Cherif, A., Amirat, Y. "Combined Multi-layer Perceptron Neural Network and Sliding Mode Technique for parallel robots control: An Adaptive Approach", *In Proceedings of the International Joint Conference on Neural Networks*, pp. 28–35, 2009.

Aitken, A.C. "Statistical Mathematics", 8th Edition, Oliver & Boyd, 1957.

Al-Faiz, M.Z., Sabry, S.S. "Optimal Linear Quadratic Controller Based on Genetic Algorithm for TCP/AQM Router", *In Proceedings of the International Conference on Future Communication and Networks*, pp. 78–83, 2012.

Ariely, D. "The Upside of Irrationality: The Unexpected Benefits of Defying Logic at Work and at Home", HarperCollins Publishers, 2010a.

Ariely, D. "Predictably Irrational", Harper Perennial Publishers, 2010b.

Azar, A.T., El-Said, S.A. "Probabilistic neural network for breast cancer classification", *Neural Computing and Applications*, Vol. 23, No. 6, pp. 1737–1751, 2013.

Babaie-Kafaki, S. "A note on the global convergence theorem of the scaled conjugate gradient algorithms proposed by Andrei", *Computational Optimization and Applications*, Vol. 52, No. 2, pp. 409–414, 2012.

Ballester, C., Hernández, P. "Bounded rationality", *Revista Internacional de Sociologia, 70 (EXTRA 1)*, pp. 27–38, 2012.

Bentham, J. "The Works of Jeremy Bentham", *Published under the Superintendence of His Executor, John Bowring, Adamant Media Corporation*, Vol. 1, 2001.

Bentham, J., Dumont, E., Hildreth, R. "Theory of Legislation: Translated from the French of Etienne Dumont", Adamant Media Corporation, November 2005.

Bordes, L., Chauveau, D., Vandekerkhove, P. "An EM algorithm for a semiparametric mixture model", *Computational Statistics and Data Analysis*, Vol. 51, pp. 5429–5443, 2007.

Brahmana, R., Hooy, C.W., Ahmad, Z. "The role of herd behaviour in determining the investor's Monday irrationality", *Asian Academy of Management Journal of Accounting and Finance*, Vol. 8, No. 2, pp. 1–20, 2012.

Brandt, R.B. "A Theory of the Good and the Right", Clarendon Press, 1979.

Bredeson, D. "Utilitarianism vs. Dentological Ethics", *Applied Business Ethics: A Skills-Based Approach. Cengage Learning*, 2011.

Byrne, R.M.J. "The Rational Imagination: How People Create Counterfactual Alternatives to Reality", Cambridge, MA: MIT Press, 2005.

Campanella, G., Ribeiro, R.A. "A framework for dynamic multiple-criteria decision making", *Decision Support Systems*, Vol. 52, No. 1, pp. 52–60, December 2011.

Chao, Yu, Jian Yu. "Bounded rationality in multiobjective games", *Nonlinear Analysis: Theory, Methods & Applications*, Vol. 67, No. 3, pp. 930–937, 2007.

Chel, H., Majumder, A., Nandi, D. "Scaled conjugate gradient algorithm in neural network based approach for handwritten text recognition", *Communications in Computer and Information Science, 204 CCIS*, pp. 196–210, 2011.

Chen, J.Q., Lee, S.M. An exploratory cognitive DSS for strategic decision making", *Decision Support Systems*, Vol. 36, No. 2, pp. 147–160, October 2003.

Chen, M.-H. "Pattern recognition of business failure by autoassociative neural networks in considering the missing values", *ICS 2010 — International Computer Symposium,* art. no. 5685421, pp. 711–715, 2010.

Choma, M.A., Sarunic, M.V., Yang, C., Izatt, J.A. "Sensitivity advantage of swept source and Fourier domain optical coherence tomography", *Optics Express*, Vol. 11, No. 18, September 2003.

Chung, I., Rhee, K.H. "Multi-layer perceptron neural network for grouping of XOR-collusion", *International Journal of Information Processing and Management*, Vol. 4, No. 4, pp. 109–120, 2013.

Dempster, A.P., Laird, N.M., Rubin, D.B. "Maximum likelihood from incomplete data via the EM Algorithm", *Journal of the Royal Statistical Society, Series B*, Vol. 39, No. 1, pp. 1–38, 1977.

Dowdy, S., Wearden, S. "Statistics for Research", Wiley, 1983.

Earle, W.J. "Rationality/irrationality: Elster/bourdieu", *Philosophical Forum*, Vol. 44, No. 3, pp. 295–326, 2013.

Farouk, N. "Genetic algorithm and fuzzy tuning PID controller applied on speed control system for marine diesel engines", *Research Journal of Applied Sciences, Engineering and Technology*, Vol. 4, pp. 4350–4357, 2012.

Foss, N.J. "Bounded rationality in the economics of organization: "Much cited and little used", *Journal of Economic Psychology*, Vol. 24, No. 2, pp. 245–264, 2003.

Fuhrmann, J.T. "Rasputin: A Life (illustrated ed.)", New York: Praeger, 1990.

Fuhrmann, J.T. "Rasputin, the Untold Story (illustrated ed.)", Hoboken, New Jersey: John Wiley & Sons, Inc, 2013.

Gasking, D. "Causation and Recipes", *Mind*, Vol. 64, pp. 479–487, 1955.

Gayathri, K., Kumarappan, N. "Comparison of fault location on extra high voltage lines using support vector machine and scaled conjugate gradient with ANN", *Modelling, Measurement and Control A*, Vol. 83, No. 1–2, pp. 1–19, 2010.

Ghosh S., Gude, S. "A genetic algorithm tuned optimal controller for glucose regulation in type 1 diabetic subjects", *International Journal for Numerical Methods in Biomedical Engineering*, Vol. 28, pp. 877–889, 2012.

González, R.C., Woods, R.E. "Digital image processing", Prentice Hall, p. 354, 2008.

Haghbin, H., Nematollahi, A.R. "Likelihood-based inference in autoregressive models with scaled t-distributed innovations by means of EM-based algorithms", *Communications in Statistics: Simulation and Computation*, Vol. 42, No. 10, pp. 2239–2252, 2013.

Horaguchi, H. "The role of information processing cost as the foundation of bounded rationality in game theory", *Economics Letters*, Vol. 51, No. 3, pp. 287–294, 1996.

Ikuta, C., Uwate, Y., Nishio, Y., Yang, G. "Multi-Layer Perceptron including glial pulse and switching between learning and non-learning", *Proceedings — IEEE International Symposium on Circuits and Systems,* art. no. 6572290, pp. 2107–2110, 2013.

Kaplan, A. "Irrationality in decision-making," *Mathematical Social Sciences*, Vol. 13, No. 3, pp. 299–300, 1987.

Kauermann, G., Xu, R., Vaida, F. "Nonlinear random effects mixture models: Maximum likelihood estimation via the EM algorithm", *Computational Statistics & Data Analysis*, Vol. 51, pp. 6614–6623, 2007.

Koyuncu, H., Ceylan, R. "Artificial neural network based on rotation forest for biomedical pattern classification", *2013 36th International Conference on Telecommunications and Signal Processing, TSP 2013,* art. no. 6614001, pp. 581–585, 2013.

Lee, C.-H., Chen, J.-S. "Proper orthogonal decomposition-based model order reduction via radial basis functions for molecular dynamics systems", *International Journal for Numerical Methods in Engineering*, Vol. 96, No. 10, pp. 599–627, 2013.

Li, M., Huang, X., Liu, H., Liu, B., Wu, Y. "Prediction of the gas solubility in polymers by a radial basis function neural network based on chaotic self-adaptive particle swarm optimization and a clustering method", *Journal of Applied Polymer Science*, Vol. 130, No. 5, pp. 3825–3832, 2013.

Lian, R.-J. "Adaptive self-organizing fuzzy sliding-mode radial basis-function neural-network controller for robotic systems", *IEEE Transactions on Industrial Electronics*, art. no. 6502699, Vol. 61, No. 3, pp. 1493–1503, 2014.

Luo, G.Y. "Irrationality and monopolistic competition: An evolutionary approach," *European Economic Review*, Vol. 53, No. 5, pp. 512–526, 2002.

Manapat, M.L., Nowak, M.A., Rand, D.G. "Information, irrationality, and the evolution of trust", *Journal of Economic Behavior and Organization*, Vol. 90, pp. S57–S75, 2013.

Mao, Y., Zeng, G.L. "A tailored ML-EM algorithm for reconstruction of truncated projection data using few view angles", *Physics in Medicine and Biology*, Vol. 58, No. 12, pp. 157–169, 2013.

Mill, J.S. Crisp, Roger (ed.). Utilitarianism, Oxford University Press, 1998.

Pearl, J. "Causality: Models, Reasoning, and Inference", Cambridge University Press, 2000.

Peirce, C.S. "The Essential Peirce", *Selected Philosophical Writings*, Vol. 2, pp. 1893–1913, Peirce Edition Project (eds.), Indiana University Press, Bloomington and Indianapolis, IN, 1998.

Peires, J.B. "The Dead Will Arise: Nongqawuse and the Great Xhosa Cattle-Killing Movement of 1856–7", Indiana University Press, 1989.

Polman, E. "Self–other decision making and loss aversion", *Organizational Behavior and Human Decision Processes*, Vol. 119, No. 2, pp. 141–150, November 2012.

Quine, W.V. "From a Logical Point of View", Logico-Philosophical Essays, 2nd Edition, Harvard University Press, Cambridge, MA, 1980.

Quine, W.V. "Two Dogmas of Empiricism", Philosophical Review (January 1951). Reprinted, pp. 20–46, in W.V. Quine, From a Logical Point of View, 1980.

Radicchi, F., Baronchelli, A., Amaral, L.A.N. "Rationality, irrationality and escalating behavior in lowest unique bid auctions", *PLoS ONE*, art. no. e29910, Vol. 7, No. 1, 2012.

Ramsey, F.P. "Facts and Propositions", *Aristotelian Society Supplementary*, in F.P. Ramsey, *Philosophical Papers*, David Hugh Mellor (ed.), Vol. 7, pp. 153–170. Reprinted, pp. 34–51, 1927, Cambridge University Press, Cambridge, UK, 1990.

Raol, J.R. "Multi-Sensor Data Fusion", *Theory and Practice*. CRC Press, 2009.

Rescher, N. "Methodological Pragmatism", Oxford: Blackwell, 1977.

Rescher, N. "Realistic Pragmatism", Albany, SUNY Press, 2000.

Reyes, J., Vellasco, M., Tanscheit, R. "Fault detection and measurements correction for multiple sensors using a modified autoassociative neural network", *Neural Computing and Applications*, Vol. 24, Nos. 7–8, pp. 1929–1941, 2013.

Riverol, C., Pilipovik, V. "Assessing the failure frequency of potential hazardous incidents using radial basis function networks (RBFN)", *A Milk Pasteurization Unit as Study Case Food Control*, Vol. 35, No. 1, pp. 18–21, 2014.

Rodgers, J.L., Nicewander, W.A. "Thirteen ways to look at the correlation coefficient", *The American Statistician*, Vol. 42, No. 1, pp. 59–66, 1988.

Rose, K.H. "Framing decisions: Decision making that accounts for irrationality, people, and constraints", *Project Management Journal*, Vol. 44, No. 4, p. e4, 2013.

Russ, J.C. "The image processing handbook", CRC Press, 2007.

Russell, S., Norvig P. "Artificial Intelligence: A Modern Approach", 3rd Edition, Prentice Hall, 2009.

Samuels, R., Stich, S. "Irrationality: Philosophical Aspects, In: Neil J. Smelser, Paul B. Baltes, Editor(s)-in-Chief", *International Encyclopedia of the Social & Behavioral Sciences, Pergamon, Oxford*, pp. 7906–7910, 2001.

Sarma, K.K., Mitra, A. "Multiple-input–multiple-output channel modelling using multi-layer perceptron with finite impulse response and infinite impulse response synapses", *IET Communications*, Vol. 7, No. 14, pp. 1540–1549, 2013.

Schroeder, D.J. "Astronomical Optics", 2nd Edition, Academic Press. p. 433, 1999.

Schwartz, H. "The role of aspirations and aspirations adaptation in explaining satisficing and bounded rationality", *The Journal of Socio-Economics*, Vol. 37, No. 3, pp. 949–957, 2008.

Simon, H., Rescher, N. "Cause and Counterfactual", *Philosophy of Science*, Vol. 33, pp. 323–340, 1966.

Stamoulias, I, Manolakos, E.S. "Parallel architectures for the kNN classifier", *Design of soft IP cores and FPGA implementations Transactions on Embedded Computing Systems*, art. no. 22, Vol. 13, No. 2, 2013.

Stapleton, T.J. "They No Longer Care for Their Chiefs': Another Look at the Xhosa Cattle-Killing of 1856–1857", *The International Journal of African Historical Studies*, Vol. 24, No. 2, pp. 383–392, 1991.

Švecová, L., Fotr, J.P., Renner, P. "The influence of irrationality on the innovativeness of variants and the quality of decision making", *Procedia — Social and Behavioral Sciences*, Vol. 41, pp. 570–576, 2012.

Uzer, M.S., Inan, O., Yilmaz, N. "A hybrid breast cancer detection system via neural network and feature selection based on SBS, SFS and PCA", *Neural Computing and Applications*, Vol. 23, Nos. 3–4, pp. 719–728, 2013.

Valle, M.E., Vicente, D.M.G. "Sparsely connected autoassociative lattice memories with an application for the reconstruction of color images", *Journal of Mathematical Imaging and Vision*, Vol. 44, No. 3, pp. 195–222, 2012.

Vogt, K.M. "Are Human Beings Rational? Theory of Action in Plato's Symposium Seminar presentation for Sam Scheffler's class", NYU Philosophy, 2010.

Wang, X., Schumitzky, A., D'Argenio, D.Z. "Constrained Monotone EM Algorithms for Finite Mixture of Multivariate Gaussians", *Comput Statistics & Data Analysis*, Vol. 51, pp. 5339–5351, 2007.

Welsh, F. "A History of South Africa", HarperCollins, 2000.

Wolberg, W.H., Mangasarian, O.L. "Multisurface method of pattern separation for medical diagnosis applied to breast cytology", *In Proceedings of the National Academy of Sciences*, Vol. 87, pp. 9193–9196, 1990.

Wu, Z., Xu, J. "A consistency and consensus based decision support model for group decision making with multiplicative preference relations", *Decision Support Systems*, Vol. 52, No. 3, pp. 757–767, February 2012.

Yang, B., Lester, D. "Reflections on rational choice — The existence of systematic irrationality", *The Journal of Socio-Economics*, Vol. 37, No. 3, pp. 1218–1233, 2008.

Yu, L., Lai, K.K. "A distance-based group decision-making methodology for multi-person multi-criteria emergency decision support", *Decision Support Systems*, Vol. 51, No. 2, pp. 307–315, May 2011.

Zhang, J. "Selecting typical instances in instance-based learning", *In Proceedings of the Ninth International Machine Learning Conference Aberdeen, Scotland: Morgan Kaufmann*, pp. 470–479, 1992.

Chapter 10

Conclusions and Further Work

10.1 Introduction

This book is on causality, correlation and artificial intelligence for rational decision making. Causality was defined as a function that maps variable x to variable y provided that x is connected to y, x happens before y and that there is a flow of information from x to y. This book also proposes that if one can identify a function that maps variable x to variable y where x is not connected to y or x does not happen before y or there is no flow of information from x to y then this relationship is merely a correlation. Furthermore, this book proposes that the flow of information from the cause to the effect can be visualized as a projectile where information either undershoots, reaches or overshoots the target. The projectile theory of causality allows one to build a probability distribution that defines the probability of x causing y.

Two models were proposed which were the causal and correlation machines. In causal machines a function is identified which relates x to y where x is connected to y, x happens before y and there is a flow of information from x to y. In this regard, the multi-layer perceptron (MLP), radial basis function (RBF), and fuzzy systems were used to construct a causal function (Bishop, 1995). The MLP, RBF, and fuzzy systems techniques were successfully used to model militarized interstate disputes, condition monitoring, and steam flow rate respectively. Furthermore, an auto-associative network, principal component analysis and expectation maximization were used to construct the correlation machine.

An auto-associative network is a network which is trained to map a variable nonlinearly to itself and then use it to estimate missing data using optimization methods was proposed to construct a correlation machine. In this regard, optimization methods such as genetic algorithm, simulated annealing and particle swarm optimization methods were used in conjunction with the MLP to construct a missing data estimation approach. These methods were successfully used to model an artificial taster and a mechanical system.

This book also describes directed acyclic graph (DAG) to model causal relations amongst variables. The directed arrow in the graph indicates a causal model with characteristics described above. The connection between the nodes (variables) can be established using correlation detection methods such as Granger causality model which is described in this book. The fact that the cause happens before the effect can be detected using experimental observation and the flow of information from the cause to the effect is detected through the use of the Neyman-Rubin causal models. Pearl causality is used to relate interventional probabilities from conditional probability.

This book also compares automatic relevance determination (ARD) method based on the MLP, the MLP causal model as well as the auto-associative network based on the MLP and missing data framework for modeling Granger causality (Granger, 1969). When these methods were tested it was found that the correlation machine models Granger causality better than the causal machine while the ARD performs well. The complex nature of the correlation machine (inference using auto-associative neural networks) compared to the MLP causal machine renders the correlation machine more sensitive to Granger causality than the causal machine.

This book also introduces the concept of flexibly-bounded rationality for decision making which basically states that artificial intelligence causal model and missing data estimation methods make the bounds which are prescribed by Herbert Simon's original idea of bounded rationality flexible (Simon, 1991). The idea of flexibly bounded rationality is based on the principles of the indivisibility of rationality as well as a distinction between rational actions versus processes. It aims to complete to some limited extent missing information and uses artificial intelligence to bring consistency into decision making. This method was successfully implemented to estimate the risk of HIV given the fact that not all information is available.

Given the fact that decision making is effectively irrational, this book proposes the theory of the marginalization of irrationality for decision making and applies this to the diagnosis of breast cancer. Given all that was discussed in this book, Section 10.2 describes the way forward.

10.2 Way Forward

In this book, the theories of flexibly-bounded rationality and the marginalization of irrationality for decision making are largely applied within the context of individuals or a specific process whether a breast cancer diagnosis system or condition monitoring system. Future studies should focus on applying these theories in organizations. In this regard, questions such as what the meaning of the concepts flexibly-bounded rationality and the marginalization of irrationality within the context of organizations should be studied. Studies on the impact of these concepts on the effectiveness of organizations should be studied. The relationships between the collective rationality within organizations and the long term survival of organizations should be studied. Techniques of how to construct internal systems within organizations that are able to self-marginalize irrationality should be explored. The concept of satisficing (making satisfactory and sufficient decisions within the general framework of irrationality) and satisffective (making satisfactory and effective decisions within the context of irrationality) should be explored within the context of organizations.

References

Bishop, C.M. Neural Networks for Pattern Recognition, Oxford: Oxford University Press, 1995.

Granger, C.W.J. "Investigating causal relations by econometric models and cross-spectral methods", *Econometrica*, Vol. 37, No. 3, pp. 424–438, 1969.

Simon, H. "Bounded rationality and organizational learning", *Organization Science*, Vol. 2, No. 1, pp. 125–134, 1991.

Index